PENGUIN [illegible]

POI[illegible]E GRAVE

'A true-life thriller' *Sunday Times*

'[illegible]einberg writes vividly and fluently' *Sunday Telegraph*

'[illegible]fully told, rigorously researched, contains a fascinating twist' *Catholic Herald*

'A dizzyingly original twist in a true-life thriller' *Marie Claire*

'Gripping account of the death of British DNA scientist in LA and how her own research helped to solve her murder' *Tatler*

'An enthralling biography of a young woman, intertwined with the most fascinating breakthrough in scientific circles for decades. Beautifully crafted' *Spectrum*

'[illegible]mbines the suspense of true crime with scientific history and examines the power, potential abuses and ethical implications' *New Statesman*

'Impeccably researched and fluently written, the best kind of non-fiction: straightforward enough for the layman, but with the intellectual rigour and balance of authentic scholarship' *Mail on Sunday*

'Those wanting a good crime yarn combined with an evening class in forensic science will find a [illegible]atch

ABOUT THE AUTHOR

Samantha Weinberg was born in London and now lives in Wiltshire. She has worked as a journalist in southern Africa, the United States and London. She is the author of *Last of the Pirates: the Search for Bob Denard* and *A Fish Caught in Time: the Search for the Coelacanth*. *Pointing from the Grave* won the Crime Writers' Association Gold Dagger for Non-Fiction 2003.

Pointing from the Grave

A True Story of Murder and DNA

SAMANTHA WEINBERG

PENGUIN BOOKS

PENGUIN BOOKS

Published by the Penguin Group
Penguin Books Ltd, 80 Strand, London WC2R 0RL, England
Penguin Group (USA), Inc., 375 Hudson Street, New York, New York 10014, USA
Penguin Books Australia Ltd, 250 Camberwell Road,
Camberwell, Victoria 3124, Australia
Penguin Books Canada Ltd, 10 Alcorn Avenue, Toronto, Ontario, Canada M4V 3B2
Penguin Books India (P) Ltd, 11 Community Centre,
Panchsheel Park, New Delhi – 110 017, India
Penguin Books (NZ) Ltd, Cnr Rosedale and Airborne Roads,
Albany, Auckland, New Zealand
Penguin Books (South Africa) (Pty) Ltd, 24 Sturdee Avenue,
Rosebank 2196, South Africa

Penguin Books Ltd, Registered Offices: 80 Strand, London WC2R 0RL, England

www.penguin.com

Published by Hamish Hamilton 2003
Published in Penguin Books 2004
2

Typeset by Rowland Phototypesetting Ltd, Bury St Edmunds, Suffolk
Printed in England by Clays Ltd, St Ives plc

To my father and son, the two men whose
DNA I most closely share.

Acknowledgements

Thank you to Fred Dickey, whose article in the *LA Times Magazine* set me off on this quest, and who became a real friend and courtroom companion. To David Bartick for his help and limitless patience, Valerie Summers at the San Diego DA's office for answering countless questions, the incomparable Detective Laura Heilig for trusting me with her files and taking me through her investigation in painstaking detail; thank you to Detectives Dave Decker in San Diego and Stephen Chaput in Atherton for unlocking their memories of the events of the mid-1980s, and to ADA Martin Murray for bringing the sexual assault trials to life.

Sam Morishima welcomed me into his house and was of vital assistance in introducing me to Helena Greenwood, as were Robbi Harvey, Howard Birndorf, Professor Mark Pepys and Denise Apcar. Thank you to Woody Clark, Toni Blake, Mary Alcoba-Buglio, Donna Lilly, Kelly Niknijad, Onell Soto and DA Paul Pfingst in San Diego for their time and help; to Bernard Esposito, and to Craig Collins, Jim Thoren and Barbara Kenney in San Francisco. To Paul Frediani's loyal friends, Kathy Clark and Diane Christiansen, both great women, thank you for showing me the other side of Paul. And to my pen pal, Paul himself, the centre of this book, who was brave enough to talk to me, and has now to ride the consequences.

I started this journey with only the vaguest idea of what DNA is and does, and it is in large part thanks to Matt Ridley's erudite and informative *Genome* that I made it out of the starting gates. Thanks so much to the slew of scientists who welcomed me into their labs and homes and gently corrected my ignorance on matters molecular and forensic: Professor Sir Alec Jeffreys at the University of Leicester, Dr Peter Gill at the FSS, Dr Ed Blake and Dr Henry Erlich up in the Bay area, and the cosmic and extraordinary Kary Mullis. Thank you to Professor Bill Thompson at UC Irvine, who taught me a great deal about DNA and the law in the US, and to Graham Cooke, who shared his expertise of English DNA law.

It is impossible to look at the subject of forensic DNA without acknowledging the huge role played by Barry Scheck, who took time out of his frantic schedule for coffee and a pastry with me, and whose book – with Peter Neufeld – *Actual Innocence*, tells the often horrifying stories of the people who served prison sentences totalling nearly a millennium before DNA proved their innocence. Thank you also to Jane Siegel Greene of the Innocence Project and to Herman Atkins, who spent twelve years in a cell for a crime he did not commit, and remains amazingly upbeat.

Above all, thank you to the people who have suffered so much from these tragic events, and who have acted with unfailing dignity and trust; the brave Sydney Greenwood, and Mr and Mrs Frediani.

Thank you to my agent and friend, Gillon Aitken, for believing in me all these years, and for his encouragement and support in this project, and to Lesley Shaw and Clare Alexander, and my editors, Simon Prosser at Hamish Hamilton and Jonathan Burnham at Miramax, for their enthusiasm and wise editing.

On a more personal level, I could not have written this book without the help and support of friends and family. Our neighbours and friends and emergency babysitters in Del Mar, the McCulloughs and Halls; cousins in Los Angeles, the Simons; in England, Jac Giddings for giving me no excuse not to work, Stuart Webster and Wendy Wood for keeping the home fires burning, Sam Neale for transcribing hours of interviews, and my wonderful family of readers, my father, sisters Joanna and Kate, and John and Tana Fletcher. To Amber, who grew in tandem with the completed pages, and arrived just as the last chapter was finished, and, most of all, the two main men in my life: my brilliant husband, editor and co-conspirator, Mark Fletcher, who lived through every second of this book and without whom I would not have the courage or confidence to write a single word, and my son, Alfie, who was born two days after this book idea was sold, and is only now beginning to learn what it is like not to have to share his mother with a word processor.

The names of several characters have been changed for legal reasons, or to protect their identity.

Prologue

A helix is a coil; a double helix, two interlocking spirals, chasing each other yet never touching. It is fifty years since the structure of deoxyribonucleic acid was first described by two Cambridge scientists, yet in that half century, this mortal coil has spun itself into almost every area of our lives. We test our foetuses for susceptibility to genetic disorders, our corpses for cause of death; rare animals are screened for DNA compatibility before breeding, sheep cloned, organs transplanted, babies born to two mothers. If we wanted to, we could predict our life expectancy before birth, our intellectual capacity, hair colour, even our ability to run a marathon. DNA has found its way into commerce, insurance, education and art: Salvador Dali used the double helix as a motif in a series of pictures, and when he died, his embalmed body was buried in a tunic with the double helix embroidered on its border.

It has also shaken up the world of crime.

This is a story about a murder and a molecule. It is both the history of a science, overlaid with human drama, and a human tragedy inextricably entwined with science. It is about two lives, made and destroyed by DNA and by each other. Many people have been affected along the journey. I am one of those. I came into this story knowing only what television crime dramas taught me; I leave having opened a small window on to a bewildering future. I came as an observer; I leave as a participant.

15 March 2000. A sparkling day in southern California. I am pregnant – growing a unique combination of my husband's and my genes in my belly, living here, 6,000 miles away from home in England, while my husband works on a film about the murderous tendencies of lions. I drive down the coastal highway to a modern courthouse on the northern edge of San Diego County. I am late for a hearing; I only discovered it was happening early this morning. I read an article about this case the day before; it pricked my attention and I wanted to learn more. I squeeze my ancient car into one of the few free spaces in a parking lot the size of two football fields and enter the building. No one knows where the case I am looking for is being heard; I do not know the judge's name. I have never been in an American court before.

I eventually find the right court, and slip into the back of the gallery. The atmosphere is still, like long-settled dust, and I am conscious of disturbing it. A lady judge presides over a spacious, modern court-room. With their backs to me, at one table, a large man in a navy cotton T-shirt, with 'San Diego Jail' stamped in faded white print across his broad back, sits next to a neater figure, smart-suited and shiny-shoed: the defendant and his attorney. Across the aisle, a wavy-haired woman is walking towards the witness box, in which another woman sits. The witness is diminutive, not more than five foot tall, blonde hair tied back, wearing wire-rimmed spectacles.

She is asked to state her name.

'Laura Jean Heilig.'

'By whom are you employed?'

'I am employed by the County of San Diego. I am a deputy sheriff.'

'And are you on a particular team with the Sheriff's unit?'

'I am currently assigned to the homicide detail.'

'And are you on a specific team on the homicide detail?'

'Yes, I am on the archive team. We're the team that looks at all of our unsolved homicides dating back to 1934,' she says in a slow, attractive voice. 'I try to review as many cases as I can in our files, and I knew that in this case there was some physical evidence that we could possibly work on.'

'And in the course of your duties on this archive team, did you have the opportunity to review the unsolved case of the homicide involving Helena Greenwood?'

'Yes, I did.'

Over the next half an hour, as she is addressed first by the prosecuting attorney, and then the defendant, I learn about the case, about the role DNA will play.

It is as though the central characters are turning round, one by one, to reveal themselves to me, swirling into flesh and bone, motion and emotion. They have been playing in this drama for fifteen years; I have known about it for a mere two days. I am starting to see the unfolding events of the last decade through their eyes; I will talk to those who have survived, bury myself in reports and letters, and in time, I will come to see it through my own. But already I am involved in this case, as surely as any participant. I have been sucked into the spinning spirals, and even if I wanted to jump out, I do not think I could.

To learn more, I need to go back to a different era, to a different science, to the mid-1980s: 60,000 British coal miners were striking against Margaret Thatcher's plans to close down their pits, Ronald Reagan was campaigning for re-election. In Europe, Germany was still divided by the Berlin Wall and Yugoslavia was a nation united. To me at least, deoxyribonucleic acid was as alien as the life cycle of the nematode. But to another English woman in America, the same age then as I am now, DNA was as important as ABC. Helena Greenwood knew the power of the twisted molecule: she could see its potential.

1

7 May 1985. The double doors swing open on a worn courtroom in a southern suburb of San Francisco. A tall woman makes her way to the witness stand. She is thirty-five, but looks younger, pale-faced, lightly freckled, shoulder-length hair the colour of mink. She is wearing a navy cotton suit, expensive but poorly pressed. She climbs the two steps to the stand, raises her right hand and swears to tell the truth, the whole truth and nothing but the truth. She says her name:

'Helena Greenwood. H-E-L-E-N-A G-R-E-E-N-W-O-O-D.' Her voice is clipped, precise, as English as a chintz-covered sofa.

She sits, nods faintly at the judge, turns to the prosecuting attorney, standing behind his table, ahead and to her left.

The courtroom feels tired, stained with the knowledge of ten thousand crimes. There are few people present, the jury box is empty, this is a preliminary hearing only.

'Miss Greenwood, on April 7th 1984, were you a resident of 90 Walnut Avenue in the city of Atherton?'

'Yes I was.'

'At approximately 10.20 p.m. were you in your residence?'

'Yes I was.'

'Do you remember where you were at that time?'

'I was in bed. I read a little then I went to sleep.'

It had been a long, slow Californian day, the sun lazy in the spring sky. President Reagan was on the radio taking credit for the economic boom. Roger, her husband, was in Washington, leaving her alone on a Saturday for only the second time in five years. She sat on the deck under the acacia tree, and waded through piles of financial reports and the latest scientific journals. Occasionally she would slip back into the house to make a pot of tea or grab a sandwich. It was strange to be without Roger – most weekends he would be leading the way to the nearest mountain, beach or desert. He was happiest outdoors, hiking or sailing, or just digging the garden of their pretty cottage, mending the white picket fence or retraining the roses. They would do everything together, and in the evenings, they might invite friends over and she would cook – sometimes twelve-course meals which took an entire evening to eat.

This Saturday, she was content to work. She had recently been promoted to marketing director of a biotechnology company on the front line of an industry in the grip of growing pains. She was a rare woman in her position, and she knew that she had enemies in her department, men waiting for her to make a mistake, so they could bury her snub English nose in it.

As the sun started its slide into the trees, she moved

to her desk in the study and drew the blinds. She made herself a quick dinner and ate it watching television, had a cup of tea, washed and dried the teapot and put it back on the window sill above the sink in the kitchen. Then she checked all the doors were locked, clipped the mosquito screen shut and went to bed with a book.

'Some time after you fell asleep were you awakened by something in your home?'

'Yes I was, by a man in my room.' This in a quiet voice.

She opened her eyes, and just made out a tall man moving through the shadows, obscured by the half-light, and by a hood, pulled tight to cover most of his face. He was holding long objects in both of his hands; one appeared to be a gun, the other a torch.

She was wide awake in an instant, kneeling in the bed, clutching the sheets tight to her.

'Did the man say anything to you?'

'Yes. He said, "Take off your clothes."'

'What did you do?'

She peeled off her T-shirt and a pair of Roger's baggy boxer shorts. The man demanded money. She said he could have anything she had. Her purse was in the study. He told her to get it, then followed as she walked, naked, through the house. She knelt down, pulled her purse from her bag, opened the clasp and shook the contents on to the carpet. They fell with barely a tinkle; there was less than a dollar in coins. Too little. The man did not bend to take it.

He ordered her back into the bedroom, told her to switch on the light at the wall and sit on the side of the bed, Roger's side. The spotlight was dim, pooling the upper half of the bed in an old gold glow. He tucked the gun into his pocket and walked towards her. For the first time she saw his eyes, dark, smooth-skinned round the edge, shadowed by the hood. He stood looming over her and put his hands on her shoulders.

'I stood up and pushed him back and I said, "No, I can't go through with this. I don't want to do this."'

'Did he say anything to you at that time?'

'He said, "Come on now. Don't get awkward or I will have to get my gun out again."'

'Did he touch you at that point?'

'He pushed me back towards the bed. We were somewhat struggling.'

'After he pushed you back on the bed, did he say anything else?'

'He said – as he was pushing me back, he said, "Come on now, I am as afraid as you are in this."'

'And what happened?'

'He quickly undid his trousers and pulled out his penis and asked me to suck his penis.'

The prosecutor nods reassuringly. They had met for the first time that morning, when he had warned her that she would have to describe what had happened as clearly and explicitly as she could, that most sexual assault victims choke up when they come to relive the experience in court, can't describe the very private horror in explicit terms. She had just nodded. She could do that, and she had. She had described being sexually assaulted almost as if she were explaining new laboratory protocols to a clutch of trainee technicians.

'What did you do?'

'I put his penis in my mouth.'

'How long did that activity continue?'

'It was very short.'

'And what happened?'

'He pushed my head back on to the pillow and he ejaculated on my face and on to the pillow.'

It had been the worst bit, but at the same time, a sign that her ordeal might soon be over. The man was pulling up his trousers, backing out of the room, warning her not to tell the cops. As soon as she could no longer hear him, she rushed into the bathroom and locked the door, splashed water on her face, over and over, soap, a rough towel, brushed her teeth. She pulled on a clean white shirt and a pair of trousers, then took a step out of the bedroom. She checked the study, the sitting room, the kitchen. She noticed that the sliding window over the sink was wide open, the mosquito screen had gone. But there was no sign of the man. She opened the front door; the short, tree-lined street was quiet, muffled by a carpet of blossoms. She stepped out; what had always seemed friendly now was a threatening maze of shadows. She ran to the next-door house, banged on the door. No one answered. Nor at the next one.

The third door she tried was opened by a young man. She knew him by sight. 'Would you mind if I came in for a minute? A man has just broken into my house and attacked me.' She sat down with his girlfriend while he called the police. The station was only a couple of blocks away. They would be right over. Then she called a friend and asked him to come and take her away.

Next to the prosecutor, a compact, round-headed man scribbles notes on the pad in front of him. He is a familiar face to Helena Greenwood, Detective Steve Chaput, the investigating officer in the case. They had met first two days after the assault, when the taste of her attacker, like foul metal, stuck to the back of her mouth; when she could still see his eyes if she closed hers. She had told the detective then that she was prepared to pursue the case – and over the following weeks and months, that resolve had not wavered.

'I would like to direct your attention to the man who is seated in front of me – I would ask that the record reflect I am standing behind the defendant. Have you ever invited this man into your home?'

The District Attorney is talking again, but she is forced to drag her eyes to his – the defendant, David Paul Frediani's – face. It is the first time she has seen the man the police believe to be her assailant, and she finds it hard to look at him without prejudice. All she can see are her memories of two dark eyes, piercing through the shadow of a hood. She pulls herself back and looks again; he is staring at her, sitting back in his chair, with an expression that conveys a complete lack of interest. She notices that he has scratched his right cheek, so hard it has left red marks.

'No.'

'To your knowledge has he ever been in your home?'

'No.'

'Do you know this man?'

'No.'

She keeps looking, but she cannot even recognize the eyes, not in the whole face. But maybe she *has* seen him before? Or is this just a trick of the brain, dating an instant memory like a tea-stained piece of parchment? She is finding it hard to trust her mind these days. She is more jumpy, less sure of herself. She starts at falling leaves where before she used to chase them, sees ghosts in every shadow. She hates being alone. She has been to see a counsellor, who said she had 'fears regarding her vulnerability'. She has never considered her vulnerability before, but if she isn't safe in her own locked house on a quiet street in one of the wealthiest suburbs of San Francisco, then where is she? Not on her frequent business tours of Europe, staying in strange hotels, being driven by unknown taxi drivers. Maybe not even hiking in the Sierras with Roger – what match is he for a man with a gun?

She glances at her husband, sitting in the gallery behind the prosecutor's table, on an old, cheap wood chair. The pain and confusion of the last year is embedded in his brow. He is looking at her intently. She knows he was nervous before the hearing, even though he tried to hide it, had felt powerless in his spectator's role, angry at what she had to go through, what she had been through, was still going through. In a way, it was easier for her, sitting here, answering the questions put to her, hiding her emotions beneath a cloak of scientific detachment and precision. At least now, in this courtroom, she is doing something to try to bring a halt to the nightmares, recriminations, uncertainties that had followed her ordeal. It is not that simple, of course; every time she looks at the man who has been fingered as her attacker, she feels a part of her freeze. His stare bores into her stomach, crawls along her arms and down her back.

'After he left, did you examine your residence?' The DA is still asking questions, in his gentle voice, almost caressing in its matter-of-factness.

'Yes.'

'Did you notice anything different?'

'The kitchen window was wide open and the mosquito screen had been removed.'

'Were there any other items that you normally kept near the kitchen window?'

'Yes . . . Our teapot and other small items with flowers in them.'

He picks a white teapot off his desk, brings it over to the witness stand and asks her if she can identify it. Even though she hasn't seen it for over a year, it is as familiar as her cream MG roadster. She and

Roger had brought the teapot back after a visit to England just two years before, and they had used it constantly. Seven years in California had not dented their addiction to tannin and the customs of home.

They had taught the love of tea to Thomas and Patricia Christopher, their closest friends, like family in a country where they had none. It was to the Christophers that she had turned in the absence of her husband, frightened and disturbed, after the attack by the armed intruder. She had called them from her neighbour's house. Patricia had answered – she was pregnant, due any week – and when Helena had told her what had happened, she passed the phone to Thomas, who was already out of bed and half dressed by the time she had a chance to explain. 'I'm coming right over,' he had told her.

When he walked through the door, barely forty minutes later, she was flooded with emotion. She was sitting on the sofa, giving a statement to the woman police officer; the sight of a familiar face was almost too much – all she wanted was for him to take her away from the house, across the Bay, to somewhere she felt safe. He sat down and held her hand, and when the policewoman had finished, Helena got in his car to go to the hospital, where she was subjected to a sexual examination. It was like a reprise of the indignity. She was told to strip, then poked and pried by strange fingers, this time under antiseptic hospital lights, surrounded by figures dressed in green. Swabs and samples were taken of her blood and saliva, she was sent over to talk to the on-duty crisis counsellor, made to fill out sheaves of forms before she was allowed to leave. It was three in the morning when they got back to the Christophers' house in Oakland.

Sleep was not really an option, but she went through the motions, and the next morning, the three of them had breakfast in the garden. It was another sunny day, the San Francisco weather out of sympathy with her feelings. 'Why', she asked over and over, 'did it have to happen when Roger was away?' And 'The gun. He had a gun. What could I do?' The Christophers were gentle, unprying, but she wanted to talk about it.

'And after April 7th, when was the next time you saw that teapot?'

'I went back to the house the next morning to collect some clothes, and in walking around the outside of the house, found it on the deck outside the kitchen window.'

She was determined not to stay another night at 90 Walnut – but she had to go back to pick up some clothes and papers she would need for work the next day. She was focusing on the practicalities almost obsessively, the figures that needed to be in before the weekly department meeting that afternoon. Thomas Christopher drove her home. He fiddled about in the kitchen while she was in the bedroom packing, then wandered outside on to the deck. She heard him call through the kitchen window. 'Is this meant to be here?' She went through the sliding glass study door to join him. He was pointing at the teapot, sitting squat on the wood in the shade of a tree.

'What did you do when you saw it there?' the DA is asking.

'I immediately called the police.'

'Thank you. I have no further questions of this witness.'

She waits in the witness box, breathes deeply. She is almost half-way through, though the harder bit is now to come. She sees the defence attorney rise from his seat beside the accused. He is a stocky man, bearded and short. He introduces himself politely to Helena Greenwood. His voice is surprisingly small for a man of his appearance, almost apologetic.

'I would like to ask you a few questions, if I may do so, with your permission. I would like to back up and ask you if prior to April 7th of 1984, had you held your house open to members of the public for any reason?'

'The house was on the market for sale at the time we are speaking of.'

It had been a wrench, but they had decided to sell 90 Walnut that spring and buy somewhere bigger. They had worked hard on the cottage, practically rebuilding it by hand, working weekends and evenings painting walls, sanding floors. Roger had nurtured the garden from a patch of bare earth, and turned it into a lush yet ordered tangle of blooms and bowers, essentially English in feel, despite the exotic trees and shrubs. They were proud of their house and garden, but it was time to move on: with Roger's job and her promotion, they could afford somewhere bigger.

She explains to the attorney that the house had been on the market for about three weeks at the time of the attack. Their estate agent had a spare key, which, according to custom, was kept in a lock box hanging from the front door. Visiting agents could open the box, to show the house to clients. Helena and Roger insisted that there should always be an agent present when someone was shown around, and that they should leave their business card. Few people came to see the house, however, as an offer was quickly made – and accepted.

'Would you be able to describe the gun at all, either by colour or – you may be an expert gunsmith, for all I know . . .'

She shakes her head. 'I'm not an expert gunsmith. I know nothing about guns. It was grey, and whatever the word – where the barrel would be . . . it was more like one of the flat, elongated type . . . with an elongated end to it.' She picks her pen off the table with the tips of her fingers, as if removing a dead insect from her half-eaten lunch.

By the time the police arrived, she was feeling 'very distraught. I was eager to get out of my house and move to my friend's house.'

'Would you tell the court the physical description of the assailant that you gave to the first officer that you spoke with about the identity of the person?'

'That he was tall, of a slim build, somewhat athletic.'

'Did you render any kind of opinion about the race of the individual?'

'I said that he had dark hair.'

The defence attorney has noticeably shifted a gear, discarding the 'Ma'ams', 'If you pleases' and 'With your permissions' for a barrage of jabs, barely giving her time to parry:

'My question was: did you render an opinion about the person's race?'

'Well, I would say that he wasn't a fair-haired, fair-skinned person.'

'Did you render an opinion about the assailant's race? Yes or no?'

'I said that I couldn't positively identify the person.'

'I understand that. Did you say the person was a black man?'

'No, I said that the person's skin wasn't totally white.'

'Do you recall the words that you used to identify and physically describe the assailant?'

'Yes. All along I said I could not positively identify the person because I didn't see anything. I saw his eyes . . . that he was a tall, athletic person . . .'

'Did you say that the assailant was', he persists, '– and I am quoting from a report – "possibly Mexican or partially black male adult"?'

'Yes.'

'I want you to look at the defendant for a moment, please. I want you to look at his skin colour, that which you can now see. Would you describe the defendant as a partially black male adult?'

'He has the type of skin colour that I was trying to describe when I spoke those words.'

Her answer is delivered in an emphatic tone, and for a while, it seems to have worked. The lawyer backs off, moves on to other aspects of her identification; her attacker had appeared to be well spoken, the area of his face that she could see was unwrinkled, smooth, she was fairly sure he was circumcised.

But it is only a temporary respite. He has the race issue in front of him and is picking away at it like a child at a scab.

'Did you utter the words . . . "half-black"?'

'I never said half-black. What I was trying to describe, and again it was very subjective, was that the nature of his skin colour did not seem to be completely white. It had sort of a yellowish tinge to it.'

'Are you at all influenced by the fact that the person who is sitting in the courtroom today has that particular skin tone and you are now a year later thinking that's probably the person because of some other incident?'

'I've always said that I couldn't positively identify the person.'

'Would you describe the defendant . . . as light brown? . . . If you knew Mr Frediani and he was a friend of yours and you were trying to describe his skin colour to me, would you use the words light brown?'

'I would in the sense that he doesn't have the same colour as you or Mr Chaput. Yes.'

'As you sit here today, is there anything about Mr Frediani that suggests to you that he either is or is not the assailant?'

'His height and his build.'

She asks if the defendant can stand up. He is noticeably several inches taller than anyone else in the courtroom. She can look at him in the eyes now, return his stare.

'All I can say is that he has the height and type of build but nothing more than that . . . he's athletic and yet somewhat slender. He doesn't have a pot-belly stomach . . .'

'You would concede', says the attorney, 'that there are hundreds of thousands of males in California with Mr Frediani's height and build?'

'Probably yes.'

'I have no further questions.'

The judge turns to Helena Greenwood: 'Thank you. You are free to step down. You are free to go back to your home.'

2

Sydney Greenwood raises himself from his armchair, in his boxy brick house down a quiet street in Lymington, a pretty town on the south coast of England, and fetches a pile of photographs of his daughter Helena from a walnut box. They slither through his dry hands and on to a rickety side table. They are mainly black and white, taken by a professional photographer when Helena was in her mid-teens. She is in a slightly different position in each picture, and looking at them together, they appear like an animated film, or one of those childhood flick-books, which come alive when you ruffle through them. The overwhelming impression given by these photographs is of serenity – she is looking away from the camera with large, steady eyes, her lips are parted slightly and there is a gap between her front teeth wide enough for an old shilling coin; her hair is long, worn parted on the right, with wisps straying across her forehead. 'She never told us about the sexual assault. She said she had been burgled, but nothing else. Her mother was ill and she didn't want to worry us, you know,' he explains.

Helena Greenwood was born in the summer of 1949, in Southampton, not far from where her father lives now. She grew up under the pale English sun, with a bucket and spade and floppy hats, adored by her parents, two gentle academics. 'She was always a very happy young girl,' Sydney says. 'She was gregarious, full of the wonders of the world. We took her everywhere. We had this little cottage in Wales, very basic, no electricity, near a stream, where we would watch the kingfishers, and the sea trout come up in autumn. Helena would walk down to the stream to collect water and come back with two heavy buckets. She was only a mite then, but she was always very determined, oh yes.'

He sinks back into his chair, closes his eyes, as if replaying the scene on the blank space behind his lids. Sydney Greenwood is eighty-seven. The passing years and tragedies have etched their stories on his face, gaunt but still handsome. At certain angles and with certain expressions, he could be mistaken for Peter O'Toole. He is warm and welcoming, and when he smiles, a whiff of mischief passes over his features. But inside his body, cancer is nibbling away at his organs; he knows his time is near.

'We doted on her, Marjorie and I. Marjorie was a geologist, y'know, a very clever woman.' He points to a silver-framed photograph across the room, of a scruffy-haired woman, standing on a moor in winter, looking at the camera with dark-eyed intensity. 'That is where Helena got her brains from. We were very concerned that she would miss out on a lot, as an only child, so we tried to get her to meet other young children. She was a bit of a ruffian, really, she was quite one of the bosses of the gang. But she was a very good girl.

'She wasn't outstanding at school, mind. Not at first. She was just a typical girl of her age. She loved going to parties, shopping for clothes with her friends, oh, she was probably the best-dressed girl in Europe in her teens. Then she moved to another school, which had the staff to cope with science. It really fired her interest. Suddenly, we couldn't stop her doing her homework.' He laughs, a genuine ho-ho chuckle. 'I think she was always interested in science – she loved playing with bits of dirt and pebbles and things like that, a puddle in the wild west of Ireland, or a stream in Iceland. And she could read a map and take us through the city when she was six.'

Over several days, between cups of tea and impromptu snoozes, Sydney Greenwood paints a verbal picture of his daughter, every bit as vivid and vibrant as his oils and watercolours of sea- and land-scapes that hang around the house, and rest stacked against the wall in his lean-to studio. Helena was determined, strong-willed, kind and loyal. She loved to cook, to make jewellery. She was scared of water: on a sailing trip with her parents when she was four, she had dropped her doll, hand-knitted by Marjorie, over the edge of the boat. The doll was rescued, but it shrank when it dried, and its eyes fell off. For many years after that, she would only walk above the high-water mark.

She met Roger Franklin when she was fourteen, a

gangly grammar-school girl in a blue pleated skirt. He was two years older, at the boys' school along the road, soft-spoken, gentle, with a shy, toothy smile that made him look younger than his age. Perhaps not Helena's equal academically, he was rugged and courageous, a first-team sportsman. He adored her from the moment they met, and once their romance had been kindled three years later, there was no way he was going to let her go. On weekends, they would go for walks in the New Forest, and after a while, Roger persuaded her out of her fear of water and into a sailing boat with him. Sydney and Marjorie liked him, but 'Well, who is ever good enough for your only daughter?' they would say.

When she went up to Sheffield University, Roger completed his degree in town planning, but their relationship survived the geographical separation. Helena buried herself in her studies. She was a hard worker, ambitious, sure of herself and of her vision of the world. As she progressed up the educational ladder, her talent for science became increasingly obvious; by the time she was twenty-four, she was working on a Ph.D. in chemical pathology at St Bartholomew's Hospital in London and had sent articles to several prestigious academic journals. She knew her future lay in science, and already she was turning her attention to DNA, the molecule that was reorienting the worlds of biology and chemistry, smashing preconceptions and opening vistas that spread from pre-birth to eternal life.

Roger was also part of her future. When she moved to London, he came with her. But it was their landlady who persuaded them to get married; she refused to let them a flat unless they were wearing rings on the appropriate fingers.

Silver invitations were sent out. Inside, Sydney had drawn a map of the route from the village church in Boldre to the Greenwoods' house, illustrated with ponies and cows and fish by the stream. On 20 September 1975, at noon, the same year as Helena became Dr Greenwood, they were married. It was a wonderful ceremony, and afterwards they celebrated in a large marquee on the lawn. Helena wore flowers in her hair and laughed when they cut the cake.

It was soon afterwards that they emigrated. Five years earlier, before Helena had started her Ph.D., they had worked their way across the United States with three friends, and from that moment, they had started talking about moving across the Atlantic. It was Helena's enthusiasm and fervour for her work that finally persuaded them; on that first trip she had seen that in America it was possible for a woman to make a career out of science. So a year after she had collected her doctorate, they packed everything they owned and flew west. The Bay area of San Francisco was a natural choice. It was the seed bed of the budding biotechnology industry, and Helena had found a job in Palo Alto, in the research laboratories of Syva, one of the leading firms in the field of medical diagnostics. The salary was many times what she could have hoped for in England – so she paid the bills while Roger completed his master's degree in Landscape Architecture at the University of California in Berkeley.

As a couple, they complemented each other, and had little need for friends. Many people who met them thought they were reserved, even stand-offish, by affable American standards. But a few managed to break through and saw a different side. Thomas and Patricia Christopher met Roger and Helena soon after they arrived, and the four of them struck up a close friendship. When Helena's and Roger's lease expired on their first house in Berkeley, they moved to an apartment near the Christophers' in Oakland, and when they eventually bought 90 Walnut Avenue, their first house, across the bay in Atherton, the Christophers helped them move. They went to jazz clubs, skiing and on camping holidays in the state parks of California and in Hawaii. The Christophers learned to laugh at Helena's organizational fetishes – she never travelled without a full library of guidebooks and would arrive at breakfast with a daily agenda.

Helena was doing well at Syva, working her way up towards the top bench. She soon realized, however, that she did not want to spend the rest of her career hunched over a microscope. There were scientific geniuses aplenty, constantly coming up with new and exciting ideas – but where the company fell down was in marketing and selling them. They were two different communities; the white coats and the suits. Helena believed she could be a bridge between the two.

She moved into product development, and from there to marketing. Denise Apcar, who joined the marketing department two weeks after Helena's appointment, thought highly of her. 'I was small fry then, but I watched Helena and I was very impressed by her professional demeanour. Yes, she was aloof, but I put that down to her British style.' It wasn't a very biotech style, though. This was an industry in its infancy, and most of the people employed in it had barely removed the braces from their teeth. They came to work in jeans, joshed each other and sprawled on sofas in their coffee break. Helena, with her nylon tights, bad haircuts and clipped vowels, was an outsider. And she made no effort to change that. When she felt that members of her team weren't pulling their weight, she was not shy to tell them, which rankles among some, to this day.

Sam Morishima, however, saw beneath the professional patina, and quickly became devoted to Helena. He had been raised in the strawberry fields of northern California by his Japanese immigrant parents, and was used to getting up with the sun for fifteen back-breaking hours filling plastic punnets. 'I always just felt lucky to be working in a temperature-controlled environment.' He first met her when he joined her international marketing team, and soon afterwards, she asked him out to lunch. 'I was so surprised. Helena was strictly business, and kind of separated from the group. I was in awe of her, but I didn't know her at all. Then she took me to this German restaurant, The Black Forest. I saw a completely different Helena. I had always thought she was really beautiful, but she had seemed so serious. That day I saw another side. When she smiled it was like you were playing in a playground with swings,' he says now, with a wide smile of his own. 'When she explained her philosophy it really made sense to me. She taught me that marketing was like shining a spotlight on your product, showing what it could do. For her it was not about deception, or making money, it was about helping millions of people. She believed that. It was her philosophy and she passed it on to me.'

Syva's main product was a system, known as Emit, used to detect the presence of drugs – both therapeutic and abused – in the blood chemistry. Its primary markets were hospitals and hospital labs, but Emit was increasingly being sought by forensic laboratories, to test for cocaine and barbiturates in urine. It was a tense time. Syva had poured more money than it could afford into a new, automated drug-testing machine. If it worked, it would have dominated the field. But there were technical hitches and Abbott, Syva's main competitor, got their product out first. It was a disaster for Syva – they were forced to lay off hundreds of staff and cancel future projects. In a highly geared industry, one expensive mistake is enough to make you drown. But Helena was determined not to let that happen. With Sam Morishima, she worked through weeks of nights, reconfiguring the instrument until it passed international standards. 'We broke every rule,' Sam remembers, 'rewrote the software and got it into the international market. Helena loved that.' And the Syva board loved her: the strong international sales were a life raft for Syva, they saved the company. Helena was riding high. Her staff might not all like her, but they now knew they needed her.

Then there was the sexual assault. It was as if a curtain had been drawn across Helena's eight years at Syva. She told no one at her office – it wasn't her habit to chit-chat, and she would have hated the curiosity, the pity, the knowing looks. She was determined to act as if nothing had happened. So, on Monday 9 April, she went into work. She may have looked a little more tired, seemed withdrawn, but even if they had noticed, no one would have commented. She just swathed herself in an untouchable air and got down to work. Business as usual.

The Monday evening after the assault, Roger went with Helena to Atherton police station to meet Detective Stephen Chaput. Roger had jumped on the first plane back from Washington, and when Helena met him at the airport, the day after the assault, and Roger held out his arms, she had crumpled into them.

Although Detective Steve Chaput hadn't been on duty on Saturday night, he was assigned the case. It was a big deal for Atherton PD, and Chaput took it seriously. He was a ten-year veteran at the small station. He lived for his job, and his precinct. Atherton was then – still is – a quiet place, tucked between the cosmopolitan glamour of San Francisco and the glass business parks of Silicon Valley. Most of Atherton is extremely wealthy – foot by foot, multi-million-dollar pay packet by billion-dollar stock option one of the richest pockets of real estate in America. There are tree-shaded streets, tall gates sheltering huge mansions. Even the small cottages on Walnut Avenue are now approaching the seven-figure bracket. Violent crime was minimal on Chaput's beat. The sexual assault on Helena Greenwood was the first such attack in years. Nobody wanted a rapist prowling through the blossom, and it was Detective Steve Chaput's job to make sure he was caught – and quickly.

He liked the English couple immediately. 'A real lady and gentleman,' is how he describes them. There was never any question of Helena not pressing charges. In her calm way, she was 100 per cent determined to see her attacker brought to justice.

Chaput took her through her statement from the night of the assault. She had been shaken at the time, but that hadn't prevented her from recalling the most minute observations. The man had smelled of cologne and well-laundered clothes. His voice was educated. He wore faded blue tennis shoes with a white flash on them. She had initially estimated his age to be around the same as her own – thirty-four – but on thinking about it, revised her estimate down a few years, mid-twenties maybe.

Chaput thanked her, and assured her that he would pull out all the stops in his search for her assailant. His department had already put out a telex message to all the local PDs, describing the crime and appealing for help; the neighbours were being interviewed, and a description of the assailant had been released under the Secret Witness Program – appealing for anonymous leads. But their main hopes lay with the physical evidence. On the night of the crime, the police had taken away with them three pubic hairs, and the flowery sheets and pillowcases, hoping to find semen stains which they could then test for blood type. The following day, after Helena called, Officer Patrick Akana came around to collect the white teapot which Thomas Christopher had found on the deck. Wearing gloves, he wrapped it in a brown paper bag and carried it back to the station, where he dusted it with fine fingerprint powder. The powder clings to the microscopic droplets of sweat that we excrete through the pores of our fingertips, revealing any latent – invisible – fingerprints on the surface. A couple of prints and some smudges showed up, so rather than trying to lift them himself – Akana was a rookie policeman, fresh from the academy – he sent the teapot along to the County forensic lab. There a fingerprint examiner photographed the teapot before lifting the prints carefully off the surface of the pot using a strip of transparent tape, and examining them under a magnifying glass. Only one of the prints was complete and unsmudged. A copy of it was sent to

Atherton police station, where it was fed into the central computer containing the FBI's database of known offenders. No match. The semen stains and pubic hairs could also only come into play once they had a suspect.

But as the months slipped by, the clues petered out. Leads were followed, but came to nothing. Chaput kept doggedly snuffling away, but he was beginning to lose hope. As far as he knew, the man did not strike again, in Atherton at least.

A few miles north in Belmont, Detective Joe Farmer was also on the lookout for a sex offender. His beat was another small town, that bit closer to San Francisco, haunt of a younger crowd, well-to-do but less so than the Athertonians. On 27 July 1984, three and a half months after the attack on Helena Greenwood, his station received a panicky call from a young nurse. At quarter to three in the morning, Catherine Scott had been asleep in her bedroom in her first-floor apartment in the French Village complex. She awoke to see a man in the doorway, his face half-muffled in a pale T-shirt. He said: 'Don't make a noise, I have a gun. Do you understand that?'

'Yes.'

'Is there anyone else here?'

'My sister is next door.'

He walked behind her into the other bedroom.

Lyssa Scott woke as soon as they came in. The man ordered them to take their clothes off, then opened his trousers. He was wearing nothing underneath.

'I am not going to rape you, I just want someone to suck me.'

'No, I'm not going to do that,' Lyssa replied.

He spoke in a monotone and never attempted to touch them, and when they refused oral copulation, he asked about the possibility of manual relief. Minutes passed when he just stood there looking at them with his zip open. He never seemed to get sexually aroused.

The sisters' flatmate, Jennifer Jones, was still asleep. They shook her awake, and she opened her eyes to see the tall man standing over her with his zip open. She screamed at him to get out, repeatedly. She saw what appeared to be a knife in his right hand, but she continued to scream and charged towards him, kicking and hitting the walls. It appeared to shake him. Still holding the T-shirt to his face, he turned and fled through the sliding glass doors on to the balcony.

Farmer interviewed the three girls the following day. They described the intruder as athletically built, with broad shoulders, a narrow waist and long legs. He was well-groomed and clean looking, with collar-length wavy brown hair, wide cheek bones and large brown eyes set far apart. His face was smooth-shaven and tanned, and he had a hairy chest and pubic area. He was wearing dark jeans, possibly Levi 501s, with a blue T-shirt wrapped around the lower part of his face.

The girls were shown mug shots from books, but

didn't recognize any of them. Working with a police artist, they tried unsuccessfully to come up with a portrait of their assailant.

Six weeks later, on 7 September 1984, again in the French Village apartment complex, a man broke into Roseanne Melia's apartment. He grabbed one of her butcher's knives from the kitchen and pointed it at her with one hand, while holding his T-shirt over his face with the other. He shoved her to the floor, then pulled his white shorts down, saying: 'I have something for you.' She pushed him away and ran for the front door, screaming. He dropped the knife on the living room floor and fled. Her six-year-old daughter had been in the bath all the time.

Melia's description was consistent with that of the girls. The Belmont police were sure it was the same man, but had no leads to go on. In neither of the cases had they found a useable fingerprint. All the attempted assaults occurred in the same complex: there was a good chance that the man was local, and if so, it was only a matter of time before he struck again.

Chaput, however, was unaware of this series of attacks. He checked in with Helena and Roger now and then over the first few months, but with time he stopped calling. He had nothing to say. Had he tried their number, he might not have received a response anyway.

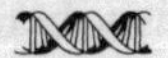

Towards the end of 1984, Helena Greenwood was head-hunted by a new biotechnology start-up based in San Diego. Tom Adams, one of the co-founders of Gen-Probe, had met her several times at the major international markets, conferences and fairs. He had seen her present papers to scientists and salesmen alike and was impressed. She seemed the ideal person to head up his marketing department. He called her at Syva and invited her down to San Diego to meet the core team: Adams, Howard Birndorf, the sharp-talking entrepreneur, and David Kohne, the resident scientific genius. It was Kohne who had developed a revolutionary new method for diagnosing infectious diseases, using DNA probes instead of traditional cultures. Helena liked them, and needed little persuading to accept their offer. She was excited about the technology – she had been following the developments in DNA as they rolled through the scientific literature like a snowball on virgin snow, and she knew that it was the way the biotech industry was heading, with Gen-Probe leading the rush. The job involved a promotion, a seat on the board and, perhaps most importantly, San Diego was 450 miles south of San Francisco, far enough to give her a chance to banish the silhouette imprint of the hooded man in her bedroom shadows.

She flew back up to San Francisco and talked it over with Roger. It would take him some time to sell the new house, leave his job and find another, but he was happy to do whatever would make her happy.

The next day, she went to see the president of Syva, and resigned. Of her team, only Sam Morishima was genuinely upset to see her go. At the beginning of 1985, she was back on a plane to San Diego, this time, she hoped, for good. Roger would be following in a few months, once he had safely knotted the loose ends.

The southernmost city in California, with its broad beaches, palm-lined avenues and sunny atmosphere, brought with it the promise of a new start for Helena. She would be able to throw herself head-first into the new venture, bury deep beneath a mound of new colleagues, a new city, a new technology. DNA probes were the new new thing, and it was going to be a challenge to sell them to a conservative market.

Instantly, she had more to think about than minutes in the day, and slowly, almost without her noticing, the horrors of the assault got squeezed out. She was still careful – Adams had offered her a beachside apartment until she found a place of her own, but she declined: it was on the ground floor. Instead, she answered an advertisement for a lodger which she found on the notice board at the university in La Jolla. Marylin Johns was a motherly woman, and Helena quickly became one of her many children. At weekends, she and Roger would meet – either in San Francisco or San Diego, but it was the latter, with its sunny climate and relaxed beach life, that was already feeling more like home.

*

At the beginning of February it was still winter in San Francisco. The weak sun was setting over the French Village apartments at six on the evening of 6 February 1985, when thirteen-year-old Chantal Clark looked up from the television to see a man standing in front of the window with his trousers open. He was masturbating. She called the police and described what was happening in terms that belied her age.

Shortly afterwards, she heard a male voice yell, 'Police officer, stop!' It had taken Officer Halleran only minutes to respond to the 911 call. As he rounded the corner of the building, he saw a silhouette of a man standing outside the Clarks' apartment, backlit by the glow from the neighbouring windows. As he approached, the man began to walk away. Halleran shone his torch at him and called out. The man started walking faster and, when Halleran yelled, 'Police officer, stop!', he broke into a sprint. Halleran radioed for help. His partner met him in the car park, and after a chase, caught the fugitive in the next-door complex, searched him and cuffed him.

Halleran went back to fetch Chantal Clark. He drove her by the spot where his partner was holding the man. She had no hesitation in identifying him. Halleran dropped her home, then picked up his partner and their prisoner and took them back to Belmont police station.

They sat in an interview room, note pad open.

'Name?'

'David Paul Frediani, but there's some mistake. Please let me explain.'

He said that he had picked up his car from the garage that evening, then driven to the French Village apartments to see if there were any vacancies. He went to the management office, but there were people inside, so he walked around the complex checking for rental signs. He saw a girl inside one apartment who 'looked startled'. Then he suddenly had to go to the bathroom, so urinated on the ground. As he was finishing, he heard a male voice shouting, and thinking that he would get into trouble for urinating, took off.

'Can you explain this open bottle we found in your coat pocket?'

'Yes. It's hair conditioner. I got it yesterday. My hairdresser recommended it.'

Halleran read over the statement, took the bottle, Frediani's trousers and handkerchief away for serological analysis. Then he said he would drive to Frediani's apartment, only a few hundred yards from the French Village, off the same street, to pick up a spare pair of trousers, after which Frediani would be allowed to leave.

At 1.30 in the morning, Officer Halleran knocked on the door of Frediani's apartment. A pretty redhead answered. She said she was his girlfriend, Andrea Goodhart. He asked when they had met. In June 1984, she said. They had started dating immediately, and had moved in together in November. She confirmed his story of the evening's events.

Did they have sexual problems? No. Not at all. Did she know why he might be carrying a Silkience conditioner bottle in his jacket? No, she had no idea what it was for, but Paul, as she called him, has 'dry skin and requires body lotion at times', she told them. 'He is very particular about his appearance and keeps a toiletries kit with him at all times. He is concerned about hair loss and is going to a place in San Francisco for treatment,' she offered. The policemen left, and soon afterwards, Paul Frediani came home.

The following night, Officer Halleran was telephoned by Chantal Clark's mother, Carrie. Earlier that evening, she told him, a woman had come round to her apartment and identified herself as Andrea Goodhart. She was, she said, the girlfriend of 'the man from the other night'. She tried to persuade Carrie Clark that Frediani was innocent, and appealed to her compassion. She left a letter explaining what had happened.

Dear Concerned Neighbours,

. . . My boyfriend and I live about a half-mile away. We have been saving since I moved in, in November, for a larger apartment with some outdoor space for my cats . . . On February 6th, I picked up my boyfriend at work . . . I was very excited about the new place and asked him if he'd go and inquire at the rental office if there were any availabilities . . . [Paul] was snooping around, waiting for the woman at the rental office to finish with the clients in her office at that

time, and decided, of all things, to go to the bathroom right there rather than wait to get home!

It is the most unfortunate thing in the world that your daughter saw him, because he was so embarrassed, he couldn't go . . . He had been holding it in a long time, since I picked him up at work, so he tried to force himself to urinate. I can imagine it must have looked extremely curious to a child to view a man physically trying to make himself urinate . . . The situation is out of proportion now, though. Paul is facing criminal charges, punishable by two years in jail! We are so broke saving for a new apartment that $3,000 for an attorney seems like a million.

I realize your little girl was scared . . . but Paul did not intend to scare anyone. We just love that little complex and visit it . . . to give us incentive to save, from time to time. Around Christmas time I must have gone there every time I was tempted to splurge on gifts! I am so sorry this had to happen at all. Now, however, things are even worse. I can't believe this is all happening . . .

Very truly yours,
Andrea Goodhart

Carrie Clark was not moved. She declined to withdraw charges and Andrea was warned not to contact her again.

Detective Joe Farmer heard about the man his colleagues had arrested for indecent exposure at the French Village apartments. It sounded like he could be the same person he was looking for in connection with the attempted assaults. At his local bar, one night,

Farmer ran into two men who lived in the same George Avenue complex as Paul Frediani. Jim Thoren and Art Settlemeyer were staples of the Belmont bar and nightclub scene. They were always to be found sitting on some stool, buying drinks and chatting up barmaids. Jim was the leader – tall, boots, belt buckle and big ego, he distributed nuts and beef jerk for a living. Art was a building contractor. They were 'good value', 'always up for a laugh'.

Farmer asked if they knew Frediani.

'Sure,' Art said. 'He used to room with Jim.'

'I put an ad in the paper for a roommate and Paul called up,' Thoren explained. 'He stayed for a couple of hours, liked the apartment and decided to move in. We were pretty good friends at one point. Why?'

Farmer answered obliquely. 'Do you think he might be involved in sexual assaults?'

Jim shrugged. 'Maybe. He was always into sex, but would he force himself on someone? I don't know. The girls always liked him. When we lived together, we were out every night, howlin' at the moon. There would be women everywhere, waiting at the bar, tons of women. We were in our thirties, thin, handsome and tan, with money to blow. The women loved us. We had at least a couple of girls every week.

'Then Paul started to change. He didn't want to go out howling with us any more. He wasn't much fun. We weren't hitting it off that great, and in the end, I said, "Get your own place," so he moved into another apartment in the complex. We still saw him around, but not so much. He'd always be out at night, on his bike. Yeah, if you're looking for someone who's into weird sex stuff, it might be Paul.'

Farmer was not going to put too much weight on the gossip of a drinker like Jim Thoren, but Frediani was worth following up. He compiled a photo line-up of a selection of dark-haired men, then called up the Scott sisters and their roommate, Jennifer Jones, Roseanne Melia and two women who had complained of a man exposing himself, and asked them to come over to see if they could identify a suspect.

Jennifer Jones studied the pictures for about a minute then picked out the one numbered 5. 'If I had to pick one, it would be this one,' she said, pointing to a photograph of Frediani. 'That looks exactly like the face structure, the eyes are exact, and his eyebrows went that way.' But she couldn't be positive; the man who had broken in had covered the lower part of his face throughout. She asked to see a whole body picture, and after looking at it for about five seconds said, 'This is spooky, he really looks like the guy.'

Her roommate, Catherine Scott, again thought that photo 5 looked like the man from the nose area up, but she also said she couldn't be positive. Her sister, Lyssa, wasn't sure it was any of the men in the photographs. Roseanne Melia thought that number 5 was the closest, though the two women who had been exposed to picked out different men.

It wasn't enough. With no physical evidence, Joe

Farmer knew he was going to have problems persuading the District Attorney's office to prosecute Frediani for anything other than the indecent exposure. It was a misdemeanour. In all likelihood, Frediani would get away with a slap on the wrist and a $50 fine. Farmer was pretty sure he was the man responsible for the attempted sexual assaults – felonies with a mandatory prison term. But a case built on shaky eye-witness identifications, in the dark, of a man with his face part-covered, was going to be laughed out of court.

3

The company that Helena Greenwood joined was a whirlwind of creativity. It was still tiny – no more than fifteen people crammed into a couple of small rooms in a dingy building in an unfashionable part of town. But everyone there was swept along on the absolute belief that their product was a winner: Birndorf and Adams wooing the investors, Kohne, more like a scruffy student than a high-powered scientist, scooting around in his VW Beetle, spouting probes and primers, adenine and cytosine, to secretaries and clients alike. From her first day, Helena loved it, but she knew she had a huge amount of work ahead of her. It was front-line science. She was aware that, to most people, the very mention of DNA was enough to snap shutters over their eyes. Her challenge was to make it appear simple. DNA probes could do in minutes what before took days. The whole company knew their product worked miracles, and had laid the responsibility of showing this to the world at Helena's feet. To do so, she had first to get intimately acquainted with the technology.

She already had a working knowledge of the fundamentals of DNA, what it was and how it had been discovered. She had been three and a half years old when a precocious American and a bumptious, fast-talking Brit had effectively changed the face of science, and by the time she started biology at school, the story of Watson's and Crick's triumphant assault on the structure of DNA was the stuff of every young scientist's dreams. Watson had probably not understated it when he told his sister at the time that she was 'participating in perhaps the most famous event in biology since Darwin's book'.

When Charles Darwin and Alfred Wallace first proposed the theory of evolution by natural selection almost 100 years earlier, they drew a thick line between the old and new biology. It is possible to imagine, across the world, lab benches being swept clean, pages of data torn up, test tubes and petri dishes flung out of sash windows, as the scientists scrambled to embark upon the new challenge. But what Darwin and Wallace had proposed was an external theory; what was needed was an internal chemical mechanism.

At that time, in the second half of the nineteenth century, there was not even a name for this study of inheritance. Yet only a few countries away, in an Austrian monastery, a fat and amiable monk had already – literally – planted the first seeds of what came to be called genetics. Brother Gregor Johann Mendel was born in northern Moravia in 1822, to a family of peasant farmers. He was a clever, sickly child, and his parents and sisters scrimped and saved to pay for his education. He went to theological college in Brünn, in what is now Austria, where – after failing as a science teacher and parish priest (he was too shy to preach effectively, and crumpled in exams) – he settled into the slow rhythms of life as an Augustinian friar.

He was good at maths, enjoyed chess and eating, but his real passion was husbandry. He wanted to know how and why breeding works; what it is that makes things look like they do. For a short time Mendel kept mice in his small flat at the monastery, albinos and browns. His aim was to breed one with the other, to see what colour their offspring would turn out. Unfortunately for him, however, his breeding centre was discovered and promptly banned by the visiting bishop, who thought the experiments in procreation unbefitting of a place of worship and celibacy.

Brother Gregor was undeterred. He got rid of the mice, and turned his attention to peas. His father had taught him how to plant and graft trees, and he used the same techniques on his small round subjects. He appropriated the monastery greenhouse, and started cultivation. The first year he planted seven different varieties of *Pisum* – tall, dwarf, yellow, green, and so on – first ensuring that they bred true (the yellow pea plants produced yellow peas, the dwarf dwarves, etc.). When they flowered, he took over nature's job, and pollinated one variety with another, carefully labelling them (yellow dwarf, tall green, and so on).

The first generation of hybrids, he noted, were

like one of their 'parent' peas – which he called the 'dominant' – not a mixture of both: a tall pea matched to a dwarf, for example, always produced tall rather than average-height offspring; a yellow crossed with a green did not give rise to striped pods. Mendel recorded his observations in large leather-bound books. The hybrids were then allowed to self-seed, while Mendel waited anxiously, like a father pacing outside a hospital delivery room. He had a hunch that he was on to something important, and he was already planning to spread out of the small greenhouse and into the extensive monastery courtyard gardens if his progeny proved to be interesting scientifically. The next generation duly emerged, and he systematically bagged, labelled and analysed them. He found, to his excitement, that in almost exactly one-quarter of the cases, the characteristics of the 'lost grandparent' – the 'recessive' – re-emerged. Thus a dwarf pea mixed with a tall one might produce tall offspring in the first generation, but when these self-fertilized, they each gave rise to a dwarf plant from one in every four seeds.

It was definitely worth moving outside. Mendel repeated the experiments, using more and more varieties of pea, and, with growing excitement, noted that the results held true. One in four plants reverted to the characteristics of their grandparent. He moved on to broad beans, fuchsias, maize and eighteen further species. Over an eight-year period, he sowed 30,000 seeds, and found that in each case – each species – there was a similar pattern, a reproducible mathematical formula.

Brother Gregor Mendel recognized what this meant, and that it was indeed both interesting and important. It was written in the peas: inheritance is passed down in entire units rather than, as was generally thought at the time, blended characteristics of father and mother. Each inherited characteristic is determined by one of two distinct particles carried by the seed (egg) and pollen (sperm). And both of these are passed down through the generations, although at any one time, only one is displayed. It explained so much: why sibling humans can differ in hair and eye colour, for example, why two brown-eyed parents can have a blue-eyed child, but not the other way around; it is the way individualism is preserved.

He was excited by his experiments, and eagerly wrote up the results, which he presented in a two-part lecture to the local scientific society in 1865. The audience clapped politely, but left without asking questions. He was surprised by their lack of enthusiasm for a subject that he thought so fundamental to our understanding of life. For a while, he carried on in private, and two years later submitted his paper, 'The Hybridization of the Garden Pea', to the *Proceedings of the Brünn Society for the Study of Natural Science*. This less-than-mainstream publication was nevertheless sent to 120 of the major European universities and societies, to Vienna, Berlin, Uppsala, Paris, Rome, St Petersburg, to the Royal, Royal Horticultural and

Linnaean Societies in London, where it was filed, unread, in large leather folders. Mendel ordered forty offprints, which he presumably sent to more distinguished botanists. But there was no reaction. No response. No recognition. The academic world apparently did not have enough time to read a paper on peas written by an unknown monk and published in an obscure journal.

In time, Brother Gregor lost heart and eventually interest in his garden. He rose to become abbot of Brünn, and on 6 January 1884, he died. The world had not recognized his work, but he knew they would. He had frequently told one of his friends, a professor of astronomy and fellow botanist, '*Meine Zeit wird schon kommen*' (My time will surely come).

It took the dawning of a new century for Mendel's experiments to be appreciated. In the spring of 1900, three botanists, working separately in three countries, simultaneously stumbled upon Mendel's paper, and credited it in their own writings on patterns of inheritance. William Bateson, a Cambridge zoologist, was inspired by their references to dig out the original work, and when he read it, on a train journey to London, something clicked; the old monk had been on the right track. As Bateson said in a lecture that evening, 'An exact determination of the laws of heredity will probably work more change in man's outlook on the world, and in his power over nature, than any other advance in natural knowledge that can be foreseen. There is no doubt whatever that these laws can be determined.' He can not have known quite how prophetic his words would prove to be.

Bateson subsequently immersed himself in the life and work of Gregor Mendel, translating his paper into English, and lecturing on its significance around the world. In 1909, one of his fellow disciples, the Danish evolutionary biologist Wilhelm Johannsen, gave a name to Mendel's units of inheritance – 'genes' – and the science of their study became known as genetics.

In the space of a few years, the forgotten monk became a scientific giant – revered and reviled. While his dissenters were determined and vocal – the Stalinist director of the Soviet Academy of Sciences, Trofim Denisovich Lysenko, even went so far as to ban the teaching of his theories and send Mendelian geneticists to the gulags – none could dismiss the impact of his work.

The search was on for the physical form of inheritance. Sperm and eggs were put under the microscope, but the gene – a notional idea, a mysterious beast – remained inaccessible. It wasn't long before scientists arrived at the theory that genes might be composed of protein. Proteins they knew to be the engines of the body; they make our hair grow, our bodies fight infection, they help us to digest, breathe, walk, run, almost everything. If genes were so important, and proteins so all-pervasive, then surely, the scientists believed, protein must form the body of genes. They already knew some proteins – enzymes – acted as switches, turning chemical reactions on and off, controlling every part of our body.

The human body is comprised of approximately 100 trillion cells, each less than 0.1 mm across. They make up every last bit of the body: brain cells, liver cells, muscle, blood and so on. Examined under intense magnification, most cells seemed to contain a small, dark bag, a nucleus. Inside each bag, it was possible to make out twenty-three pairs of short ribbons, which the German biologist, Walther Flemming, named chromosomes. In 1869, a young, modest Swiss scientist called Johann Friedrich Miescher discovered that the chromosomes in each cell nucleus were composed of more than protein. Barred from his original ambition of practising as a doctor by deafness, he had turned instead to research. He went to Germany, to study under Ernst Felix Hoppe-Seyler, the man who named haemoglobin and published the first journal of biochemistry, and under his watchful eye, set to work on the chemistry of the cell nucleus. It was a task of monumental importance, conducted at a microscopic level. Miescher started by collecting the pus-soaked bandages of wounded soldiers from a local hospital, and from these, he managed to soak out the white blood cells, and to separate their nuclei from the rest. He then teased the chromosomes from the nuclei and subjected them to intense scrutiny. These short ribbons, he discovered, were composed of an acidic, phosphate-rich mixture of protein and acid which he named nuclein.

Curious as to the chemical composition of the compound, he returned to his native Basel, to work with salmon sperm, which were known to have exceptionally large cell nuclei, from which he aimed to separate the acid from the protein. With much soaking and centrifuging, chemical dissection and manipulation, he managed to extract the pure acid, to which a pupil of his later gave a name: deoxyribonucleic acid, DNA. Miescher never publicly speculated about the function of DNA, though in a letter to his uncle Wilhelm, a doctor and his closest mentor, he mentioned his inkling that this acid might carry the hereditary message, 'just as the words and concepts of all languages can find expression in 24–30 letters of the alphabet'. But, as with Mendel, he was ahead of his time; his peers failed to follow up on his findings, and in 1895, Johann Miescher died of tuberculosis, aged fifty-one.

Even in 1944 the world was not ready for DNA. The chemist Oswald Avery was sixty-seven when, with colleagues from the Rockefeller Institute of Science in New York, he published a paper about the transforming role of DNA in inheritable pneumonia bacteria. To him, and a small band of believers, this was definite proof that the gene was composed of DNA, but again, the scientific establishment was slow to catch on. While Avery had suggested a role for DNA – as the carrier of hereditary specificity – he did not speculate as to how. Many contemporary scientists preferred to believe that DNA did not cause the transformation itself, but acted as a sort of physiological switch – a dumb molecule – that enabled protein to pass down the inherited message. What was needed was a deeper understanding of nucleic acids at the molecular level: perhaps that would inform its function? The majority of geneticists, however, were still concentrating on protein at the time, and were apparently loath to abandon something into which they had poured so much time and intellectual energy. Few turned their attention to DNA, few saw its potential; the world into which Helena Greenwood would leap with such optimism and enthusiasm just thirty years later was, to most scientists, just an obscure, uninspiring, closed book.

Fortunately – for him and for science – James Watson was attracted by the arcane. His family home in South Shore, Chicago, was filled with books, and young Jim – a pint-sized, scruffy, goofy-grinned lad who day-dreamed of becoming a famous scientist – particularly loved reading about evolution. It was with his nose stuck in a book that he first came across the gene. He was a student at the time, precocious and quick-witted. He had only been fifteen when he entered the University of Chicago, on a special fast-track experiment. At first, he displayed no outstanding ability, coasting along with B grades, preferring to spend more time in the fields with his binoculars studying birds than in the lecture theatre. He already displayed a scant respect for authority: 'You were never held back by manners, and crap was best called crap,' he wrote about himself. 'Offending somebody was always preferable to avoiding the truth, though such bluntness did not make me a social success with most of my classmates. It is lucky that for most of my college life I was still too short to see the need to effectively move outside the security of my family home.'

At home one day, he was captivated by a slim volume by the physicist Erwin Schrödinger (perhaps most popularly known for his eponymous cat) called *What is Life?*, which speculated about the physical secret of life: the so-called gene. Schrödinger knew it was encoded somehow in the chromosomes, but how and where, he was not sure. It was a challenge that caught the imagination of Jim Watson – and, on the other side of the Atlantic, a physicist called Francis Crick.

'From that point I became polarized towards finding out the secret of the gene,' Watson recalled. 'The gene being the essence of life was clearly a more important objective than how birds migrate.' By the time he was eighteen, 'I had made the decision to have the gene as my life's principal objective.'

He went to the University of Bloomington as a postgraduate, where he turned twenty-one in 1949, the year Helena Greenwood was born, and shortly afterwards, cruised to a doctorate in genetics. His research focused on the effect of X-rays on tiny viruses – phages – but he never lost sight of his central conviction, that genes were made of DNA rather than protein, that DNA was the information that describes how you build a device that looks like a human, or a horse, dog, plant, amoeba. From Indiana, Watson went to Copenhagen, but found his research there rather boring. He itched to get to work on DNA.

Maurice Wilkins inadvertently showed him the way. Watson was idling around at a seminar in Naples, when he heard Wilkins, an earnest biochemist from King's College, London, give a talk, and, still more enthrallingly, show his X-ray diffraction picture of DNA. 'Suddenly I was excited about chemistry,' Watson later wrote. He was so impressed, and so keen to meet the Englishman, that he even fantasized about his sister marrying him. But Wilkins sloped away from the meeting before Watson had a match-making opportunity.

It was not long, however, before James Watson found himself attached to the Cavendish Laboratory in Cambridge, where he found the unruly, unfocused, at times irritating – at others irritatingly brilliant – Francis Crick.

Crick's academic career had thus far been less shining. When they met, Watson was twenty-three, with his Ph.D. almost an event from prehistory, while Crick was twelve years older, and showing no signs of even settling on a subject for his. Born to a family of Northamptonshire boot-makers, Crick had determined at an early age to become a scientist. But he foresaw one snag: 'By the time I grew up . . . everything would have been discovered.' He decided to risk it anyway and emerged from London University with an unexceptional second-class degree in physics. Unable to think what else to do, he opted for further education, and found himself enmired in a research project into the viscosity of water, 'the dullest problem imaginable'.

Thankfully, the war interrupted his study, and for a time he was happily employed devising weapons of mass destruction for the Mine Design Department. With peace, however, came the necessity of finding something else to do. His interest, he decided, was in 'the borderline between the living and the non-living', what others might describe more prosaically as molecular biology. He knew little about the subject – again, Schrödinger's *What is Life?* had provided the inspiration – but he nevertheless managed to ensconce himself at the Cavendish, to the growing irritation of its director, Sir Lawrence Bragg.

'He did not have the patience to stick to his own problems, or the humility to stick to small questions,' Matt Ridley wrote of Crick. 'His laugh, his confident intelligence and his knack of telling people the answers to their own scientific questions, were getting on nerves at the Cavendish.' Watson and Crick hit it off immediately, Crick recalled in his book, *What Mad Pursuit*, 'partly because our interests were astonishingly similar and partly, I suspect, because a certain youthful arrogance, a ruthlessness, and an impatience with sloppy thinking came naturally to both of us'. They talked and talked – to the point where the rest of the unit pushed them to the front of the queue for the first available office, just to shut their ceaseless chatter and laughter behind a closed door.

Their main topic of conversation, inevitably, was the structure of DNA. They dreamed of solving the enigma, and of winning a Nobel prize for their discovery. They were spurred on by the knowledge that Wilkins and his King's College colleague, Rosalind Franklin, were closing in on the answer, through their X-ray pictures.

The Londoners were an odd, mismatched coupling: Wilkins, lean, bespectacled, a talented cook; Franklin, fiercely determined, intelligent and ambitious, and fighting to be accepted as a serious scientist in an overwhelmingly male world – much as Helena Greenwood would be twenty years later. They were less a team than a push-me-pull-you, to the extent that Franklin refused to show Wilkins her work out of irritation at being treated as a subordinate, while he was consumed to the point of virtual unproductivity by her lack of cooperation. Wilkins believed that Franklin had been hired as his technical assistant. Franklin, with a doctorate from Cambridge in physical chemistry under her belt, and four years of practical experience in X-ray diffraction and crystallography at the central chemistry laboratory in Paris, thought otherwise. So instead of pooling their resources – Wilkins' theoretical advances, and Franklin's photographs of DNA (described as 'the most beautiful

X-ray photographs of any substance ever taken') – they huddled in separate labs, and moved far more slowly than they should have.

This was fortunate for Watson and Crick. They decided to take a different approach. Instead of fiddling about with X-rays and mathematical equations, their main working tools were 'a set of molecular models superficially resembling the toys of preschool children,' Watson wrote, in *The Double Helix*. 'We could . . . see no reason why we should not solve DNA in [that] way. All we had to do was to construct a set of molecular models and begin to play . . .' They cut sheets of cardboard into hexagons of varying sizes, stocked up on drinking straws and plasticine, and set about trying to build a DNA molecule.

Their blocks were the four nitrogenous bases of DNA: adenine (A), guanine (G), thymine (T) and cytosine (C), which they believed would be linked together by a sugar-phosphate backbone. By fiddling with the different shapes, they aimed to piece them together into an attractive and regular structure.

They were convinced that this structure was somehow helical – spiral-like. It would be the neatest solution, apart from anything else, and the triple-Nobel-winning chemist and Crick's hero Linus Pauling (using the model-constructing approach) had already shown how proteins tended towards a structure that he described as an 'alpha helix'. They were shuffling the options when, in 1952, two American researchers, Alfred Hershey and Martha Chase, experimenting with bacteria, phages and a kitchen blender, announced that they had managed to prove that DNA was the unit of inheritance. But still, not how. Watson's and Crick's quest for its structure assumed a greater importance and urgency.

They fiddled and talked. They went to King's, London, to see how the opposition was doing. There, Watson met Franklin for the first time. He did not instantly take to her. To him she appeared determinedly unglamorous – as if that would somehow make her intellect more palatable – a far cry from the foreign language students occupying his fancies back in Cambridge. 'By choice she did not emphasize her feminine qualities,' he wrote. 'Though her features were strong, she was not unattractive and might have been quite stunning had she taken even a mild interest in clothes. This she did not. There was never a lipstick to contrast with her straight black hair, while at the age of 31 her dresses showed all the imagination of English blue-stocking adolescents . . . The thought could not be avoided that the best place for a feminist was in another person's lab.'

Her X-ray photographs of DNA impressed him far more, and gave the Cambridge pair the competitive impetus and inspiration they needed to redouble their efforts. More earnest manipulation of their models, a few wrong turns, and with a flash – some say of luck – Watson hit on a possible solution. Using the chemist Erwin Chargraff's data showing that there was almost exactly the same amount of A and T in each DNA molecule, and an equally similar proportion of C and G, he constructed a model which paired them together in a double helix. Miraculously, everything then fell into shape. Crick saw it and no matter how hard he tried, could not come up with a reason why it should not be the solution.

'From the start we hoped for some chemical revelation that would lead to the correct structure,' Watson wrote. 'But we never anticipated that the answer would come so suddenly in one swoop and with such finality.'

It was a true Eureka moment. What the two had discovered with their cardboard cut-out models was that DNA was like a staircase, the rungs being the AT and CG pairs, held together by hydrogen bonds; the banisters, alternating sugar and phosphate chains, climbing up in a perfectly proportioned and potentially endless spiral. For Watson and Crick, it was a stairway to scientific heaven. Each side reflected the other – like the photographic positive and negative – an A on one strand facing a T on the other (and vice-versa), a G facing a C, with each running in opposite directions. If the rungs – the hydrogen bonds – were broken in two, the A separated from the T, for instance, the ladder would peel apart, and the bases could make an attachment to a new partner – the A to a new T, the T to a new A – acting as a template for two identical ladders. DNA could copy itself infinitely using the chemical affinities between the paired letters. It showed how we are made.

Watson's and Crick's famous *Nature* article was published on 25 April 1953, a month before the coronation of Queen Elizabeth II and three and a half years after Helena Greenwood was born. The last sentence of their paper is often described as the greatest scientific understatement of all time: 'It has not escaped our notice,' they wrote, 'that the specific pairing we have postulated immediately suggests a possible copying mechanism for the genetic material.' Or, as Crick had more characteristically put it to a crowd of friends at the Eagle pub a few weeks earlier, 'We've discovered the secret of life.' It was a discovery of monumental importance, and while it hardly grabbed the attention of the headline writers, who were more captivated by the imminent royal celebrations and Edmund Hillary's first successful ascent of Mount Everest, by the time Helena had moved to her new school, Watson's and Crick's description of the structure of DNA was to be found in every biology textbook, alongside Mendel and his peas, Miescher's bandages, Chargraff and Avery.

These were the people that inspired Helena Greenwood, none more than Rosalind Franklin, who died of cancer when she was thirty-nine, before she could share the Nobel prize with Watson, Crick and Wilkins. It was their work, their discoveries, that marked the start of a new era, the birth of modern biochemistry, the impetus for a revolution in medicine. From this initial flash of inspiration flowed a deluge of discoveries. In time, came the language of inheritance, spelled out in three-letter words. These words (different combinations of the four bases, A, C, G and T) are strung together to make sentences, and thousands of these little sentences are organized into chapters: genes. In humans, 30–40,000 of these gene-chapters come together in a massive, 23-volume book, the genome. And this massive amount of information is coiled up into a double helix and repeated, in identical form, in each of the 100 trillion or so cells in our body. According to estimates, if the DNA molecules were stretched out and laid end to end, the chromosomes in a single cell would cover six foot; the chromosomes in a single body would stretch 100 billion miles.

Geneticists, with Francis Crick leading the charge, learned how the genome can both copy itself and turn itself – through the agency of RNA (ribonucleic acid) – into a protein. The original orthodoxy had been turned on its head: instead of proteins making genes, genes in fact make proteins. With remarkable speed, the decoding of the language of life began to unfurl. The science spilled out of the laboratories and into industry. Biotechnology firms raced to turn the results of pure research into applicable technology. By luring some of the best scientific brains with salaries that academia couldn't hope to match, they too started to push back the frontiers of knowledge, driving the work of the universities, much as they had originally been driven.

Gen-Probe was one of the crusaders. By the 1980s, DNA probes had become one of the most fundamental tools in genetic research. Using the knowledge unlocked by Watson's and Crick's revelations, scientists had developed the technology to create short, single-stranded chains of synthetic DNA – probes – that were mirror images of the sequence that they wanted to isolate: for every adenine, there would be a thymine; for every guanine a cytosine, and vice-versa. It was well known by then that the key to almost every biological function was encoded in DNA. Bacteria, viruses and all diseases use DNA – or its simpler analogue, RNA – to build themselves, in exactly the same way as humans do. In many cases, it is the only way in which they are identifiable. What David Kohne at Gen-Probe and scientists like him realized was that it should be possible to employ DNA probes to test a person's blood for infectious diseases by looking for alien DNA or RNA sequences.

The blood they tested contained millions of genes; human, bacterial and viral, all composed of DNA. The DNA would be first heated, to split the strands, then cut into millions of fragments using a restriction enzyme – a protein that cleaves the DNA strands at designated positions. These lengths would be immobilized by dropping them on one end of a dish of agarose gel, to which an electric current would be applied. The smaller fragments would move through the gel more rapidly than the larger ones, ending up at different positions, and this pattern would then be transferred from the gel to a nylon membrane –

via a method known as Southern blotting (after its inventor, Ed Southern).

This is where probes came into action. Primed with the correct chemicals, tagged with radioactive isotopes, they worked as tiny sequence-seeking missiles, which would first nose out and then identify targeted stretches of DNA – where the disease-causing anomalies were believed to lurk, and which were often buried anonymously in a much larger section of DNA or RNA. When the membrane was washed, only the probes that had found their images – the targeted sequences of DNA – and bound to them, would be left, making the affected sections immediately visible.

David Kohne at Gen-Probe had developed probes targeted at common infectious disorders, such as those caused by streptococcae, Hemophilius influenzae, and several sexually transmitted diseases. It was one of the first times that probe technology had been successfully applied to medical use. The process was fantastically efficient: what had previously taken weeks to diagnose through traditional culture techniques could now be identified in a matter of hours.

Helena Greenwood's challenge at Gen-Probe was to make this revolutionary technology acceptable to the marketplace – the hospitals and clinics of the world.

4

The months passed. Roger joined Helena in San Diego and they moved into a small rented cottage near the beach in Del Mar, an alluring village twenty miles north of the city centre, inhabited by the sort of rich young people who show their wealth in straight teeth, tight bodies and year-round tans. They soon settled into the typical Del Mar rhythm of long weekend walks along the wildly beautiful beach, Sunday brunch at one of a handful of pavement cafés, sailing in San Diego bay (Helena's fear of water was firmly behind her), year-round blossoming flowers and citrus trees in the garden. Immersed and inspired by her job, she grew stronger and more like her old, confident self. As spring started to squeeze up from every crevice, she began to believe that she had managed to put the events of the previous year firmly behind her.

Work was going well, especially since Sam Morishima had come down to join the team. She had called soon after she joined Gen-Probe to offer him a job. He refused. Two days later, she called again. 'Sam,' she said, 'you know you can surf down here?' It was a done deal.

'After the first call, I had done some research and

saw that this was going to be the future: antibodies in DNA,' he said. 'I told the president of Syva that I wanted to be with Helena and work in DNA probes.' Within weeks, the boy from the strawberry farms of northern California was ensconced in Helena's old room at Marylin Johns' house in La Jolla.

He immediately noticed a change in his boss: 'She looked different. At Syva, she had reported to Richard Leute and he didn't care for looks. He wanted results and she produced. At Gen-Probe, she was a vice-president, an executive, and she was taking on that role; she knew she had to look good. Her clothes were more ironed, and although she still didn't wear make-up, she combed her hair. She was very excited and very happy. Gen-Probe was on the front line of the new technology – it was like surfing, we were flying in front of a wave.'

Sam became part of Helena's family. He met Roger for the first time, went to their house on many occasions. 'At Syva, I wondered about Helena's husband. At first, I didn't even know she was married – she never talked about her life outside work. Roger reminded me of a British explorer in Africa – you know, tanned, fit, very handsome, in a safari shirt. He was friendly, but they weren't the types that were always hugging. You could tell, though, that they were on a matching frequency. I bet Helena didn't talk about work with Roger – he was like the balance to that area of her life. Her work was everything to her when she was there, and Roger was her release.'

To Helena, San Diego was the present and the future and she loved it. She started looking for a house to buy and soon found one they both loved. It was modern and white, up on the bluff with an uninterrupted view of the ocean and the little lagoon full of fresh water from the mountains to the east. The price tag was half a million dollars, but they had money from the sale of the San Francisco house as a deposit, and Helena's new salary at Gen-Probe was easily enough to cover the mortgage. Terms were agreed – the sale was due to go through in mid-summer.

In San Francisco, the file on Helena's assault was still open on Sergeant Steve Chaput's desk. He had exhausted all his leads but not given up hope. There was always the fingerprint. In March 1985, nearly a year after the assault, he got his breakthrough. Among the intelligence reports that were sent through the inter-station 'PONY' mail from Belmont Police Department, Chaput noticed a page about a suspected sex offender called David Paul Frediani. There were photographs and a written description. Even in the typical police booking shots, Frediani contrived to look both unimpressed and arrogant, as if watching a particularly boring play. He had been picked up six weeks earlier, while exposing himself to a thirteen-year-old girl through the window of her apartment. He was also being looked at for three other incidents in the same complex, the second of which caught Chaput's attention:

On 27/7/84 @ 0300hrs. a suspect similar in description entered an apartment via an unlocked balcony building and confronted 3 female tenants while sleeping, partially covering his face, and demanded they orally copulate him. He was dressed in blue jeans, with a shirt wrapped around his face.

The modus operandi was too similar to be discounted. The next day, 26 March 1985, Chaput picked up a copy of Frediani's fingerprints from the records division of the local sheriff's office. He dropped them off at the crime lab, along with the latent print lifted from the teapot found on Helena Greenwood's deck.

Three days later, the fingerprint analyst called. The prints matched; her written report was in the post.

Chaput was thrilled. At last. On 3 April, he phoned Del Mar to let Helena know. Roger answered the phone. 'We've got him,' Chaput said.

'Thank you. I'll let Helena know. I am sure she will be relieved.'

Chaput's next call was to Joe Farmer at Belmont, who was similarly delighted. It looked as if they were going to get a habitual sex offender off the streets. They arranged to meet that afternoon to discuss their next move. They collated their evidence and shared what they knew about the crimes and their suspect. Farmer had questioned Frediani following the indecent exposure charge, and knew he was not the easiest of customers. Their next step was to present their evidence to the District Attorney's sex crimes unit. The case was assigned to Martin Murray, a young high-flyer with a growing reputation.

Murray agreed that they had enough to proceed, and on 19 April 1985, obtained a warrant for David Paul Frediani's arrest on charges of burglary and the forced oral copulation of Helena Greenwood. Three days later, at ten past seven in the evening, Detectives Chaput and Farmer rang the bell of Frediani's George Avenue apartment – just half a mile down the street from the French Village.

Frediani answered the door. He was a good half a foot taller than the policemen. Chaput identified himself, and said he was investigating an incident in Atherton a little over a year before. He said he would like Frediani to come down to the station to discuss it. Frediani agreed, but asked to change his trousers first. Chaput followed him into his bedroom, trying to catch a glimpse of a hooded dark sweatshirt, or faded blue sneakers. 'I watched Frediani as he removed his trousers,' Chaput recalled in his detailed report. 'He was not wearing any underpants and there wasn't any pronounced "tan line" around his waist or legs. He then proceeded to put on a pair of blue jeans, again without any underpants.' The three of them drove back to Belmont PD.

They went into a small interview room and sat around a table, Chaput at the head, with Frediani on his left and Joe Farmer on his right. Farmer read Frediani his rights from a card: 'You have the right to remain silent. Anything you say can and will be used against you in a court of law. You have the right to talk to a lawyer and have him present while you are being questioned. If you cannot afford to hire a lawyer one will be appointed to represent you before any questioning if you wish. If you desire a lawyer at any time during my questioning, inform me of that, and further questions will not be asked until your lawyer is present. Do you understand each of these rights I have explained to you?'

'I understand.'

Chaput got up to use the telephone and when he returned, started asking questions. His scribbled notes show Frediani sparring with the detectives, denying knowledge of any assault in Atherton.

'Do you know where Atherton is?' Chaput asked.

'I know where it is but I am not familiar with it,' Frediani replied.

'Do you know anyone who lives in Atherton . . . friends, relatives?'

'No, well, the vice-president of my company lives in Atherton but I don't know where exactly.'

'Have you ever entered a house in Atherton without permission?'

'No.'

'Have you ever had any sexual contact with a female in a house in Atherton?'

'No.'

'Do you have any idea of what incident I am talking about?'

'No.'

Detective Farmer took over the questioning, asking about the incidents in the French Village. According to Chaput's formal, typed notes, 'While the two of them were in dialogue, I noticed that Frediani's hands and legs were shaking markedly. A few minutes later, even his stomach and chest were vibrating noticeably.'

The Atherton detective recalls that at that point he regained the baton. 'I hit him with it, sudden like: "We've got your fingerprints." It was like I had slugged him. His face went flush, his shoulders dropped and he started frantically gabbling: "I was drunk when I did those things. I was really drunk . . . I was so drunk I honestly didn't remember . . ."'

According to Chaput's contemporary notes, he then said, 'Sometimes I get so drunk I don't know how I made it home.'

Frediani then appeared to come to his senses. Chaput's next notes read:

Wanted lawyer.
Phoned lawyer.
Said he would like to clear it up but had to be assured anything he said wouldn't be used in court.

The policemen told him that they wanted to record any future conversations, and reread Frediani his rights. This time, he refused to waive his right to an attorney.

The interview was over. They collected a saliva sample, plucked hairs from his head, took him into the bathroom and combed through his pubic area for more hair samples, then drove him to the San Mateo County jail in Redwood City. There, phials of blood were drawn, and Frediani was formally booked for the offence, with bail set at $100,000. At 10.30 p.m. on 22 April 1985 – fifty-four weeks after the attack on Helena Greenwood – David Paul Frediani was locked in a cell to await the preliminary hearing that would determine whether he would stand trial for burglary, forced oral copulation and gun use. The only evidence that linked him to the case was a single fingerprint, but that could be enough. In the courtrooms of the world, fingerprints and blood and semen stains were increasingly playing the dominant role. Forensic science was leaping from the test tube to tap criminals on their shoulders like a triumphant child in a life or death game of grandmother's footsteps.

It was in the eighteenth century that forensic science – the study and application of science to the law – came into practice in the Western world. It developed in parallel – occasionally in conflict – with the formation of the modern detective force. The challenges faced by Steve Chaput in 1985 were essentially the same then: the issue of identity – how to connect a finger's smudge or a stain on a pillowcase to a face in the crowd.

The discovery in the mid-nineteenth century that no two people had the same fingerprint – each possessed a unique maze of ridges, whorls and swirls – gave rise to the science of fingerprinting, the first great leap forward in crime detection since the early law enforcers faced off against their criminal prey. In 1892, Charles Darwin's cousin, the mutton-chopped eugenicist, Francis Galton, published a detailed study of the new science, *Finger Prints*. By the turn of the century, Edward Henry, a former civil servant in India who had been using fingerprinting with great success on the sub-continent, persuaded the Metropolitan Police of its efficacy and in 1901, it became Scotland Yard's official method of identification.

Fingerprinting was quickly adopted around the world. In 1902, Germany, Switzerland, Hungary, Austria, Denmark and Spain took it on board followed, in 1903, by the United States. In well over a century of examination, in police investigation after investigation, case upon case, there has yet to be an example of any two persons having matching fingerprints, even identical twins. Now practically every policeman is trained in the art of collecting fingerprints, and every police crime lab has a fingerprint analyst. The techniques employed to reveal – and identify – fingerprints have become increasingly sophisticated. Chemicals like ninhydrin can stain absorbed fingerprint sweat patterns on paper, making them visible, while superglue fumes can lift prints off human skin. At the end of the 1970s, the Federal Bureau of Investigation in the United States started developing its Automated Fingerprint Identification System (AFIS), which these days scans 85,000 fingerprints each year into a massive central computer, designed to hold up to 65 million sets of prints.

Even from the early days of fingerprinting, however, it was abundantly clear to the clever criminal that detection could be avoided by taking the simple precaution of wearing gloves. It became increasingly obvious that detectives could not rely on fingerprints alone. Perhaps bodily fluids could identify a criminal as reliably?

Bizarrely, it was a fictional detective, the incomparable Sherlock Holmes, who inspired the so-called 'scientific detectives'. In 1887, when Holmes made his first appearance on the printed page in *A Study in Scarlet*, he was in a chemical laboratory, brandishing a test tube, and claiming that he had 'found a re-agent which is precipitated by chemistry and by nothing else'. It was, he asserted to Dr Watson, 'the most practical medico-legal discovery for years. Don't you see that it gives us an infallible test for blood stains?'

It was a clear case of fiction pre-dating reality, this time by more than a decade. When Conan Doyle wrote this, there was no way to determine whether a dried bloodstain was human or animal. Microscopic analysis was of little use, as blood cells lose their shape and clump together when they dry. Attempts at reconstitution by mixing the dried blood into a solution of caustic potash and alcohol failed if the stains were too old or too small. Criminals across the world were escaping the net of justice by claiming that bloodstains found on their clothing came from their Sunday joint, while there appeared to be a definite statistical link between poachers and chronic nosebleed sufferers.

The turn of the century brought two discoveries that would underpin the new discipline of forensic serology. In Germany in the summer of 1900, Paul Uhlenhuth, an assistant professor at the Institute of Hygiene in Griefswald, found a method of determining the origin of unknown blood using a precipitating antiserum. (A known animal's serum – the clear substance left when the red and white cells are extracted from blood – is imbued with antibodies, and then mixed with an unknown blood sample. If the species match, the serum reacts and the proteins from the sample float to the bottom of the solution in a cloudy white precipitate. If they do not, nothing happens.)

Uhlenhuth realized the forensic potential of his discovery. He produced a range of serums from different animals, against which blood could be tested: if it precipitated the dog serum, for example, then the unknown blood came from a dog, and so on for cats, pheasants, human beings . . .

In December 1900, he tried his method on bloodstains of different ages. He dissolved them in a saline solution, then tested them with his range of serums containing the antibodies of different animals. It worked just as it had with fresh blood: the whitish precipitate would form in the serum containing antibodies from that animal, and that animal alone. In the future, murderers would not be able to claim bloodstains on their shirts came from the family's dinner. Forensic science had caught up with the imagination of Arthur Conan Doyle.

Uhlenhuth's work was greeted with fanfare by the criminological world, who immediately set out to develop a set of practices and controls to guard against errors. Over the years, the 'precipitin test', and derivations of it, became standard practice in every serological and forensic laboratory in the world.

Across the border in Austria, the fundamental importance to crime detection of the almost simultaneous discovery of Dr Karl Landsteiner was not so readily recognized. Landsteiner, a shy man in his early thirties, an assistant professor of Pathology at the University of Vienna, had been drawn from medical practice and back into research out of frustration at the shortcomings of medicines in dealing with many illnesses. Particularly, he wanted to find out why so many blood transfusions – more than 60 per cent – resulted in blood clots and death. He suspected that blood contained properties which were not universally shared, and set out to devise an experiment mixing human blood cells and serum together. He drew samples of his own blood, and that of five fellow doctors in his department. He separated the cells from the serum, then carefully mixed samples of each with the other.

Some mixtures clumped together – agglutinated – while others didn't. He analysed the different reactions, and came to the conclusion that blood could be broken down into four groups (now known as 'A', 'B', 'AB' and 'O', after the antigens found in the red blood cells). Blood serum contains antibodies, known as 'anti-A' and 'anti-B'. People with blood group A have the anti-B antibody and vice-versa; people with AB have neither antibody, while O people have both anti-A and anti-B antibodies in their serum. What this means, in effect, is that a person's blood group can be easily determined by injecting a small amount of a known antibody. If, say, anti-A is added to the blood sample, and the blood cells clump, then the blood comes from someone who is group A, and so on.

Landsteiner published his findings on 14 November 1901 in an Austrian journal. There was little immediate acclaim. It was only twenty years later, after failing to get tenure at the University of Vienna and moving to the Rockefeller Foundation in New York, that his work was truly appreciated, and another decade before he was awarded his Nobel prize. His work had made it possible, among other things, to give a blood transfusion without the danger of serious clotting. It also led to the discovery that blood groups are among the traits inherited according to Mendelian genetic laws. But it would be several more years before blood-typing would be applied in the forensic field.

It took a suspicious Italian wife to provide the impetus. On 7 September 1915, a small, stooped man walked into the Institute of Forensic Medicine at the University of Turin and asked to be directed to the office of Dr Leon Lattes. He was wearing his best suit and a brown hat, and carrying a flat package neatly wrapped in newspaper and tied up with string. He found himself in the lab where Lattes spent much of his time working on blood groupings, particularly in exploring their potential in criminal work.

The small man introduced himself as Renzo Girardi, a construction worker from one of the poorer areas of the city. He handed his package to Lattes. Inside was a white shirt, with two brownish spots on its tails. 'Have you been involved in a crime?' Lattes asked Girardi, who shook his head. His story soon came tumbling out. Three months previously, at the beginning of June, Girardi had gone to visit friends in his home village, a few miles outside Turin. They had ended up in a tavern, and he only returned late to his house in the city. There he found his chronically jealous wife waiting up and clearly spoiling for a fight. She accused him of infidelity and he was up half the night protesting his innocence. He eventually fell asleep fully clothed.

The next morning, when he took off his white shirt, he saw the two stains for the first time. He had no idea where they came from, but his wife thought she did: they were another woman's blood, she screamed, she had been right. From that moment on, his life had been hell. His wife had consulted soothsayers and fortune tellers, all of whom agreed that her husband had been philandering. He left for work in the morning in a shower of insults and returned to a barrage of accusations. But he refused to admit his guilt.

He was a poor man, Girardi told Lattes, but he would give everything he had if the good dottore could prove that the blood spots did not come from marital infidelity. Lattes felt sorry for Girardi, as well as bemused at the manner of practical opportunity that fate had served him to test Landsteiner's blood grouping theories on dried stains. He agreed to take the case.

Lattes' first job was to try to discover the blood group of the dried stains. First, he carefully restored the blood to its original liquid consistency – he cut the fabric around the stain and weighed it, then subtracted the weight of an identical swatch of fabric. He dropped the stained cloth into a test tube containing the appropriate amount of distilled water and saline solution, and left it overnight. The stain dissolved into the solution, and the next morning, Lattes was able to remove the tiny piece of white cloth from the dark solution.

He first ran Uhlenhuth's precipitin test, which showed the blood was human. He then placed a drop of the solution on each of two dimpled slides and added fresh A cells to one and B to the other. Within half an hour, the B cells had agglutinated: the serum was clearly from group A blood.

Lattes then ran Landsteiner's tests on a sample of Girardi's blood: he was also type A. He had a sense that the little man was innocent, so before going any further, he invited him to come in for a medical examination. He quickly found the problem: Girardi suffered not from a roving eye, but intermittent prostate trouble, which led to occasional bleeding of the urethra. Girardi, nevertheless, was delighted, and as Lattes wrote in his account of the case, 'The result restored peace to the family.'

Over the following years, Lattes, and a growing band of fellow forensic serologists, were called in to use both the precipitin test and blood grouping in an increasing numbers of cases. Although they acknowledged that they were nowhere near being able to tell whether a bloodstain came from a particular person – the groupings were far too large for that – and it was of no help if the victim and suspect shared the same blood type, the techniques proved to be powerful in excluding suspects, narrowing down the list of potential culprits, and above all, as tools to produce a confession.

Their work was made easier when, in 1925, Karl Landsteiner and a Japanese team from the Imperial University of Hokkaido simultaneously discovered that the same blood antigens are secreted into other bodily fluids – semen, saliva, tears and sweat – by 80 per cent of the population. Not only could a murderer be tracked by his blood, but a rapist could be identified by his semen.

Once Paul Frediani had been arrested, Chaput sent his blood and urine samples off to the lab, in an attempt to determine whether they were of the same blood group as the semen stain that had been found on Helena's blue flowery sheets. If they matched, as well as the fingerprint, it would be another important pointer to his suspect's guilt.

Martin Murray telephoned Helena the following week from the San Mateo DA's office. 'Would you be willing to testify at the preliminary hearing?' he asked.

'Yes, of course.'

'Would you be available on May 7th?'

It was sooner than she had expected. 'I had better check at work, but yes, I am sure that would be all right.'

The next day, Helena went in to see Tom Adams. She was clearly uncomfortable.

'I need to go up to San Francisco for a couple of days,' she said.

Adams looked at her. 'Sure,' he replied.

But instead of leaving, Helena sat down, and the whole story tumbled out, the attack, her fears, the counselling, moving down to San Diego.

'I had the distinct impression she was really afraid of the guy,' Adams says. He asked her if she was sure she wanted to testify, and she nodded. 'She was determined.'

She and Roger flew up to San Francisco the night before the preliminary hearing, and stayed with the Christophers. She met with Martin Murray in the morning and that afternoon, dressed in a navy cotton suit, Helena walked into the courtroom in Redwood City.

5

8 May 1985. The double doors swing open on the worn courtroom in the southern suburb of San Francisco. David Paul Frediani makes his way to the defence table on the second day of the preliminary hearing into his sexual assault case. He is tall, built like an American football star with strong shoulders and long legs. His face is broad, almost flat, and tanned, dark hair curls over the collar of his grey sports jacket, an inch too long for Waspy respectability. He has full lips, and dark eyes with thick lashes. He looks like an advertising executive, or a property developer, or the womanizing son of a Hollywood mafia don.

The prosecution has not finished presenting its case. The previous day had seen Helena Greenwood; today, Martin Murray calls Patrick Akana. The young Atherton police officer describes in a soft voice how he had been called over to 90 Walnut Avenue on Sunday 8 April 1984 by Helena Greenwood and Thomas Christopher. They had shown him the teapot, he had pulled on latex gloves, picked it up and taken it back to the station, along with a brass pot found near by. He had dusted both objects for fingerprints, then sent the teapot off to the lab for analysis.

Carl Hill, the supervising evidence technician at the

San Mateo Sheriff's forensic lab, explains, as he has many hundreds of times – to people who have heard them as often – the underlying principles of fingerprint identification: 'They are based on the fact that fingerprints are formed in the first three to four months of the foetal period; they remain the same throughout life unless permanently scarred or decomposition sets in after death.'

He had overseen the analysis of the fingerprints taken from the white teapot and the crime scene. These he had compared to the card of Frediani's prints, taken after his arrest for indecent exposure.

'Were you able to make a comparison?'

'Yes, I was.'

'Were you able to form an opinion based on the comparison?'

'I found that the latent was the right middle finger of the card marked Frediani, David Paul.'

'Is that a positive identification?'

'Yes.'

Collins' cross-examination only manages to elicit that, of all the fingerprints Hill had examined from the scene, only one was clear enough for full analysis, a single print found under the lip of the teapot. After studying it using a microscope, he found sixteen separate points of comparison, all of which matched.

The prosecution rests. Frediani leans over to talk to his attorney. They have learned nothing new – the case rests on that single fingerprint found outside Helena Greenwood's house, together with her testimony that he has the same 'height and type of build' as the man who had attacked her thirteen months previously. He cannot believe that he will be convicted on such flimsy evidence, but Collins has warned him that he must be prepared to go to trial. He does not know his lawyer well – he found Craig Collins' name in the yellow pages at the time of his arrest for the indecent exposure. When they met the first time, the attorney had told him that he had worked as an assistant district attorney before starting his own practice, argued from the opposing table more times than he could count, knew the courtroom from both sides. Collins had never asked whether he had committed the sexual assault – only whether he had an alibi to his whereabouts at the time it occurred. They would discuss his defence in detail once they knew for sure whether the case was going to court.

Sitting in the gallery behind them is Andrea. She had been adamant about taking time off from work to support Frediani. Helena Greenwood is not in court: on the witness stand the previous day, she was calm, detached almost, in the way she had recounted the cold facts of what had happened. Does she really think Frediani was her attacker? She is the cause of his current uncomfortable predicament, yet she did not point to his face and say, 'That's the man.'

Collins calls Detective Stephen Chaput as his first witness. Frediani watches as the policeman crosses the floor from the prosecution table, to climb to the witness stand. Despite a naturally jolly face, he looks serious, much as he had when Frediani first met him, outside his door, on the evening of his arrest. The policeman, it appears, finds it galling to be standing there as a defence witness.

They start with the formalities, but Collins is soon straddling his favourite harp.

'For the record, would you personally refer to the defendant sitting next to me as a half-black?' he asks Chaput.

Murray objects. 'Irrelevant.'

'Sustained.'

'I don't think it's irrelevant. Pardon me . . .' Collins starts again, but the judge is having none of it.

'Sustained. That's a conclusion for the trier of fact . . .'

'I understand. You are probably right – all right. You are right.'

'You don't have to agree with me,' the judge tells him, 'as long as you abide by what I say.'

Beside Collins, Frediani looks down at his fingernails.

'All right. Do you observe any Negroid features of Mr Frediani?'

'Objection. Irrelevant.'

'Sustained.'

Collins then reads out the bulletin released through the Secret Witness Program on 13 April 1984. 'Suspect description: Hispanic or light-complected black male, 22–28 years, 6–0 tall, slim build, dark hair, dark eyes.' Collins goes through those characteristics one by one: his client is 6–3, white, thirty-one years old.

'Do you know the colour of his eyes?' he asks, indicating Frediani.

'Well, I thought they were brown. But . . . I am told they are hazel.'

'Have you looked at his eyes?'

'Not real closely.'

'Do you see the blue rim around the iris of the eye? And then it gets green as it gets toward the pupil . . . As you were sitting next to the defendant yesterday, did you ever look into his face?'

'I glanced a couple of times. It was more the profile I saw, though, because he was always looking straight ahead.'

Chaput concedes that no weapon had been found at Frediani's apartment, that no car identified with Frediani was seen near the scene, that none of the prints found inside the house matched those of Frediani. 'I believe there were some [prints] taken, either around the doorknob or on the front door. All the prints that we did take, smudges, whatever, were lifted, were sent up to the laboratory to see if any could be identified. The only prints that were identifiable out of everything that went up there were the ones taken off the teapot.'

Chaput reports that analysis of the semen found on the flowery pillowcase and sheets is underway at the San Mateo crime lab, as is a comparison between the pubic hairs found beside the bed and a sample taken from Frediani on the evening of his arrest. 'I spoke to Mona Ng, who is the criminalist doing the testing . . . She had completed two of the tests that I requested on the serological samples. She did the ABO types, which did match the defendant. She also did PGM types, which was the same as the defendant. But she said it put him as a type O secretor, which is not a terribly uncommon situation among adult males. I asked her if she could do any further testing of any other enzymes and she said she would attempt to do that.'

Craig Collins immediately moves for a continuance of the preliminary hearing pending the results of the enzyme tests and hair analysis. He is trying to buy time. Judge Judith Koslowski, however, is not keen. 'Well, first of all, the pubic hairs – the value of that, I think, is minimal. We don't know whose pubic hairs they are. The husband had access, the wife had access to the bed. Maybe guests have been in that bedroom. So the value of the pubic hair comparison is minimal.'

'Yes. I think the semen is a little stronger,' Collins suggests.

'He's an O secretor,' maintains the judge. 'You have got fingerprints with sixteen points of identification.'

'On a teapot *outside* the house.'

'Well, but the obvious implication of the circumstantial evidence is that it was moved by the assailant who was entering.'

'I certainly understand that, Judge. I make the motion because this is a mandatory state prison case and I just want to exert extreme caution to do what I am required to do to fulfil my role to the defendant.'

'Motion denied. Would you stand, Mr Frediani?' He once more rises to his feet. Despite Collins' warnings, he still believes the case will be dismissed, evaporate, be forgotten. He appears calm as the judge makes her ruling:

'It appears to me that the offences alleged in the complaint have been committed. To wit, a one count violation of 459 of the Penal Code, which is burglary, and a one count violation of 288 (a) (c), forcible oral copulation, has been committed and that there is reasonable and probable cause to believe that you have committed these offences, therefore you are held to answer for those crimes. Further, I make the finding that there is reasonable and probable cause to believe that a firearm was used in these cases. You are ordered to appear in the superior court before the presiding judge of the criminal department on May 23rd at 9 a.m. Bail, which has previously been set at $100,000 . . .'

Martin Murray jumps up: 'Well, your Honour, it was actually set at $100,000. For some reason, I believe, it was reduced to $25,000. I don't consider that adequate bail for an offence such as this. With the mandatory prison provisions . . . the defendant is looking at a possibility of ten years . . . If a jury were to find that the burglary was committed with the intent to commit theft, he could receive an additional six years consecutive to the top of that. So we are talking about a range of possibly sixteen years in the state prison. I don't think that $25,000 bail is adequate for that type of sentencing with a mandatory provision.'

Now Collins is standing: 'If I can just indicate to the court, for the purposes of responding to Mr Murray's observations, that this was already aired extensively at Mr Frediani's arraignment. He is a lifelong resident of the Bay area. He works for Lincoln Properties as an executive.'

The judge asks: 'What is Lincoln Properties?'

'It's a property company that manages and builds large condominiums and apartment houses, and they also manage the apartment houses that they build. He has significant contacts here.

'He is before the court a second time in his life – this court, that is to say. He was arrested in February for the misdemeanour of indecent exposure. The circumstances of that are simply, for the court's purposes of setting bail, he was standing outside of an apartment house and was viewed by a young girl looking out of the window. When Mr Frediani was arrested, he claimed that he was urinating. The girl said he was masturbating . . . The $25,000 bail is very substantial. There has been no showing that he's about to flee. He has been co-operative with the police department in this case.

'. . . Mr Frediani is now seeing a Doctor Thomas Samuels, a clinical psychologist, three times a week. I can only indicate to the court that there is – if Mr Frediani were going to another place, as has been suggested by Mr Murray, it would have already happened.

'. . . There's no new information, respectfully, and Mr Murray will confirm this, that nothing was revealed in the preliminary that wasn't known to the prosecution at the time the original complaint was filed and, particularly, at the time of the original setting of bail. There's no reason to detain the defendant pre-trial here unless the court has some reasonable expectation that he is going to flee.'

'Well, what I am weighing in my mind, the crime is very serious . . .' the judge intones.

'I understand that, Judge. All I can say is that there is ongoing, three-times-a-week, intensive counselling by Dr Samuels with the defendant. It seems to me that this is a case that would probably be resolved at some point and not tried.' Collins is hinting at a pre-trial deal with the DA.

Judge Koslowski is apparently convinced: 'Bail will remain as set: $25,000.'

The trial is scheduled for 16 September.

Paul Frediani was shaken by the preliminary hearing. Everything had been going so well; he had a good job, a nice apartment in a city he loved, a pretty girlfriend and a BMW. He had come so far, and now it was like someone was walking up to the blackboard of his life, brandishing a wet cloth. He would need his parents' help with his attorney's fee. He did not like to think how they would react.

His parents live not only on the other side of the

country, but in a different world to San Francisco, cocooned in a place where respectability is a currency as valuable as Bay shore property. Paul's father is second-generation American – his parents had joined the spaghetti run from Italy in the early 1920s, and settled on the East Coast. There, they had instilled into their young son a reverence for their new culture: he would grow up not as an immigrant but as an American, speaking English and eating hamburgers with hot sauce. After graduating from high school, Frediani senior clipped his hair even shorter and did the patriotic thing: he joined the United States Air Force. It was while stationed in Denver, Colorado, in the early 1950s, that he met his future wife.

She was a southern girl from New Mexico, striking to look at, with an apple-pie American face that could have been used to sell home-baked cookies. She was smart too, and independent, working as a secretary on the base. For a time, they worked side by side in the same building. He was smitten by her, and she grew to like the big, proud man with the open smile. They started seeing each other out of working hours, and within no time, it seemed, they were married and Paul had turned up. He was born with a club foot, his toe touching his ankle. It was the worst case the doctor said he had ever seen.

Everything was going rather fast: one minute they were a handsome young couple dancing to big bands and holding hands in the movies, and the next they had a young son with a disability and no one to help them. They decided to move back to his homeland – the north-eastern border of the United States, a prospering town with plenty of work and a big Italian family, eager to embrace the new bambino. For the first years, they lived in one half of his parents' duplex. It was not always easy – the senior Fredianis had not slung off their heritage completely, and they could not hide their disappointment that their son had not married a Catholic. Paul's mother tried her best; she learned to make a lasagne to rival her mother-in-law's, but it was still frustrating living under their protective wings. Her husband had found a good job at a big industrial plant in the city, and she worked as a secretary to a doctor – the sooner they got the money together to buy a home of their own, the better.

When Paul was three, they moved to what was then countryside, about ten miles south of the city. Their house was soon immaculate, shining white clapperboard with black shutters, plumped in two and a half acres of fields and orchards. Deer and pheasant would venture out from the woods and graze on their lawn. Paul's father had always been an avid huntsman – as a child, his father had taken him shooting in the woods and to fish in the great lake just north of the city. Living in the country, he was like a kid in a fairground: he could step out of his back door with his gun and start hunting. As soon as Paul was old enough, he would go with his father on these expeditions: the big man and his limping son, always accompanied by Paul's black Labrador, Jinx.

Paul spent a lot of time with his grandmother – she would look after him while his mother was working, and he stayed with her and his grandfather sometimes at weekends. He liked it; they had a concrete drive, and he would ride his tricycle up and down and along the sidewalks, and play with his friend next door. When he was four, Donna was born and Paul started kindergarten. His mother stopped working to look after her children.

In many ways, they were the essence of the American suburban family: the Frediani parents working hard to make improvements to their house, building new rooms, taming the garden; the children running errands and playing Little League baseball. 'Throughout the years we cut down huge old apple trees,' Paul Frediani recalled. 'It seemed like there was always one being cut up for firewood. Cutting up an apple tree by hand saw and axe would take weeks. I would help however I could, cutting the small stuff and then stacking the wood piles. We'd burn the remaining branches in open fires. I can remember helping my dad plant pine saplings around the entire perimeter of the property; at least these kinds of trees didn't provide the litter of apples all over the lawn.' One summer, Paul and his father built a swimming pool together – a tall, fibreglass tub, sitting on top of the back terrace – and when his parents weren't looking, Paul would climb on to the roof of the house and dive in.

He spent long periods of his childhood wearing an

uncomfortable brace on his leg. The club foot was a problem that had to be sorted out, and from as far back as he could remember, Paul was as familiar with doctors' surgeries and children's wards as basketball hoops and cinemas. 'At age seven, I went in for major reconstructive surgery on my ankle. The plan was to open it up and reposition the heel, and also add a bone graft from my shin. I really dreaded this, even though they said it was going to help me walk better. I will always remember how much pain I was in when I woke up after the six-hour operation. I felt like they had lied to me. As they wheeled the gurney back to my room, I yelled at everyone I could see: "You lied to me." I feel terrible about it now as I remember the looks of concern on my parents' faces. I'm sure they were feeling bad enough without me blaming them.' It was only the first shot of morphine that quietened him.

A week later, and the pain was wearing off. He started racing along the corridors in his wheelchair, and visiting the other kids. 'I have a vivid memory of one baby with a head the size of a basketball. I learned really young that there were many kids much worse off than me. But I would still get bitter sometimes because all in all, although I was active and athletic, I was always in pain. The more I ran, the greater the pain, but I would try to hide the limp as much as possible as I got older. I was very self-conscious of it. My lower leg was skinny, my ankle thicker and my foot shorter by four sizes.' He stopped wearing shorts when he didn't have to: his mother told him that he was lucky he wasn't a girl and didn't have to wear a dress every day.

Paul and Donna shared a room for years, but they didn't get on well in those days. Donna had her own health problems – she was diagnosed with rheumatoid arthritis at an early age, and spent years wearing a back brace and going through painful treatments and operations. She was the glint in her father's eye – Paul was closer to his mother. He felt his father was too strict, demanding that he work hard, mow the lawn – a job he hated – shovel snow from the sidewalk. Paul would complain to his mother, but she just advised him to do what his father asked.

As he grew older, he became increasingly rebellious. He began to resent the conservative clothes he was made to wear, the ultra-short haircuts, the enforced Sunday trip to the local Methodist church (his mother had prevailed in the question of family religion). He was always being told to set a good example to Donna, and later Steve, who was born when Paul was ten. Steve did not escape the health problems that seemed to plague the family – he was born with no colon, and so it was back to the hospital for more operations. Paul remembers when he was in his teens, at junior high school, the three Frediani children had the same bedtime – eight o'clock – and were all forced to drink milk at every meal. He did not like milk.

Paul's father had not been an exceptional student

– he was a doer rather than a thinker. But he hoped that, through his son, he could find academic achievement, success in a white-collar world. He knew Paul had the ability – his son had inherited his wife's brains, he was proud to say. But he felt it was his job to chivvy him along. He used more stick than carrot to do this. Paul remembers once getting a 'C' grade, where he had been accustomed to only 'A's: his father went straight to his basketball game and, in front of everyone, demanded that the coach release him from the team until the 'C' was corrected. Why, thought Paul, humiliated, couldn't he have come to talk to me in private to hear my side of what happened?

The Fredianis were ambitious, particularly Paul's mother. She had been cleaved from her childhood on the plains of New Mexico, to live in a sophisticated eastern city which for months each year was buried under snow. She had thrown herself into the Frediani clan's world, but she wanted more for her children – a life of travel, culture and friends whose names did not necessarily end with 'i' or 'o'. She dreamed of a house in the northern suburbs, made of stone, and set in formal gardens. Her children were all good-looking, well-spoken and bright – she wanted them to conquer the world.

Paul became increasingly resentful of his parents and the demands he felt they were placing on his life. He had never liked being told what to do, and as he grew older, into his mid-teens, he confronted his parents' demands on him with resistance or aloofness, in an attempt to convey the impression, at least, that he was in control. At the same time, at high school, he was becoming increasingly confident, and with this came popularity. With his mother's sharp brain, schoolwork was easy. 'I was either first or second in all my classes until junior high. Then I guess I realized that the cool kids did not get the best grades. By high school, I was a "B" student. I knew I could have done better, but I also had no idea of what I wanted to be, or in what to major at college.'

His parents could not understand what had happened. They knew he was capable of better, but any discussion of his grades turned into a confrontation, usually ending by Paul stalking out of the room. Those final years of academic lassitude blew his chance of getting into a top-notch college, but Paul was more concerned about friends than grades when he was seventeen, and he needed a way to prove that he was cool during school hours. His parents refused to allow him to date, and he was the only one among his friends with a curfew – now 9 p.m. on week nights – and so when they all went to the drive-in movies, he had to beg someone to make a special trip to drop him home.

'Throughout high school, I was outgoing with the guys, and terribly shy around the girls. My first date was the senior prom. About a week before, I was walking along with Linda Breiner, the student body president. I was just casually asking who she was going with. It had never occurred to me that no one had asked her. I mean, she was very pretty and outgoing, head cheerleader and all that. She just says she's going by herself as no one has asked her. So I said, "Well, do you want to go with me?" I really didn't expect her to accept, but she was ecstatic and I was pleasantly shocked. She made me feel great. If not for her, I probably would not have gone – that's how shy I was. The whole night was a blast. I got home around 6 a.m., and my parents never said a word.'

Paul's choice of college was governed by his grades and by geography: he wanted to be far from home. He applied to his mother's alma mater, Eastern New Mexico University, and in August 1972, flew for the first time to school, with two suitcases. Everything was new: the landscape, the faces, the smell of the heat. Used to being part of a close-knit community – he graduated from high school with 80 per cent of his kindergarten class – he was now the outsider among childhood friends. It gave him the freedom to reinvent himself; no longer was he the guy with the straight clothes and early curfew. He could grow his hair and wear what he liked; for the first time, he felt free. His initial plan was to major in engineering, but when he discovered that the workload was nearly half as much again as regular courses, and joined a fraternity which promised to take up much of his energy, he switched to business administration.

He took to collegiate life like a tiger to the jungle. The fraternity was his focal point, and he loved the new family it provided him with. They had parties, played sports together, went for wild midnight jaunts across the New Mexican plains. Paul felt truly happy; at last he was becoming the person he wanted to be.

A decade later, and he was contemplating how to approach his parents to ask for money to pay an attorney to represent him in a sexual assault case. It would be humiliating, even though he knew they would stand by him, believe him when he said that it was all just a terrible mistake that would be resolved when the case came to trial.

That is what he believed himself most days. In the months following the preliminary hearing, his life had returned to something approaching normality. He had tried to avoid telling his friends that he had been arrested, though he had been forced to tell his office – he knew the police would be contacting them. His supervisor had believed his assurance that it would all be resolved; Paul had always been an excellent employee, hard-working, effective, and responsible. While he could not continue working under these conditions, it was arranged for him to be put on administrative leave pending the result of the trial. If he was found innocent, his job would be waiting for him the day after the verdict.

In the meantime, he was on what amounted to a holiday. He lay beside the pool at his apartment complex, played tennis, went for bike rides, to the gym, the movies, to see that pointless Dr Samuels.

And then, just as he was trying to come to terms with the ordeal ahead, Andrea sprang her surprise.

Their relationship had been under strain since his arrest. The apartment they had been sharing had been sold, and she had moved back into her townhouse, though they continued to see each other a few evenings a week and on weekends. He had answered an advertisement for a flatmate in another apartment in his complex. It was a two-bedroom, two-bathroom apartment, and the landlady, a quiet young teacher called Barbara Powell, seemed decent enough, different to his normal set. After checking his references, she had accepted him and he moved in. One evening a few weeks later, Andrea bounded up the stairs with her news.

'I'm pregnant,' she told him. 'I'm going to have twins.'

She was clearly delighted, but for Paul it was like another heavy weight landing on the seesaw of his life.

6

In the height of the summer, the races come to Del Mar. Six days a week for six weeks a year, the streets of Del Mar village are crammed with Range Rovers, BMWs and jaunty open-topped sports cars, the restaurants and shops overflowing with out-of-towners. The small cottage that Helena and Roger rented while they waited to complete on their new house was only a couple of hundred yards from the main gate of the Fairgrounds racetrack. It was a tiny brick bungalow, painted a murky green, with glass windows that reached from ceiling to floor. Faded blue director's chairs stood on the expanse of wooden deck which hugged the front and side of the house. With little time to transform the garden, they placed terracotta pots, filled with bright red and pink geraniums, in every corner. A tall bamboo fence surrounded the house and deck. The sailing boat lived on a trailer in the large dirt parking lot. The cottage was simple inside and out. They slept on a mattress on the floor, in mismatched sheets.

The glitziness and scrum of the races was not particularly Helena's and Roger's scene, and so, in their first summer in Del Mar, they oriented themselves towards the beach, where they swam and went for long walks. Their cottage was on 23rd Street, just across the coastal highway from the ocean, and although it was a short, dead-end road, bordered to the east by the railway, there was plenty of human traffic. Theirs was the last house on the north side of the street. Beyond it, a drainage channel ran through scrubland beside the railway. There was a heavy sleeper across the channel, and a path worn over the tracks, leading between the bus stop on the coast road, and the race course, a favourite route for carless gamblers. The trains ran at walking speed here, tooting pedestrians off the line.

22 August 1985. Four days before Helena's thirty-sixth birthday, the sun rose in a cloudless sky, as it almost always does on the southern border of California. The alarm went off as usual at 6.15. Roger got up first, showered, and went to the kitchen to make toast and tea, while Helena was in the bathroom. They ate breakfast together and discussed their plans for the evening. At eight o'clock, when Roger left for work in San Clemente – a pleasant hour's drive along the coast to the north – Helena was in her underwear, ironing a royal blue cotton suit. She normally left later than he did: her office was closer, and she often telephoned Europe from home – before close of business east of the Atlantic.

After a series of calls to London, at 8.37 she dialled her old boss, Richard Leute, in San Francisco. They talked for eighteen minutes. She was due to drop in to see her realtor, Donna Lilly, to look over the loan documents for the new house, on her way to work. She gathered those papers, her things for the office and a yoghurt for lunch, and headed towards her cream MG, parked in the drive beyond the bamboo fence.

But she didn't turn up for her meeting with Donna Lilly, nor for a business conference at Gen-Probe scheduled for 10 a.m. Her secretary, Robbi Loiterton, was surprised at this most uncharacteristic behaviour. Initially she thought that Helena must have been having car problems – the MG was notoriously unreliable. Sam Morishima had a gut feeling that something was wrong. 'I had been to her house the previous night for a barbecue,' he recalls. 'We were there to celebrate the team being, at last, in place. Helena was excited and full of plans for the future. She talked about the possibilities that DNA technology was opening up. That next morning, I drove on the freeway past the Del Mar exit, and I had this strong feeling that I should drop by 23rd Street on my way. But I told myself that was stupid – I would see Helena as soon as I got to the office.'

Sam hovered over Robbi's shoulder most of the morning, urging her to call Helena at home, again and again. But the phone was never answered. Most members of the small staff dropped by Robbi's desk at some point during the morning, to find out whether Helena had showed up yet, and when she was still not there for her one o'clock meeting with the vice-presidents and staff of Gen-Probe, they called Roger. He raced home. He turned into their dead-end street, parked, got out and walked to the tall, bamboo gate. But he couldn't open it: something was blocking the way. Peering over, he saw his wife, slumped on the ground. Her royal blue skirt was hoiked up over her hips; office papers were scattered across the lawn, fluttering in the early afternoon breeze.

Helena was dead. Strangled. Aged thirty-five. Her face, arms and legs were covered in cuts, her tights were torn. Her wallet and other valuables were strewn around her, the unopened yoghurt lay beside one ear.

Roger clambered over the high fence and rushed into the house, dropping his keys on the floor inside the front door. He called Robbi in a frantic state. 'I think Helena's dead,' he told her. 'Call the police.' A few seconds later he called back, 'No, don't, I will call them.'

His 911 call sounds almost absurdly English: 'This is an emergency. My wife has been attacked. She's lying in the garden. I think she's been killed,' he told the operator. She connected him to the paramedics, and the Sheriff's office. 'My name is Roger Franklin. The address is 260 23rd Street in Del Mar. My phone number is 481–0144. I think my wife has been murdered.'

'Did you see anybody?' A woman from the Sheriff's office cut in.

'My wife's secretary called me . . .'

'The Sheriff will be right there.'

When the first officers arrived, Roger was sitting beside Helena, crying, gently brushing flies from her eyes.

The fire department paramedics were there in minutes. They pushed down a section of the bamboo fence as Helena's body still blocked the gate. There was no need to check her pulse: it was clearly too late for that.

Detectives and criminalists from the Sheriff's Department arrived soon afterwards. Detective David Decker, who led the investigation, remembers seeing Roger sitting on the ground in front of the house, his head in his hands, very distressed.

The house was quickly cordoned off with yellow crime-scene tape, while the detectives, police photographers and criminalists got to work. They took endless pictures of Helena's lifeless body, searched every inch of the yard, looking for clues as to how the killer might have got in, how Helena had died, tiny scraps of evidence that might link any future suspect to the scene of the crime.

They were looking particularly for hairs and fibres from clothing or other materials. Back in 1985, this was the new hot technology, state-of-the-art investigation technique – and together with fingerprint evidence represented a detective's best chance for solving a murder with no first-hand witnesses, as this appeared to be. The contents of Helena's bag and her papers were collected carefully – each item would be taken to the lab and minutely examined for unexplainable fingerprints.

Helena's hands were wrapped in white polythene bags, sealed with elastic bands, and her body covered and taken to the coroner's office. Where it had been lying, the detectives found one broken fingernail – and another under an upturned pot beside the gate. These they bagged and labelled.

To Detective Decker, it was immediately apparent that Helena had not died quietly. 'My first thought, when I came through that hole in the fence was, "Wow, there's been a hell of a fight." Then I noticed that she was in a strange and somewhat compromising position. It was bizarre – I had never before or since seen a victim who had died and stayed in that position. It was clearly not natural. She was lying on her back with her legs propped up symmetrically, in a frog-like pose.'

Decker searched the grounds for a clue as to how the murderer might have got in. Roger had told him that Helena always kept the bamboo gate locked, and that the killer could not have left that way because her knee was propped against the inside of the gate. He looked for footprints, and found some small ones to the west of the house, where the dirt had been raked. But there was a covering of leaves over the dirt, and the footprints weren't clear enough to take an impression.

He noticed some scrape marks on a section of the bamboo fence on the eastern perimeter of the property, beside an unusual 'jog' in the fence made of round terracotta drainage bricks – the type often used to store wine bottles – which could be peeked through to see into the inner courtyard, or used as a foothold to climb the fence. This was a possible entry or exit point – it was on the most secluded and heavily vegetated side of the house, where the garden backed on to the scrubland beside the railway tracks – but if it was, the killer had left nothing behind.

News spread quickly that something terrible had happened on 23rd Street. Crowds began to gather. Donna Lilly had been surprised when Helena failed to turn up for her meeting with the Escrow agents, and when she heard from a colleague that there were police cars outside the cottage she had rented to Helena and Roger, she went along to see for herself. 'There was yellow tape everywhere,' she recalls. 'I asked one of the deputies what had happened, but they wouldn't discuss it. The Coroner's vehicle arrived and brought out a body in a bag on a gurney. I asked a person with a trench coat on, "Is it Helena?" He didn't answer. "Is Roger dead?" I asked him. He replied no. I burst out crying. I was so upset for my friend and client.'

At Gen-Probe, everyone had gathered around Robbi Loiterton's desk, waiting for news. When she turned, shocked, and told them that Helena was dead, there was silence. The president of Gen-Probe, John Bishop, immediately got into his car to go round to 23rd Street. Sam Morishima followed. One of

Helena's colleagues, Barry Epstein, was conducting an interview when he heard. 'I couldn't continue. It was like the day Kennedy was killed.'

The company's co-founders, Howard Birndorf and Tom Adams, had taken their girlfriends to the races. 'I remember the day she was killed like it was yesterday,' says Birndorf. 'We were at the racetrack and we had this hot tip for the last race. I can't remember its name, but it came from dead last to first, and we won a lot of money, I mean a lot, thousands of dollars. We had this huge wad of cash and were tipping everyone in sight.

'We got home about six or seven p.m., to find this message from the office: Helena had been murdered. It was like we came from a huge high to a complete low.'

If they were on a low, Roger was plumbing the depths of devastation. Decker's partner, Detective Charlie Kelly, had taken him back to the Encinitas Sheriff's station, where they were joined, once he had finished at the house, by Decker. He was not the typical, doughnut-eating deputy of a million TV series. Even when he was in his thirties, Decker dressed sharply and conservatively, smoked a pipe and gave off the air of a gentle academic.

At 8.30 p.m., they ushered Roger Franklin into a small interview room, and started what became a marathon, four-hour interview. 'At that stage, we knew nothing about the background to this crime,' Decker recounts. 'Statistically, there are a large number of spouses involved in the demise of their mate, so spouses have to be interviewed early on. Until you look, you don't know what you are going to find. We didn't detain Roger Franklin as such, but he couldn't return to the house, which was tied up by the investigation, and he didn't have many places to go, so he stayed around at the station until his friends arrived late that night to collect him.

'We asked Roger his movements that morning. He said that when he had left for the office, Helena was alive and preparing to make her morning calls. Then, you see, we still didn't know exactly what time she died, whether he was telling the truth. I was reasonably convinced that he was, but you never know until you have corroboration. He appeared to be a creative, sincere – at that time mourning – husband. All of his emotions seemed to be real. He demonstrated the classic symptoms: first of all, "I don't believe it, it's not happening, it's a trick, she's going to come back." Then, "No, it's real, I'm sitting here at the police station." And lastly, the emotion comes flowing out: "She's not here, not coming back – what am I going to do?"

'You see this over and over again, it goes in waves. When interviewing the recently bereaved, you have to wait until they get through these stages – there is no sense in trying if they are crying and devastated.'

Detectives Decker and Kelly learned a lot about Helena Greenwood in the last hours of the day she was murdered. They took down names of her friends and business associates, found out about her activities of the previous twenty-four hours, her normal routine. And for the first time, they heard the name David Paul Frediani.

'Very soon, Roger told us about the sexual assault. That immediately turned our thoughts to Frediani. But we didn't know if he was in jail, or whether he had an alibi. You don't focus on one person until you have done all the interviews and read all the lab reports. At that point there was a list of several potential suspects.'

After midnight, they let Roger go. Sam Morishima was waiting outside to take Roger back to stay with him and his wife, Mae. 'They think I did it, Sam,' Roger said. 'They think *I* killed Helena.'

The grieving husband, Roger Franklin, was pushed down the suspect list over the next couple of days, after Decker and Kelly had confirmed that he had arrived at work at around nine o'clock on the morning of the murder, and interviewed his co-workers in San Clemente to ascertain that he behaved in a suitably natural fashion before and after he received Robbi's phone call. They drove his route to and from work, and even with no traffic, it took the best part of forty-five minutes. When, several days later, they received copies of Helena's calling card phone bill from Gen-Probe, which showed she was on the phone until around 8.55 a.m., Roger was officially eliminated as a suspect.

The detectives turned their attention to Helena's

work colleagues and rivals. The stakes are high in any business which relies on inventions and once-in-a-lifetime brain flashes by brilliant people – and the biotech world was famously riddled with industrial espionage. Had she brought an important secret with her from Syva to Gen-Probe? Or was it professional jealousy? There were plenty of former colleagues and associates of Helena's who hadn't been leading lights in her fan club. As Decker put it, 'She gave the impression of being dynamic, very career-oriented, very driven in her field, and there are lots of people who feel uncomfortable around women like that.'

Here again their inquiries failed to turn up anything substantive.

The autopsy was performed the day after Helena was killed. Her body was wheeled on a stainless steel gurney, along the marble-flecked floor of the medical examiner's building, and into the morgue, where it came to a halt in front of Dr Katsuyama. He cranked it up to chest height, then peeled back first the white sheet, then the blanket of clear polythene covering the body, all the time recording his actions through the microphone which dangled from the ceiling. With Decker and Kelly watching, Mary Pierson, the criminalist who had helped collect the evidence at the crime scene, unbagged Helena's hands, then carefully clipped her fingernails, to be stored with the rest of the evidence. When a victim has died after a violent struggle, there will often have been an exchange of evidence. One of the fundamental tenets of crime detection, Locard's Exchange Principle, states that a cross transfer of evidence takes place whenever a criminal comes into contact with a victim, an object or a crime scene. When the victim has died after a violent struggle, it is almost inevitable that in the course of the fight, as they claw each other, the victim might manage to scrape vital pieces of evidence with their fingernails – skin, dirt, hair.

But there wasn't much under Helena Greenwood's fingernails; not enough body matter, in any case, to perform blood and enzyme tests.

As the pathologist worked, opening up the rib cage, weighing the organs, sawing through the cranium, checking for anything out of the ordinary, David Decker described the crime scene to him, and took notes of the autopsy findings. There was a deep gash in the back of Helena's head, caked with dried blood. She had bitten the gums inside her mouth. Blood had pooled in one of her hazel eyes. The underside of the body showed advanced lividity; it was a cerise colour, with white patches where there had been areas of pressure: on her shoulder blades, underneath her bra straps. It looked as if she had spent a day in hot sun without any protection. This petechial haemorrhaging occurs when high blood pressure causes the capillaries to snap, all over the body. To Dr Katsuyama, these were all classic signs of death by manual strangulation.

This confirmed Decker's initial suspicion that Helena's killer was a large man – strangulation is a very physical crime, and requires great strength. It is also an intensely personal way to kill, hand on neck, flesh to flesh: there are few strangulations between strangers. The detective returned to 23rd Street – he always liked to go back to the crime scene in the quiet of the following day. On his first look round, he had noticed a couple of hairs on the latch of the gate, and blood dripping down the frame. At the autopsy, he had thought that the trauma to the back of Helena's head matched the shape of the latch and wanted to check.

As he had suspected, they were almost a perfect fit – her head, it appeared, had been repeatedly and violently bashed against the metal latch. The hairs were still there, and Decker carefully collected them, and stored them in an empty cigarette packet.

He conducted careful house-to-house inquiries, to see if any of the neighbours had seen or heard anything unusual the previous morning. Two men said they had heard strange noises, possibly screams – though one thought they had been near 8.30 in the morning; the other, between 10.30 and 11. When each had looked out of the window, they noticed nothing out of the ordinary. Only three young girls were able to report having seen anything unusual. The Alton girls, Kyri, who was seven, and Kati, six, lived at 260 22nd Street, exactly opposite and one street to the south of Helena Greenwood's house. They were at home on the morning of the 22nd, watching *Inspector Gadget* on television. Kyri happened to look out of her window, at the back of the house, and noticed a black sports car – she thought it was a Porsche – pull into the driveway of 260 23rd Street. She particularly noticed that it had a Padre – the San Diego baseball team – sticker in the rear window. She called her sister to look, but the car immediately drove away. About ten to twelve minutes later, she told Decker, it was back again. Both girls heard the door slam. Kati stayed at the window watching while Kyri dressed – she saw a person wearing blue jeans, with white hair tied back, standing near the car in the drive. Decker spoke to a friend and next-door neighbour of theirs, ten-year-old Rian Alworth, who was confined at home with chicken pox. She had also seen a sports car parked at the end of the road between 9 and 10 in the morning, she told him. It was a black Porsche 925 with a Padre sticker in the rear window; her father played football for the San Diego Chargers and drove a red Porsche, so she was pretty sure.

Decker made meticulous notes of his interviews. That evening, he contacted the authorities in San Mateo to tell them what had happened. Martin Murray, the prosecutor assigned to the sexual assault case, was horrified when he heard that Helena was dead. He immediately suspected Frediani: he knew as well as anyone that Frediani was not in jail, but out on $25,000 bail. 'I quite frankly kept hoping it wasn't him. I was hoping that the fact he was being prosecuted was not the motive; the fact that he was out on bail had nothing to do with it. When someone comes to you with something as personal as having been sexually assaulted, they're putting a lot of trust in the system and they are putting a lot of trust in you that something good will come of it. It took courage for her to come forward and participate in this prosecution – the thought that it might have been the cause of her death was a difficult thing to deal with. I was shocked, upset, and hoping, despite my fears, that it would be solved in some other fashion.'

Helena Greenwood had been murdered twenty-five days before the sexual assault case against Frediani was set to begin. Murray knew that without his star witness, the sexual assault case would be harder to prove, but he was extra-determined now to get a guilty verdict. He was counting on the judge allowing her testimony from the pre-trial hearing. In the meantime, Decker spoke to Chaput, and over the next few days, the detectives tried to determine where Frediani had been at the time Helena was killed.

The pre-trial conference for the sexual assault case was scheduled for 4 September. Murray decided not to mention Helena's death at first. He and Craig Collins had been talking about a possible plea bargain: if the gun use allegation was dropped, Collins had indicated that his client would plead guilty to the sexual assault and burglary charges. Under California law, any crime involving gun use means an automatic prison sentence. Collins was hoping that with Frediani's clean record, good job, standing in the community, he might be able to persuade the judge to give him probation. But until that point, Murray had consistently refused to accept the bargain – he thought his case was strong and that Frediani deserved to be locked up. The way he had treated his victim, forcing her to walk naked through the house, ejaculating over her face – that is what, for Martin Murray, plunged Frediani on to a level below the common sex offender. These were acts of psychological cruelty, degradation, poisoned cherries on top of a rotten cake. And there was a personal element too – he didn't like Frediani, he thought he was arrogant, smug and self-assured.

However, things had changed with Helena's death. Murray was worried that his case would be weakened considerably by her absence. He decided it would be prudent to try to nail down the reduced sentence. 'I assumed he would accept the offer,' Murray said. 'I don't have any duty to tell any attorney that I have witness problems at a plea negotiation.' To his surprise, Collins passed.

'My client isn't interested in pleading to anything,' he told Murray.

'That is when it hit me. I thought, whoa, there isn't any other motive for this crime. Why else would someone who was previously ready to plead for what probably would have ended up as a three-year prison sentence suddenly change his mind? I thought, My God, he did this. He should not know at this point that she is not available. And now he's not accepting the plea bargain that he had been pestering me for.'

It was at this point that Martin Murray informed

the judge that Helena Greenwood had been murdered in San Diego thirteen days previously. Craig Collins, in his own words, 'went white'.

'Did your client have anything to do with the death of the victim Helena Greenwood?' asked Murray.

Collins could not respond.

Chaput was having little luck in pinning down Frediani's movements on the day of the murder. He talked to Frediani's flatmate, Barbara Powell. She told him that Frediani had only moved into her apartment a month previously, after she had advertised for a roommate. He was moving out of the apartment he shared with his girlfriend in the same complex. Barbara had known who he was, of course: everyone in the complex knew Paul. He was the good-looking one by the pool. He and his friends seemed always to be partying; there were always pretty girls hanging around that set – rarely the same ones from one week to the next. Barbara wasn't part of their fast-living crowd, she told Chaput.

She hadn't seen him on 22 August, but that wasn't unusual. They lived separate lives. She remembered the day well, however: her neighbour had brought round a cutting from the local paper, about Frediani's imminent trial. She was horrified. Until that point, she had no idea that he had been accused of anything. She called her boyfriend in a panic, and he told her to pack her bags and move out. She spent the day of Helena Greenwood's murder ferrying her belongings between the apartment she shared with Frediani in

George Avenue and her boyfriend's house. She wouldn't go there alone: her boyfriend and her boss took it in turns to act as a bodyguard. She recalled seeing Frediani's white BMW parked in its usual space outside the apartment at some point – she particularly noticed it because it had a big bash on one wing.

Detective Joe Farmer ran Frediani's name through the central police computer. It showed that he had been in a traffic accident in Valencia, 300 miles south of San Francisco and just 130 miles from Del Mar, on 15 August, exactly one week before the murder. What had he been doing there? Chaput and Farmer asked his former flatmate Jim Thoren and his friend Art Settlemeyer, who said Paul had mentioned that he was taking off to Lake Tahoe for a break – a few hours' drive to the north-west. They had only found out he had gone south instead when he arrived back with a crippled car a few days later, and took a call from a breakdown service in the Valencia area. They didn't think much of it: Paul had been acting increasingly erratically and often used to disappear off at odd times, seemingly on a whim.

Chaput spoke to Frediani's boss at Lincoln Properties to be told that he had not seen him for a month. Frediani was on administrative leave to prepare for his upcoming trial. He was a fine fellow, his supervisor said, an excellent employee. He was sure he would be fully exonerated in court.

Decker began to focus his suspicions on Frediani. On the surface, he was the only man with a motive, and all the little bits and pieces of evidence were starting to form a picture: Frediani had allegedly had prior sexual contact with Helena, he was six foot three and strong, certainly capable of strangulation, from a purely physical point of view. He appeared to have no alibi for the day of the murder, and there was no logical explanation for his presence in southern California the week before. Had he driven south to try to find Helena's new home? Was he, in fact, planning to kill her on that trip, before he was thwarted by an inconvenient accident?

Decker and his sergeant, Chuck Curtis, flew to San Mateo to meet Martin Murray in his office on the third floor of the court house in Redwood City. It is an old-fashioned building, with a distinctly institutional flavour. Decker and Curtis introduced themselves to the young attorney. 'I will never forget it,' recalls Decker. 'He was just a few years out of law school, enthusiastic and aggressive. He was excited about the case; he already disliked Frediani from the preliminary hearing. He asked if we would mind if he called in a detective from the local Sheriff's office. This is normal practice, we had no problem with it. An older sergeant walked in. Murray then said, "Dave, Chuck, I would like to introduce you to Bob Morris, the world's greatest homicide detective."'

Decker laughs. 'Well, we weren't offended, but Bob was clearly embarrassed. We knew that we could hold it over him, and he went out of his way to help us, and provided tremendous assistance.'

They talked through the case. The San Diego detectives, naturally, wanted to interview Frediani, but he had legal representation, and no good attorney would have let him talk. If they had had probable cause to believe he had murdered Helena Greenwood, they could have arrested him. 'We had reasonable suspicion – but not probable cause,' said Decker. 'And the motive didn't really make sense: yes, he had one in theory, but thinking logically, you wouldn't kill her after the preliminary hearing, as anyone with a rudimentary knowledge of law would know that immediately made her preliminary hearing testimony admissible.'

7

Sydney Greenwood was devastated. His beloved wife, Marjorie, had died of leukaemia after months of pain, just months before his daughter's murder. Helena had flown over to sit at her dying mother's side, and after she was buried, persuaded her father to come back to San Diego to stay with her and Roger. Sydney was glad to be with people he loved, and thought he could be of some use. Helena had eventually told him something of the attack the previous year, emphasizing the burglary aspect and omitting the sexual element, and Sydney sensed it had affected her. Every morning, after Roger left early for work, Sydney would walk his daughter to the gate, and see her safely into her car. Then he would take his sketchbook and walk for miles and miles along the beach, in the hills, painting the cliffs and wild ocean, anything to take his mind off his grief. He was always back in time to escort her back into the house in the evening.

'I never should have left. If I had stayed, he would never have got her,' he says, with the bravado of an old man who has forgotten his weakness. 'He wouldn't have dared – not with the two of us there.' Sydney returned to England only short weeks before his only daughter was murdered. The first he heard of it was when Roger's father, Don Franklin, came round to break the news, as gently as he could. He buried his head in his hands and wept. 'Oh my beautiful daughter, what have they done to you?'

'I only knew there was a God because Marjie had died before having to go through this. He just wasn't looking after me.'

Roger could also not forgive himself for failing, for a second time, to protect his wife. When Sydney flew to California after Helena's death, the two sad men went for long walks together, each entombed in their private grief. But while Roger withdrew into his memories, Sydney was consumed with anger. 'I was furious. I met the police and peppered them with questions. We all thought we knew who had done it, but why couldn't they catch him? Roger was terribly sad – he had always believed in life, but after Helena was taken away from him, he said to me, "I don't believe in anything any more, anything at all." He wanted to plant a tree in her memory.'

Sydney Greenwood and Roger Franklin flew to England. Helena Greenwood – daughter and wife – came back with them for the last time. After another post mortem and an inquest, she was cremated, and her ashes buried in the garden of remembrance at Boldre church, a few miles from Lymington. It was at this same pretty village church, almost ten years to the day earlier, that a garlanded Helena and proud Roger had married. This time the occasion was far more sombre: many of the same people came to her funeral, and more, from California. She was buried under the same stone as her mother.

As the trial date approached, Sydney waited anxiously for news of the investigation. 'With each passing day, as the killer was not found, my heart sank to new depths of misery,' he recounts. 'One cannot describe such pain. It was a numbing ache, which gnawed away at me for years. I was determined to see her killer caught.'

Craig Collins had clearly been taken by surprise when Martin Murray revealed Helena's death at the pre-trial conference into the sexual assault. He immediately asked for – and was granted – a continuance, while he researched the legal implications.

Collins was placed in a somewhat invidious position: he knew that Frediani would be under suspicion for the murder – could possibly be a murderer – yet he was professionally bound to do his utmost to profit from Helena Greenwood's death, on his client's behalf. He hastily prepared a motion to exclude Helena Greenwood's preliminary hearing testimony from the trial, on the grounds that the description she had given to the police of her assailant was inconsistent with that of his client. With her death, he would now be unable to demonstrate to the court, as he had planned, that Frediani could not possibly have been the man.

He submitted the motion to Judge Haverty on the

first morning of the sexual assault trial, 14 October 1985. He outlined what his strategy would have been: 'As the victim was the only witness to the assault itself, and as the preliminary hearing demonstrated the inconsistencies in regard to the eye-witness investigations, the defendant had planned, at the trial of this matter, to confront the victim with a line-up of the stomach-to-knee area of male adults of varying shades of skin colour in order that the victim could pinpoint what she meant when she said that the assailant was "Mexican", or "half-black". This line-up was to be accomplished either with actual persons or through the use of photographs. Because of the unavailability of this crucial witness, a witness who, through her inconsistencies, would exonerate the defendant of the charges, this defendant cannot get a fair trial.'

Judge Haverty, however, was not as disappointed as many might have been by the enforced removal of the dramatic nub of Collins' proposed defence, and denied the motion. Martin Murray was relieved, albeit unsurprised. He had done his research, and knew that Helena's preliminary hearing testimony would be admitted. Still, it would be a hard case to win. 'I hadn't tried a case before where we didn't have a victim to describe to the jury what had happened – apart from homicides, of course. Sex assault cases are hard as it is – you not only have to prove who did the crime, but also that there had been an assault. In many cases like this, you get people raising their eyebrows and saying, "I wonder if she knew him?" People often have this crazy view that the victim asked for it, and the strength of these cases usually stands or falls on how much the jury likes your victim.'

The judge allowed Collins to stipulate that none of the witnesses refer to, allude to or suggest that Helena Greenwood was either murdered or is now dead. 'The reason for this request, Judge, is I think it would be extremely prejudicial to the jury in this case. The defendant is not charged with her death.' Murray agreed to the stipulation, and to instruct his witnesses not to refer to her death in any way. Judge Haverty particularly mentioned Roger Franklin: 'In the event he testifies with respect to the wife – in the present tense, not in the past tense.'

The next morning, the freshly chosen jury were led in, and Murray opened his case. Roger Franklin was his first witness. It was always going to be a delicate examination, and Murray started quietly.

'Good morning, Mr Franklin. What type of work do you do?'

Roger Franklin gathered his best British reserve around him, and responded quietly and concisely.

'I am a landscape architect.'

Murray could not avoid mentioning Helena for too long, and on his sixth question, 'What *is* your wife's name?' he stressed the 'is'.

Roger held up well, even when he was shown a photograph of a smiling Helena. Perhaps it was even a relief to be able to think about Helena in the present tense, living still.

'Do you recognize the person in that photograph?' Murray asked.

'Yes, that is my wife.'

Murray turned to the teapot, and Roger explained that it was their custom to drink tea several times a day, how they would boil a kettle, then swill the pot with boiling water to warm it, before putting in the tea leaves or bags and letting them steep in more boiling water. He confirmed that the pot would always be washed after use, then put back on the kitchen window sill.

'I would like to direct your attention to the man who is seated right in front of me now,' Murray pointed to Frediani. 'Did you ever give him permission to enter your home at any time?'

'No.'

Frediani was sitting back in his chair, his legs stretched out in front of him. He appeared a little bored, almost as though the proceedings unfolding in front of him were of minor import. From time to time, he looked along the two rows of the jury, as if appraising the contestants at a beauty contest, as if *he* were judging *them*.

Murray finished as quickly as he could. Craig Collins restricted his cross-examination to trying to determine when the 'For Sale' sign was removed from the lawn in front of 90 Walnut – he didn't want to have to ask too many questions about Helena for fear that Roger might break down.

The ordeal was soon over, Roger was dismissed

and Thomas Christopher called to the stand. He was nervous, more visibly upset than his friend, and again, compelled to answer questions about Helena in the present.

'Mr Christopher,' Murray began, 'you are friends of Roger Franklin and Helena Greenwood, is that correct?'

'Yes.'

He described how Helena had phoned him late on the night of the assault, how he had driven across the Bay to collect her, found the home ablaze with lights, police cars parked outside, how he had taken her back to his home, and the next day, while Helena was packing her things, he had spotted the teapot.

In response to questions from Craig Collins, he said he thought he remembered there being a 'For Sale' sign on the lawn. The garden, in his opinion, was beautifully landscaped and nicely planted.

The next witness was a young, dark-haired lady called Marsha Baca.

'Your Honour, for the jury's benefit, Marsha Baca is a secretary with the District Attorney's office. She is going to read the testimony that Helena Greenwood gave at the preliminary hearing conducted on May 7 and May 8 of 1985.'

Murray gave no further explanation: the jury were left to wonder why Helena Greenwood, the victim, Roger Franklin's wife, was unable to appear in person. The judge instructed them to consider the testimony as if it was being given in court.

Murray and Collins read their parts more or less fluently; Marsha Baca had obviously practised hers, but made no effort to try to imitate Helena's English accent. The jury heard about the intruder with a gun apparently clutched in his hand, a hood obscuring his face, and how he had forced Helena Greenwood to undress then perform a sexual act. The rigmarole of Collins' repeated questions about his skin colour was re-enacted, this time in front of a jury of twelve. They listened, took notes: nothing gave away that they were hearing this testimony from the grave.

The police were next up: Glen Neilsen, the first officer to respond to the 911 call, and Patrick Akana, who arrived the next day to collect the teapot. Collins asked once again about the state of the garden: 'Do you recall whether or not the front yard area appeared to be well groomed, manicured or average condition or unkempt and as if it was in great need of gardening and mowing the lawn and things of that nature?'

Akana's garden aesthetic was obviously different to Thomas Christopher's: 'I would say it was leading more towards the unkempt side of the scale.'

'Unkempt?'

'Yes.'

The prosecution was galloping through their witnesses. Detective Stephen Chaput was called from the prosecutor's desk – where, as investigating officer, he sat throughout the trial – and on to the stand to see them through to the noon recess. He was back in the witness box promptly at 1.30 p.m. Murray dived straight in with questions about Frediani's arrest. Chaput recounted how he had noticed a physical reaction to his interrogation: as soon as he had told Frediani that his fingerprint had been found on the teapot, 'he kind of sank – his shoulders just kind of dropped. His face turned flushed. And then he blurted out something along the lines that, "I was drunk when I did those things. I was drunk."'

'And did he tell you anything else?'

'No.'

It was over to Craig Collins. 'Do you have any information of any source that any officer entered the residence after they all left in the late hours, early morning of Sunday . . . until Officer Akana had arrived there approximately 4.52 Sunday afternoon?'

'To my knowledge nobody from our department went back between those times.'

'Was there tape or anything else put about the house?'

'Not to my knowledge. No.'

He was soon hammering Chaput on his favourite subject: Helena's description of her assailant:

'Were you left with the impression that she was trying to describe to you she had been physically assaulted by a half-black male, tall, athletic, with dark eyes?'

'When we discussed the colour of the skin, it was my impression that all she was trying to relate was the tone of the skin or pigment, when she used half-black, Mexican, Hispanic or whatever it was. I don't think she was trying to qualify that individual by any nationality or race.'

It was like a long ping-pong rally, with both sides trying, if not to win the point, at least to keep the ball on the table. While Chaput gave little way on the colour question, Collins was able to elicit that Frediani was white, with hazel eyes.

He then turned to Frediani's manner during questioning. Of the innocent people Chaput had interviewed, Collins asked, 'Can you tell the jury whether all of them are always calm and relaxed or cool as a cucumber?'

'I wouldn't say they all are, no,' the detective conceded.

'Would it be true to say most of them are visibly upset, and you can notice they're upset by their physical features?'

'There's a certain – yeah, anybody that comes into a police station is going to get that nervousness.'

'How do they show you that they're nervous?'

'Just maybe by watching legs, hands.'

'What are they doing with their hands?'

'Either shaking or sitting on them or holding them real tight, knuckles turning white or whatever.'

'Does the breathing change?'

'Sure it will . . . Might get more rapid than normal.'

'This would be because of the stress of the very environment the person is in?'

'Mm-hmm.'

'So the mere physical shaking and blushing, biting

fingernails, whatever they do when they get nervous, in itself would not suggest to you guilt or innocence, would it?'

'Not by itself.'

Collins had clawed back some ground.

Chaput was taken through the interview again, particularly the seemingly incriminating admission that 'I was drunk when I did those things . . .'

'Did you record on a tape recorder your conversation with Mr Frediani?'

'No.'

He admitted that Frediani's prints had not been found anywhere inside the house – only the print on the teapot on the deck had matched that of the accused.

Murray had only one question for Chaput on redirect: 'When Mr Collins asked you if you would describe the defendant as half-black, you said not today. What did you mean by that?'

'I've seen the defendant at the preliminary hearing and also the night of the arrest, and going back to the night of the arrest, he was a lot tanner than he is today.'

Mona Ng was the criminalist – the evidence technician – who had examined the three pubic hairs found beside Helena's bed. These she compared to the samples taken from Frediani the night of his arrest.

'What was the result of your comparison?' Murray asked.

'Two of the hairs could not be associated with the suspect Frediani. The third hair could not be excluded as possibly coming from him.'

This, she explained, was after microscopic examination of the individual characteristics of the hairs.

She was also responsible for the serological analysis of the blue flowery pillowcase, on which, she testified, she found evidence of semen. After running ABO tests, she determined that it was left by a type O secretor – the same as Frediani. PGM enzyme tests found that both Frediani and the person who ejaculated on the pillowcase were type 1+. Mona Ng explained that around 80 per cent of the population are secretors, 48 per cent are blood type O, 37 per cent PGM 1+. As these variables are independent of one another, they can then be multiplied together to achieve an approximation of the frequency of type O 1+ secretors in America.

'They occur in approximately 14 per cent of the population, or one in seven persons.'

What, Collins asked, is the most common blood type? O. The most common PGM result? 1+. Obviously there are four times as many secretors as non-secretors. 'So,' Collins continued, 'as you were testifying, I counted the number of people in this courtroom right now. And if my counting is correct there's twenty-one individuals. So three people in this courtroom would meet the specifications which you've made for us.' It was a statement, not a question. 'If the Bay area itself has 2 million people in it, we've only narrowed this down to 280,000 people. That's the best we can get in the Bay area?'

'With these blood groups, yes.'

Murray had no further questions: 'The People rest.'

It was Craig Collins' turn to present his defence. Murray still had no idea what it would be: would he try to intimate that Helena had picked Frediani up in a bar? He was an attractive man, the husband was away . . . Or would he try to argue that his client had never been there, that the fingerprint analysis was just plain wrong? Collins began his opening statement: 'Evidence has been brought forward . . . showing you that there was an attack on Helena Greenwood on April 7th of 1984 by a person that's never been identified. And that the defendant's fingerprints admittedly were on a teapot which was discovered outside of the home at approximately between two and three o'clock the next day. Essentially the defendant has no quarrel with any fact that's been presented so far. Never been an issue . . .'

Frediani was soon in the witness box, outwardly calm, smartly suited. He was asked his name and for the first time, the jury heard his voice: educated, deep, soft.

'Mr Frediani, I can appreciate the fact that you're nervous a little. I want you to speak up if you will, please,' his attorney said. He asked Frediani about himself.

'I was born in Denver, Colorado, November 27th, 1954.' He graduated from Eastern New Mexico University with a degree in Business Administration. His first job was as an accounting clerk in Rochester, and he rapidly climbed the career ladder. Two years later – just a little behind Helena and Roger – he moved to the Bay area, working in a series of accounting jobs, each better than the last. In 1980, he started at Lincoln Properties in Foster City. At the time of the trial, he was earning $31,000 a year.

It was all standard stuff, designed to show that David Paul Frediani was an upstanding member of the community, a respectable accountant. Collins then changed track. He mentioned the young, attractive, obviously pregnant redhead, who had been in and out of the courtroom during jury selection and each recess, and whom Frediani identified as Andrea Goodhart, his girlfriend. He said that they had met soon after Christmas 1983.

'I was shopping at Macy's. I remember because I had an arm full of bags and I recently just bought a bottle of cologne for my brother and it had slipped through the bags and had fallen. I was surprised at how it just shattered in a million pieces and I was creating a lot of attention and people were like "Phhhew, phhhew, phhhew", you know, stinking up the place. I was pretty embarrassed staying there at the cosmetic counter. She was there shopping . . . We met up and exchanged phone numbers.'

Their official first date, Frediani said, was 14 January 1984. 'Now up until January 14th, can you describe your social life in the prior six months?' Collins asked.

'It was basically characterized by socializing a lot. I was going out a lot with my friends. We'd go out dancing, to various pubs, meeting, travelling, going out to dinner.'

'Were you single?'

'Very much so.'

'Do you drink alcoholic beverages socially?'

'At that point I was more inclined to drink more than I do now. I consider myself a social drinker even though I rarely drink myself now. But in that point of time it was very common when I went out I drank, bar-hopped – I danced and drank.'

After meeting Andrea, however, things changed. They started seeing each other every Friday and Saturday night.

'I didn't date anyone since I met her. She hasn't either. We always kept the weekends open for each other. Even if she had other offers I believe that she would say no, hoping that we would be together in those first couple of weeks. But after the first couple of dates we sort of knew we were always going to see each other.'

'I am going to pry now . . . when did you begin to have a sexual relationship with Andrea?'

'I would say it was around a month from our first date. We never rushed it. We weren't those types. You just know when you fall in love with someone there's no rush.'

After that, they would spend all their weekends together. He painted a picture of idyllic togetherness.

Andrea had a key to his apartment, and would be waiting when he got home from work on Friday night. They would get up early on Saturday. 'It was always the morning I cooked breakfast,' Frediani said. 'She has a favourite dish that I make.' She would typically go to aerobics, while he worked out at the gym, then they would meet up, and maybe go antique shopping, to Monterey, or wine tasting in the Napa Valley. On Saturday evenings, they always went out to dinner, sometimes with another couple, then to a movie, maybe to one of the comedy shows on Chestnut in downtown San Francisco, often to Cobb's Pub.

'Sundays we'd get up early again . . . Usually go out for brunch . . . We had this nice little drive. We'd go to Portola Valley – it's way up in the woods and redwoods, very serene, very peaceful. Not many people know about it. We'd have brunch there . . . A lot of times in the beginning we sort of knew we had mutual interests in looking for homes. We just – first we'd just enjoy looking, going through open houses, commenting how this would be exactly what I would like. It was just a kind of way we broke the ice together.'

'Do you remember, as you sit here today, physically looking at 90 Walnut Avenue in Atherton?'

'Well now I do. After all the evidence . . .'

Andrea had moved into Frediani's apartment in June 1984, he said. They wanted to sell her condo and get somewhere together. They used to buy the paper and look for advertisements for 'open houses'. They talked to realtors, tried to work out what they could afford.

'Now, in April of 1985 police officers arrived at your home and placed you under arrest for this offence, correct?'

Frediani explained that he didn't realize at the time he was under arrest. But he had gone to the police station voluntarily to answer a few questions.

'Do you recall as you sit here today whether you had any recollection of having been to 90 Walnut Avenue in Atherton when you were talking to Officer Chaput?'

'No I hadn't.'

Once he learned the address – from Craig Collins – several days later, however, he had driven past the house. 'Like I say, it had been bothering me a lot. I couldn't figure out how I could have been there, so right after work one night I drove on down there . . . As soon as I saw the house I went – that was one of the houses we had seen. And I was pretty relieved at the fact that I finally had a good explanation.'

'Do you remember now, what day it was that you were there?'

'I remember it being on a Sunday morning. I can only assume now from lifting my fingerprints I'd been there that morning.'

The jury were left with this ringing in their minds when Judge Haverty cut in to adjourn the court for the night.

The jury were let in promptly at nine o'clock the

next morning. Frediani was back in the witness box, and Craig Collins picked up where he had left off. 'Why were you in that neighbourhood in the spring of 1984?'

Frediani explained that they had been going to view an open house in nearby Menlo Park that had been advertised in the *Sunday Chronicle*. They had driven down after brunch in Portola Valley, and then taken a wrong turning, into Walnut Avenue. 'As we got to the end there was this house that had a sign . . . [It] appeared from the front to be somewhat in need of attention. It was the fence – the fence really attracted us. It was kind of tilted and needed a lot of paint.' The front yard as a whole was in need of attention, he thought. They stopped the car.

'We had just basically said, "Here's the type of house we look at." And we were hoping that possibly someone might be home. It was Sunday . . . after brunch . . . some time in the morning.'

They went through the 'rickety' gate, and knocked on the front door, then decided to go round and see if anyone was in the back garden. 'It didn't seem like it was occupied. There was no car alongside the house, the drapes were pulled . . . Just didn't seem there was anyone there.' They continued round, and 'just before I took a step up on to the deck I remember that there was something laying on the ground that I practically kicked because I was basically looking at the house, and I don't remember consciously too much what it was. I just remember I picked this up and set it out of the way, because I didn't want Andrea to step on it. But I remember something being like a flower pot of some sort.'

'When you saw that teapot [in court] did you recognize it?'

'No, I definitely didn't recognize the teapot.'

They left 90 Walnut – it wasn't exactly what they were looking for, it had no garage – and saw a few more houses including the one in Menlo Park mentioned in the *Sunday Chronicle.*

Collins jumped back to the evening of the arrest.

'Did you hear [Officer Chaput's] words that you're reported to have said something to the effect that, "When I used to do those kind of things I was so drunk, I didn't know what I was doing"? Do you recall? . . . Did you utter those words?'

'No, not exactly . . . I basically said, "I have a difficult time remembering what I was doing a year ago." That was the period of time when I was going out drinking with my friends, various different people.'

He had thought initially, he explained, that it was before he had met Andrea, when he was drinking a lot.

Shortly after his arrest, the apartment he was renting was put on the market, and he answered an advertisement for a roommate in a two-bedroom apartment in the same complex. Andrea moved back in with her parents, until they found a new place to share.

'And you are now living together with her?'

'Yes.'

'For the record, is she now pregnant?'

'Why, yes, she is five and a half months along. She is a little bigger because she has twins.'

'Are you presumptively the father of those children?'

'Yes.'

'Mr Frediani, on the night of April 7th of 1984, did you break into Helena Greenwood's residence at 90 Walnut Avenue, Atherton and force her into an act of oral copulation?'

'No, I did not.'

'I have no further questions.'

Martin Murray rose quickly. He was champing to get at Frediani. This was the man he believed had murdered his witness, and now it was looking increasingly as if he might shrug off even the sexual assault charges. He had been unprepared for Frediani's defence – he had had no time to investigate whether his story added up. He would just have to stand up there and wing it. He asked about the time after his arrest, when Frediani visited Walnut.

'I immediately recognized that house as – you know. Thank God that was the house we had visited one time. I immediately went home because I couldn't wait to tell Andrea. We'd been beating our brains out that past week wondering and worrying . . . She vaguely remembered the house.'

They went back the next night. Andrea recognized the house instantly.

Murray returned to the day they first visited 90

Walnut, on to the arrest, firing questions as if from a pump-action shotgun. Where did they park? Were there any cars parked in front of the house? ('I think there may have been one car.') How much money was Frediani making at the time? How much did he have in the bank? What about the house made him think it was abandoned? Where was the teapot lying?

At one point, Craig Collins had to interject to ask Murray to slow down, in order to let his client answer one question before he was asked another. Murray was trying to get Frediani to explain his 'I was so drunk . . .' statement. But Frediani stuck to his guns: he hadn't used those words. He said that he didn't remember specifically what he was doing that particular Saturday, as he was going out and drinking a lot at the time.

'The officer's lying about that?'

'I believe he just misconstrued it,' Frediani replied.

'And then you said, "I didn't remember doing it until . . ." Do you recall saying that?'

'No.'

'So the officer's account is inaccurate?'

'I believe he has misconstrued what I said and the tone that I may have said it in.'

'Are you telling us that when you said, "I was drunk when I did those things," that you were telling the officer about some other things that you had done?'

'No I was not in any way construing that I had done anything else.'

'And you just don't recall at all saying, "I didn't

remember it at all until . . ." You just didn't make that statement, is that correct?'

'That's correct.'

'Thank you. I have no further questions.'

The court adjourned for its morning break, and when it reconvened, Andrea Goodhart was called to the stand. She should have been a sympathetic figure: intelligent, attractive, twenty-three years old and pregnant with twins to a man who was facing a prison sentence. Collins started by asking for her account of her first meeting with Paul. It matched his in every detail. She said that in March of 1984, she had started a second job at Macy's, working at the cosmetics counter. She worked the late shift – after she got off from her job in the personnel department of the local housing authority – as well as some weekends. She often worked on Sundays, but never on Saturday nights.

'Do you recall, as you sit here today, there ever being a Saturday night that you did not personally physically spend with Paul?' Collins asked.

'No, I don't recall there being a Saturday night I wasn't with him.'

'In April of 1984 would you describe your sexual relationship with Paul as complete, satisfying, incomplete – I don't want to beat you. I know it's a touchy subject.'

Murray stood up: 'I'm going to object. It's totally irrelevant . . . It's well established perverted sexuality has no relationship to normal sexual ability.'

'Sustained.'

Andrea confirmed her boyfriend's story of their visit to the house at 90 Walnut Avenue, in almost every respect. She said, however, that there were no cars parked outside: he had said he thought there had been one.

Yes, she said, she was pregnant with twins, and they were due at the beginning of 1986.

Martin Murray was looking at Frediani's alibi with the same elegant distaste he had directed at the accused. His cross-examination started with a touch of comedy: 'Does the defendant normally work alone?' he apparently asked.

Andrea looked puzzled: 'He's not a sole proprietor. No, he works for . . .'

'I'm sorry. I didn't speak clearly. Does he normally wear cologne?'

'Oh sometimes, yeah.'

'Do you know whether the defendant is circumcised?'

'Yes, he is.'

Murray started probing about when they actually met, how much they earned, whether they had enough money to buy a house and whether they really would have started house-hunting together so soon after the beginning of their relationship.

'I got a roommate. I got a second job,' Andrea explained. 'I wanted to be earning as much as – as I could so that we would qualify.'

Murray needled more, now he was back to the day

they looked around 90 Walnut. They were supposedly on their way to see an open house near by. 'Tell me something about the house in Redwood City and Middlefield that you went to look at.'

'I can't,' Andrea replied.

'You didn't go there, did you?'

'Yes, we went to a lot of houses, but I cannot remember each and every house, I'm sorry.'

'But you can remember details about the house on Walnut?'

'I've been there twice again.'

'And that's how you remember it, isn't it, the time you went with the defendant, and the time you went with the attorney. That's how you remember the house on Walnut, isn't that true?'

Andrea blustered, but Murray had got his point across. He started to question whether they had enough money for a deposit on an apartment to rent – let alone a down payment on a pretty cottage with a white picket fence. 'Isn't it true that last Christmas you avoided buying Christmas presents because you wanted to save so that you could scrape up enough money for a deposit on an apartment, isn't that true?' He had read the letter Andrea had given to Chantal Clark's mother, in an attempt to make her drop the indecent exposure charge.

'Yeah, but what we had planned to give each other were – you know, I kept saying keep it under ten dollars and we'll just bank the rest of it. And Paul bought . . . some pretty lavish gifts for me for

Christmas, and I tried to do my best, but I remember thinking it was really silly and superfluous and that we should save our money.'

The more Murray dug, the longer and more elaborate Andrea's answers became. She was obviously nettled, but she gave little away. Her testimony continued to back up Frediani's. Still, Murray got her to admit that she had put up her townhouse as collateral for his bail, that she'd been present at the preliminary hearing. He asked whether, once she heard what Paul had been arrested for, she had immediately gone to the police to tell them that he couldn't possibly have done it as she had been with him every Saturday night?

'No.'

'Sergeant Chaput yesterday asked if you would mind answering a few questions.'

'Right.'

'What did you tell him?'

'I told him I certainly wouldn't mind but that I didn't think it would be . . .'

'You didn't think it would be in his best interests to let the police know what you were going to say today?'

'No, I think I said "In *my* best interests," quite frankly.'

'I see. Because your interests are you're pregnant by this man and you don't want a father who may be in prison while your kids are being born, do you?'

'Who would?'

Murray established that Andrea had moved out of Paul's apartment soon after he was arrested. She said it was for financial reasons.

'Isn't it true that the reason you left him is that you did not want to be living with a sexual pervert any longer, isn't that true?'

'No. Because Paul's not a sexual pervert.'

'Who's Dr Samuels?'

Craig Collins jumped up to object. The judge called the lunchtime recess.

When they came back an hour and a half later, it was clear that Murray's fervour had not been damped by the break. He went straight back on the attack.

'Do you know who Dr Samuels is?'

Andrea replied that he was the clinical psychologist Paul had been seeing for stress. Andrea had accompanied him once, to see if there was something she could do to ease Paul's apprehension.

'So basically your testimony is that it had nothing to do with the offence that he is accused of, just the stress relating to it – is that your testimony?'

'That's all.'

'Did you know what the purpose of the preliminary hearing was when you attended it?' Murray asked.

'Well, I know that Mr Frediani had told his attorney that . . .'

'The question is did you know what the purpose of the preliminary hearing is?'

'It's a difficult question for me to answer. What I'm understanding you to say is what the purpose of . . .'

'Don't try to understand what I'm saying, Ma'am. Read my lips . . .'

If Martin Murray and Andrea Goodhart had been warring lions, by this point they would have stopped the snarling and leapt straight into a fight. Fortunately, after a few more cuffs to the head, Murray said he had no further questions. Andrea was soon off the stand and back in her place among the audience.

As the last defence witness had not yet arrived, Martin Murray called his rebuttal witnesses. First Thomas Christopher, then Roger Franklin returned to the stand to say that the house and garden were in great condition – nothing that anyone could have described as unkempt – that there had been lush front lawn, and that, contrary to both Paul's and Andrea's testimonies, both Helena's white MGB and Roger's tan Volvo had been parked in front of the house.

Detective Joe Farmer was called to the stand. He essentially corroborated Chaput's account of the arrest and subsequent interrogation. He described Frediani's demeanour after he was confronted with the fingerprint evidence: 'He became flushed in the face. We noticed that his breathing became very rapid and shallow. He started to slump down in his chair. He stated, "I was really drunk when I did those things." At that time I asked what it is that he wanted us to do and he stated, "All I want to do is get this thing out, to get this nightmare over with."'

Craig Collins jumped up to cross-examine. He appeared excited about something:

'Detective Farmer, did you prepare any kind of police report in connection with that interview?'

'Yes I did.'

Collins asked to see it, and immediately called for a private conference with the judge. The jury were sent into the hall.

Collins was angry. He demanded to know why he had never seen the report before – why it had not been passed to him as 'discovery', a fundamental tenet of American law. Farmer said he didn't know why. His account of the interview, Collins insisted, differed in several respects to that of Chaput.

'Your Honour,' he said. 'I would like the record to reflect that I understand that there is a standing order by the presiding judge of the criminal department that all reports shall be furnished to defence counsel as soon as they become available . . . Under those circumstances I'm going to move the court for a mistrial because this evidence is totally unwarranted. Should the court deny that, the alternative is to move to strike all of Detective Farmer's testimony, and I'm afraid you've rung a bell with the jury that we just cannot un-ring.'

Judge Haverty was grave when he said: 'Obviously this witness's testimony with respect to this statement he has related now, that Sergeant Chaput did not relate, with respect to "I want to get this thing out and get this thing over with", is very damaging testimony. Mr Frediani, your attorney has asked two things here: one, that a mistrial be declared. And the other that the court strike the testimony of this witness that was given before the jury. In terms of the mistrial, you can or cannot join in that request. If you do not join in the request and the court grants the mistrial, the case is over. Res Judicata applies. Double Jeopardy applies. You cannot be tried again. If you join in the request for mistrial the case can be tried again against you. Do you understand that difference?'

Frediani was allowed time to discuss his wishes with his lawyer, and when the court reconvened, Collins informed them that 'He told me he does not join in the motion for mistrial. I personally have no intentions of retrying the case, without further – to be crass about it – my professional arrangement with Mr Frediani does not include a second trial.'

'I hope that's not a consideration,' the judge said.

'He says it is,' Collins replied.

'Your Honour, I went through everything to come up with his fee,' Frediani explained.

The judge decided that it was an accident that the report hadn't made its way to Craig Collins. 'In view of this, Mr Collins, I think this relief you seek is too severe. The court's ruling will be as follows: the motion for mistrial will be denied. But in fairness I think, rather than instructing the jury to disregard the particular statement which we referred to many times, I'm going to order all of his testimony stricken.'

When the jury returned, he ordered them to disregard the testimony 'as though you had never heard it'.

After that tense moment, Craig Collins called his

final witness, Feng Liu, a tiny Chinese lady, who arrived with her son, who translated from Mandarin to English. The Lius, it transpired, lived at 40 Walnut Avenue. On the night of the sexual assault, around 10.30 p.m., Mrs Liu saw a black man walking down the street. Her dog barked at him, and he told it to shut up. Several days earlier, a black man had smiled at her and said hello – she didn't know whether it was the same man, but it could have been. He was fairly light-skinned.

'Do you see anybody in this courtroom that looks like that man?' Collins asked.

'She says no,' Frank Liu replied.

Murray asked how tall the black man was.

'Pretty like your size, man. A little bit shorter, but pretty like your size,' Mrs Liu – through her son – replied.

'Was he as tall as the man standing next to me right now? I'm referring to the defendant.'

'No.'

On the night of the assault, the man had been wearing blue jeans, and a jacket, which tied round the bottom, she said.

'The defence rests.'

The following morning, Martin Murray began his closing argument. He described the offences. 'Now,' he told the jury, 'the difficult part in this case is not whether the defendant did this. There is overwhelming evidence of the defendant's guilt in this. The difficult part for you is the sympathy factor that's been injected into this case by having Andrea Goodhart around all the time, pregnant. That is a powerful issue for you to have to deal with . . .' And not one, Murray stressed, that they should take into account.

He ran through the evidence against Frediani: he fitted Helena's description, in height, build, age, skin tone. She had mentioned he smelled of cologne, and Andrea Goodhart had met him while he was buying cologne. He was circumcised, well spoken. He had the same blood type, same PGM marker, he is a secretor. Then there was the fingerprint on a teapot, that had to have been put there by the assailant.

'Now that's overwhelming evidence,' Murray contended. 'But we have something else. We have a confession, an actual confession. When confronted with the facts of the case, does he say, "My God, I'd never do a thing like that. You must be crazy." What does he say? "I was drunk when I did those things. I was drunk when I did those things. I didn't even remember doing it until . . ." Does that sound like a man who's innocent? Does that sound like a man who's not capable of doing this type of thing? No, that is an actual confession.'

The defence had had to answer the question of how Frediani's fingerprints got on the teapot, some time after the police left, and before Helena and Thomas Christopher returned the next day. 'What a coincidence. What a horrible coincidence that not only does he match the physical description, have the same body type, the same type of pubic hair, not only does he confess to the crime, but he also has an explanation for how in that twelve-hour period coincidentally he just happened to be in this neighbourhood and just happened to pick up the teapot and leave his fingerprints on it. Pretty ridiculous story.'

Then Frediani had to come up with an alibi. 'Who can you get? Well either someone who loves you a lot or someone who's in a pretty desperate situation. Now Andrea Goodhart is that person . . . I understand why she did what she did. She's got a child to think of and doesn't want to have this man convicted of this crime . . . But it doesn't relieve the defendant of his responsibility for what he did.'

But their story didn't quite fit, Murray contended. They said the house looked abandoned, that the front yard was made of dirt, that there was a stump by the side of the house. 'Now, of course the defendant only saw it in the dark in April of 1984. It wasn't until '85 when he went back in again, concocting this defence and he saw this house and it wasn't in as good shape as then. Andrea Goodhart says there was a stump. There may be a stump now. But Mr Franklin said there was a tree there in 1984.

'She can remember detail after detail after detail about this house on Walnut. But when I tried to get her to talk about something that they hadn't obviously gotten together and compared notes on, she can't tell me one thing about this house they were supposedly looking for on Middlefield. Why can't she tell me? Because she wasn't in here when he testified and she wasn't sure what he may have said about that house. That's the problem when you're concocting defences. You have to be careful. She was careful. She talked about everything under the sun except the questions I asked her.'

Murray found it unbelievable that they could be house-hunting only two and a half months after they got together, and with minimal means. He found Frediani's explanation for his confession to be 'patently ridiculous', and reliant on Detective Chaput having committed perjury.

'Look at all of the things that you as a jury have to say are reasonable to find reasonable doubt, because that is what your job is. You've got to say that just because he's the same height, just because he's athletic, just because he's the same build . . . has dark eyes . . . circumcised . . . same pubic hair . . . blood type, the PGM, secretor . . . only 14 per cent of the population, fingerprint . . . because this perjurous officer is lying with his confession, that the case is wrought with reasonable doubt and that this is an adequate excuse, that this man has presented a case to you that convinces you yes, you've got the wrong man, Mr Murray, you've made a terrible mistake.

'Can you do that and still call yourselves reasonable people? Can you look yourselves in the face and say, yes, I'm a reasonable person and I think it's all just a coincidence?

'You can't do that.'

Collins knew that Murray's oratory must have

affected the jurors. The scales had been pretty fairly balanced throughout the trial, but now he had an uphill task. 'I think it's important for me to outline what Mr Murray did not say,' he told the jury. 'What he did not say was that within hours after the terrible assault on Helena Greenwood she described the suspect. Why didn't he discuss that? Why is he hiding it from you?

'She described the suspect as a Hispanic man, possibly Mexican, partially black . . . When given an opportunity to see the only person seated in the courtroom at the defence table a year and a month later, she then says that this person – I can't inject my own opinion into the case. But you can certainly look at the defendant and ask yourself whether you would in your wildest imagination describe him as partially black or half-black or light brown. Or possibly Mexican.

'The other evidence that Mr Murray did not discuss – there were fingerprints throughout that house that were not Helena Greenwood's, not Roger Franklin's . . . usable, identifiable fingerprints of an unknown person. On the screen.' They were not Paul Frediani's fingerprints.

He moved on to the blood and enzyme type. 'You know statistics can play very strange games because that 14 per cent is also the most common person. If you were to pick a person out of a crowd and put him under a microscope the odds are that's what the person would be. I thought about how you could look at that. And some of you might have gone to a forty-niner football game. Let's say there are 50,000 people present. 7,000 would fit the qualities and the characteristics that have been described. That's a small town of people . . .'

It was suspicious that the prosecution had never mentioned at the time that Mrs Liu had seen a black man in the neighbourhood on the night that Helena Greenwood was attacked. 'In all fairness do you want your government to suppress that kind of evidence? To hide it from you?

'They've a bankrupt case. It's an immoral case the way it's been presented, and I'm not accusing Mr Murray of that. It's the quality of the evidence and the way it's been presented to you. It's shameful.

'This is a circumstantial evidence case. No one saw the defendant there. Concede that.' He urged the jury to believe Paul and Andrea's story that they had been innocently house-hunting that Sunday morning. 'What evidence do you have that that is not true? Mr Murray has not produced one shred.' The stump, he said, was irrelevant, since Andrea had been back to the house several times recently. They could have been mistaken about the cars.

'You heard the defendant testify. I think you got to know him a little bit. I don't represent a saint . . . but did you get a feeling that he was – I want to say a rapist. Did you get the feeling that he's that kind of person that would do this? He's an accountant. You heard his background. Educated person. Reasonably hard-working, earns a good living. First thing the assailant says is, "I want money." I mean, Jeez.

'You have a courageous job in front of you because, you know, it's easy to find someone guilty. It's just part of the system . . . You don't do it with any kind of joy, but it's a lot tougher, it's a lot harder to say to yourself the government was wrong . . . It's a courageous person that can stand up and say to their government, "You have failed." Can you do it?'

Murray had the last word. His message played to the prejudices of the majority of Americans, the widespread desire for more law and order, stronger sentences, bigger, meaner prisons. 'If this case isn't strong enough for you to convict this man, if the standard that this jury is going to adopt in this case would be adopted by all juries, we might as well forget about our prison expansion programme, because no one is going to be convicted. This case is about as strong as they get. The evidence of guilt is overwhelming in this case. When you took the oath as jurors you became part of the criminal justice system. The criminal justice system is much maligned, much criticized, but it is the best system in the world. You are now part of that system.'

Judge Haverty turned to the jury of eight men and four women and instructed them in the law and their role in determining David Paul Frediani's guilt or innocence. He gave them verdict forms to fill in, then, at 11.30 in the morning, he sent them off to the jury room to begin their deliberations.

By mid-afternoon, they had still not reached a verdict. The foreman said they needed more time. They reconvened the next morning at 9 a.m. and by lunch, were still locked in debate. At 1.37 p.m. they asked for the instructions on circumstantial evidence and reasonable doubt to be read to them again. 'The presumption places upon the state the burden of proving him guilty beyond a reasonable doubt,' the judge read. 'Reasonable doubt is not a mere possible doubt, because everything relating to human affairs and depending on moral evidence is open to some possible or imaginary doubt. It is that state of the case which after the entire comparison and consideration of all the evidence leaves the minds of the jurors in that condition that they cannot say they feel an abiding conviction to a moral certainty of the truth of the charge.

'If after considering the circumstances of the identification and any other evidence in the case, you have a reasonable doubt whether the defendant was the person who committed the offences, you must give the defendant the benefit of that doubt and find him not guilty.'

At 3.12 p.m. – after nearly ten hours of deliberations – the jury returned to the courtroom. The foreman handed their verdict forms to the clerk, who read them out slowly. 'We the jury in the above entitled cause find the defendant, David Paul Frediani, guilty of the crime of burglary in the first degree ... guilty of the crime of forced oral copulation ... we find the allegation that at the time of the commission of the offence . . . that the defendant used a firearm . . . to be true.' As in the vast majority of cases which come to American courts, the jury had placed their trust in the system, in the police and in science, and chosen to disregard the defence's alternative explanation of the events of the previous year.

For the first time in four days, Paul Frediani showed emotion. He was visibly, physically shocked. The colour drained from his face, as he sat up straighter in his chair. The jury was excused.

Martin Murray argued vociferously for Frediani to be remanded into custody pending the sentence. He was haunted by what had happened the last time the court let him out on bail, though he could not, of course, mention that. Collins remonstrated: his client had no prior record, was not a danger to the public, and was unlikely to flee because he knew he had a strong case for a mistrial, based on the withheld police report.

The judge granted an increased bail of $75,000. Frediani stood up. 'I realize you won't change your mind, Your Honour, but 75,000, 7,000, seven dollars, I'm not going to – I can't leave Andrea. She's pregnant. I want to start a family. I'm not going anywhere.'

'The court has obviously considered that in setting bail, Mr Frediani. Quite frankly, sir, under normal circumstances there would be no bail.'

Frediani was led away.

Three weeks later, he was back in court for sentencing. Martin Murray argued strongly for the maximum term. Collins was equally vociferous in his desire for the minimum. Roger Franklin was allowed his say.

'It's unfortunate that Helena was not here to speak for herself and I just wanted to take an opportunity to say one or two words,' he began, with typical understatement. 'I think it's important to really establish Helena's character. [She] was a very successful, career-minded, professional woman. She was very involved, and has been her whole life, in medical research . . .

'She was always a very cautious person. She was never happy being alone, and travelling was a constant strain to her, and the effects upon her of this were totally devastating. She wanted to continue her career because she felt very serious about it. And it had a tremendous effect upon her, the fact that every time she had to go on a trip – often alone, staying in hotels alone, having to fly alone and move from the airport to hotel and business meetings, it was a tremendous impact upon the following of her professional career.

'It also had an effect upon our personal life. It became somewhat of a sensitive issue between us because of the psychological impact of what had happened to her. And that was not particularly a pleasant thing. And I think it just seems to me that it was an entirely premeditated event. I mean, I rarely travelled. The defendant, it seems to me, knew I was not in the house . . . and I suspect he knew that Helena was alone.

'And, finally, I think I'd just like to make a comment about the whole issue of the gun. And the term "menacing fashion" was something I picked up on. I think it's important to understand Helena's state of mind, having come from a country where guns are not freely available. We don't know anybody who even owns a gun. I don't think that Helena has ever touched a gun in her life. Just the mere mention and seeing a gun, in my mind, would have been totally devastating to her. That's all I have to say.'

He sat down. He was shaking.

The judge read through the probation report. Frediani had complained at length to the probation officer about what he regarded as the unfairness of the trial. He consistently maintained his innocence. But Judge Haverty clearly did not believe him. 'I agree with the jury's verdict. I think you committed this crime,' he said. 'If I didn't think so I would have a lot of trouble doing what I'm going to do today, because of your previously good record.'

He sentenced him to a total of nine years in state prison.

'Let me just tell you that if you didn't do this crime, a terrible injustice has been done here. And only you know in your heart whether you did it. Nobody else in this room really knows whether you did it, except you.

'Defendant will be ordered delivered by the Sheriff to the California Medical Facility at Vacaville, California.'

Murray stood up: 'Excuse me, Your Honour. Mr Franklin asked if it would be possible to have the photograph of his wife returned to him.'

8

As Paul Frediani was being locked away in prison, police 6,000 miles away in England were still grappling with an investigation that had been baffling them for over two years. On the evening of 21 November 1983 – five months before Helena Greenwood was sexually assaulted – a fifteen-year-old girl had left her home in the English village of Narborough, near Leicester, heading for her friend's house. She never arrived. By eleven, her parents had started to worry; by midnight they were frantic. They called all her friends, then the police. Her stepfather drove round and round the village, but there was no sign of her. He walked up and down the shaded footpaths, but didn't see a thing.

Her body was found the next morning, splayed in a field near the local psychiatric hospital, naked from the waist down, bloody, her head resting on her new donkey jacket, scarf pulled tightly around her neck.

The murder of Lynda Mann shocked Leicestershire like no other murder had before. The small midlands county is famous for its foxhunting, but little else. The county capital, Leicester, is the birthplace of Engelbert Humperdinck and the Attenborough brothers. The police instituted the biggest murder inquiry that Leicestershire had ever seen, marshalling a force of their best detectives with the aim of tracking the killer down quickly, before he could kill again.

The results of the autopsy provided the first clues. Lynda, slim and slight, had been strangled to death. Before she died, she had been sexually assaulted: 'Intercourse was attempted and premature ejaculation occurred,' the coroner wrote. The semen was analysed: the murderer was a secretor, and he had left behind his calling card, type A blood. Enzyme tests were performed, which revealed that he was PGM 1+. These characteristics narrowed it down to one man in every ten – but they were enough to eliminate the chief detective's early suspect, Lynda's stepfather.

The sperm count indicated that the murderer was young, and so the 150-strong murder squad focused its attentions on the thousands of men, between the ages of seventeen and thirty-four, who lived, worked or visited Narborough and the surrounding villages. They zoned in on everyone who didn't have an alibi, particularly those with a history of indecency offences, a population artificially enhanced by the presence of a hospital specializing in psychiatric disorders – including sexual ones.

The detectives rushed this way and that, nose to the ground in search of clues. They had plenty to go on – numerous sightings of strange men who subsequently appeared to have vaporized into thin air. There were red herrings aplenty, false tips and blind alleys. Someone placed a poppy on Lynda Mann's grave on the first anniversary of her death, but no one saw them do it. The local Leicester paper reported the investigation's every meander and continued to exhort the public to run a fine-tooth comb through their memories, but nothing came up. And soon, as the years passed, life in the cluster of villages on the fringe of Leicester's southern suburbs returned to more or less its normal pace.

At the same time, just six miles away in a laboratory at Leicester University, Alec Jeffreys' life was changing. Bearded, enthusiastic and a seasoned geneticist at thirty-four, Jeffreys was working on the inherited variation in genes: how Mendel's laws applied to our fundamental biological make-up, the tiny differences that make each of us individual. It was a big subject, and at that time, largely unexplored. Jeffreys was eager to make a major breakthrough.

He was genetically programmed for ingenuity; his father was an inventor in the car industry, while his grandfather had devised the 'Jeffreys 3-D sculpture method' – a way of creating literal likenesses of people, which was all the rage in London before the war. For his eighth birthday, Alec was given a microscope and a chemistry set – the former got him interested in biology, while the chemistry set resulted in domestic chaos. 'I went through a blessed period of making stinks and bangs and trashing the house,' he says. 'One day, I was on my paper round when I found a dead cat in the road. I put it into my paper boy's bag, its feet sticking out of the top, cycled home and dissected it on the dining-room table.'

The dissections and stink bombs led to Oxford, where he read biochemistry. Most of the teaching he found disappointingly dull, however, except for genetics, 'the grand union of inheritance and chemical inquiry'. He never looked back. The science of human molecular genetics – combining Watson's and Crick's structural discoveries with Mendel's theoretical postulations – was only really beginning in the mid-1970s, as Alec Jeffreys was working on his doctorate. He was there at the inception, and when he moved to Amsterdam on a two-year post-doctoral fellowship, to attempt to isolate a mammalian gene, he was working on virgin ground.

The project failed, but in the course of it, Jeffreys developed a method for detecting human genes. He moved to Leicester University, where he started up a laboratory – later funded by the Lister Institute. 'I thought, "OK, we've got this ability to look at genes, what should we do now?" There was no point in taking genes to bits to see how they worked, as everyone was doing that. It was obvious to me that the next step was to compare genes from person to person, in an attempt to pick up inherited variations in the genetic material itself. Nobody was doing it. People were looking at inherited variation in things like eye colour, height, weight or blood group, but no one had brought it to the most basic level of all – our genes.'

What Jeffreys wanted to determine was whether there was some way of distinguishing individuals through differences in their DNA. Most human DNA is identical; more than 99 per cent follows the exact same sequence of the chemical bases – A, C, G and T – like photocopied pages in a book. (In fact, humans share 98 per cent of the same DNA with chimpanzees: we have the same number of bones, teeth, organs, glands . . . We breathe, digest and reproduce in the same way.) It is that remaining fraction of 1 per cent that is capable of identifying us, of making us individual, like a passport or social security number, and we carry it with us in every cell in our body. It was that fraction of 1 per cent that Jeffreys needed to target. If he found variation at the genetic level then, he believed, it should be possible to map these positions, and thus start to chart out the physical geography of genes on the human chromosomes. The driving force for this was medical genetics; the goal, to track down the genes involved in inherited diseases.

Within months of embarking on the project, Jeffreys' laboratory had picked up its first inherited variant – like a typographical error in a paragraph of text. The mutation became known as a restriction fragment length polymorphism (RFLP), and the errors appeared to be inherited along Mendelian lines. He knew the method was right, but soon identified a snag; because they only involved a single letter change, RFLPs weren't very informative. It was a start, but what Jeffreys realized he needed to find were entire sentences of DNA that displayed more variation.

From the beginning of the 1980s the hunt was on.

'The problem was that we hadn't a clue what sort of DNA to look for, or where to look for it,' he explains. Then hints started appearing in the scientific literature: that there were certain rather peculiar bits of DNA that stuttered – repeated themselves over and over again. (For instance, one strand of DNA might contain the sequence CCG TAG TAG TAG TAG CTC, in which the three-letter sequence TAG would be the stutter, repeated three times, with its complementary strand of DNA thus containing the sequence GGC ATC ATC ATC ATC GAG.) And these were to be found not only in genes, but mainly in what is known as 'junk' DNA.

Functional genes – the devices that contain the recipe for proteins – comprise only 3 per cent of the human genome. Much of the rest is 'junk' – long, long stretches of DNA that, in the main, have either limited or no use, and are often jumbled and repetitive. (The 'junk' consists partly of now-defunct genes – which once carried instructions that are no longer relevant. For instance, in humans, the stretch of DNA that told our bodies to grow thick long hair all over is no longer useful, but, instead of being deleted, remains alongside a DNA message which disables it.) Because much of the junk DNA is not vital in the functioning of cells, it can vary more between people than working genes, without apparent effect.

Jeffreys read the articles about the stutters with interest, and decided to investigate whether the number of stutters varied between people. But where in the giant waste land of junk DNA to look for them?

The answer came in 1984 from another of the lab's projects, which looked at the evolution of genes over millions of years. 'Tucked away in one of the genes we were studying was this peculiar stuttered piece of DNA that actually gave us the golden key that unlocked the door to this. It said that not only were there a lot of these stuttered pieces of DNA – or hyper-variable minisatellites, as they became known – in human chromosomes, but that many of them shared the same chemical sequence with each other. That gave us a handle on being able to detect lots of these stuttered bits of DNA at the same time.' Junk DNA had found its use, after all.

Jeffreys set to work to devise a multi-locus probe – a radioactive piece of synthetically produced DNA – capable of looking for these stutters on all of the chromosomes at the same time. In September 1984, he decided to put it to the test. Using the same basic techniques as Helena Greenwood was helping to employ in the field of medical diagnostics, he first cut the sample human DNA into fragments using a restriction enzyme. Some of these fragments, he believed, would contain the stutters – and how many would determine their length. They could then be sorted according to length by dropping them on one end of a slab of agarose gel, to which an electric current was applied. The smaller fragments move through the gel more rapidly than the larger ones, ending up at different positions. The pattern was then transferred from the gel to a nylon membrane via Southern blotting, and a radioactive, multi-locus probe introduced to seek out and bind to all the minisatellite fragments that contained the shared chemical motif. When exposed to X-rays, the probes appear as dark bands, which indicate the positions – and hence lengths – of the varying fragments of each sample. The result looks similar to a supermarket barcode.

Jeffreys believed that the X-ray picture that is produced might just be different for every human.

For most of the late summer of 1984, Alec Jeffreys had glandular fever, but he was determined to press ahead with the exciting new avenue of his research. He popped in and out of the lab, otherwise directing operations from home. On the Monday when the results of the first test were expected, however, he was at the university almost before the sparrows. 'I went into the darkroom to get the X-ray film, and there it was! Here was the human genome crawling with what were clearly lots of extremely variable bits of DNA. When you looked at the pattern – of all these variable bits superimposed on each other – it was clear that what we had come up with was DNA fingerprinting. Not only had we accessed very large numbers of these incredibly informative genetic markers, but simultaneously, we had actually solved a completely different problem – human identification.'

Nearly two decades later, sipping coffee out of a Ministry of Silly Walks mug, Jeffreys' eyes still sparkle when he describes that Monday morning. 'It was a Eureka moment. I mean, science does not go by sudden revolutions that in five minutes flat change your life. But in my case, that is exactly what happened. Within ten minutes, we're all in the lab, talking about what we can do with this. We immediately saw the potential forensic application. Someone suggested splashing blood around the lab to see if we could type it. At that time, nobody had the faintest idea that you could do any of this: it was a sort of insane science. There was no end to the possible applications.'

In November 1984, one year after Lynda Mann's murder, and nine months before Helena Greenwood was strangled, Alec Jeffreys announced his findings to the Lister Institute of Preventive Medicine. He applied for a patent on his method, which he called 'DNA fingerprinting', and when it was safely accepted, the following March, he published an article in *Nature*, detailing the results of his research. In San Diego, Helena Greenwood read it, and the next morning, marched into a meeting of directors of Gen-Probe, brandishing the journal: 'This DNA fingerprinting is going to be big,' she said. 'I think we should get into it.'

One use of Jeffreys' method that he hadn't initially seen – but that his wife, Sue, had pointed out the evening following the Eureka moment – was in resolving immigration disputes arising from doubts over claimed family relationships. It wasn't long before Jeffreys had an opportunity to put this to the test. A Ghanaian boy born in the United Kingdom had emigrated to Ghana to live with his father. A few years later, he was put back on the plane to London to rejoin his mother, brother and two sisters. But he was stopped and detained by immigration officers at the airport, who suspected that a substitution might have occurred – that the boy was either not related to the woman claiming to be his mother, or that he was the child of one of her sisters in Ghana. Conventional serological tests – including ABO and PGM – showed that the woman and the boy appeared to be related, but could not determine whether she was his mother or his aunt.

Alec Jeffreys was asked by the putative mother's solicitor to carry out his DNA fingerprint analysis to determine the boy's maternity. From tests in the lab, he had found that his DNA fingerprint test showed a simple pattern of inheritance, with a child receiving a random selection of half his mother's fingerprint, and half his father's. This case, however, was complicated by the woman's uncertainty as to whether the man who thought he was the boy's father had definitely sired her son (and this man was unavailable for testing). The other three children, however, she knew were his. By analysing the DNA prints of the woman and her three England-based children, Alec Jeffreys was able to work out which of the characteristics came from the father. By subtracting these fragments from the returning boy's DNA fingerprint, he was able to infer 'beyond any reasonable doubt' that he was his mother's child (and that the man he thought was his father was indeed his father). This evidence was given to the immigration authorities, who dropped the case against the boy and granted him residence in the United Kingdom.

'That was the golden moment that completely changed my life,' Alec Jeffreys said. 'Most scientists will go through a whole life and will not experience that magic moment. I feel it was a great privilege, and more than that, great fun.'

The case was described in another article sent to *Nature* in August 1985, the same month that Helena Greenwood was strangled in her garden 6,000 miles away. Jeffreys received the acclaim he richly deserved: he was awarded a full professorship, and medals, prizes, fellowships to a host of prestigious societies including the Royal Society, scores of honorary doctorates and the award of the Freedom of the City of Leicester duly followed. The scruffy scientist from Leicester was on the map. Across the world, molecular biologists were back at their lab benches, using Jeffreys' discoveries as a basis from which to develop their own proprietary techniques, on variable sections of DNA that they were now searching for, and using probes they had developed.

Gen-Probe, in San Diego, was one of the first companies to use the DNA probe technology in the field of medical diagnostics. Helena Greenwood's main aim had been to present their systems in a way that would be easily understood by people without Ph.D.s. After her death, her successor pushed forward with her ideas, and their first products were launched into a receptive – and later eager – marketplace. Her legacy lived on, even while her name was lost among the hundreds of new recruits to Gen-Probe.

David Decker did not forget Helena Greenwood, however. His murder investigation had hit barren ground, and the Sheriff's Department was too understaffed and underfunded to enable him to follow his hunch up to San Francisco again, and on to Frediani's trail. He knew the outcome of the trial, knew Frediani was waiting for the results of his appeal. He still wanted to interview the man he regarded as his prime suspect, but knew he would not be able to do so until the appeal process was over. In the meantime, the file stayed open, in easy reach of his desk.

Back across the Atlantic, Leicester was in the news again, less than a year after Jeffreys had successfully sorted out the immigration case, and this time for a far less celebratory reason. On 31 July 1986, Dawn Ashworth – aged fifteen like Lynda Mann, pretty, with brown hair and a brace on her upper teeth – left her holiday job at the newsagents in Enderby, the neighbouring village to Narborough, at 4 p.m. She was wearing a thin white polo-neck under a multi-coloured shirt, a white skirt, white shoes, and carrying a denim jacket. She was last seen at 4.40 p.m., walking into Ten Pound Lane, a sheltered footpath only a psychiatric hospital away from the field where Lynda's body had been found two and a half years previously.

Her parents were panicking within hours – they knew, as every family in Leicestershire knew, that there was someone out there who had killed a fifteen-year-old girl before, and who had never been caught.

Their fears were confirmed two days later when their daughter's body was discovered under a clump of thorns, naked from the waist down and covered in insects.

The autopsy found that she had died by manual strangulation, and that this time, the assailant had been more successful in his sexual assault. Early serological results indicated that he had been a type A 1+ secretor.

The police were convinced – even before they found her body – that Dawn had been killed by the same man. They threw all their resources into a redoubled manhunt, and before long, they believed they had picked up the trail. The name of a young kitchen porter at the hospital was mentioned to them over and over again. He rode a red motorbike like the one four separate witnesses reported having seen parked under a bridge near Ten Pound Lane around the time Dawn had disappeared. He was talking to everyone who would listen about Dawn, and many of the things he was saying rang true, but he could not have learned them from the newspapers.

At five o'clock in the morning of 5 August 1986, the seventeen-year-old boy was arrested at his home in Narborough and taken to the nearby police station, where he was interrogated throughout the day. Different police officers took it in turn to try to get a statement from the boy, but it was not easy. His answers to even their most straightforward questions were rambling, frequently incoherent and often off the point. He said he knew Dawn; then that he didn't. That he had seen her that day; that he hadn't. That he had sexual experience; that he was a virgin. The police were becoming increasingly frustrated when, that night, after more than twelve hours of questioning, he confessed to killing Dawn Ashworth.

His account of what he had done was riddled with contradictions and inaccuracies, but by the end, he was fairly definite about raping, assaulting and killing Dawn Ashworth. He was formally charged with murder, and the papers duly announced that a dangerous killer had at last been taken off the streets.

The first intimation that things were not quite as they should be came with the results of the boy's blood tests. His ABO type was not A, and his PGM not 1+. Still, the police were pretty certain they had their man, even though he continued to deny any involvement in Lynda Mann's murder – nearly three years earlier, when he was fourteen years old.

The chief superintendent was more cautious than many of his force, however. He was also keen to cross the Ts and dot the Is on this case, and to tie the kitchen porter to both murders. He had seen coverage of Alec Jeffreys' DNA fingerprinting technology and phoned up to ask whether there was any chance he could apply it to this case.

Jeffreys said he would try, although he didn't think it would be possible. His technology was constantly being refined. Already, he had seen the shortfalls of DNA fingerprinting – that it couldn't deal with small or partially degraded samples of DNA (they needed an amount of blood or semen the size of a 50 pence piece), and that the complex multi-band patterns had proved to be refractory to computer databasing, making comparisons of DNA fingerprints obtained at different times, or by different labs, periodically inaccurate. To combat this, he had simplified the tests: where the original DNA fingerprinting had used multi-locus probes, with each probe detecting many minisatellite loci to produce the complex banding patterns, his new methods isolated individual, highly variable minisatellites on human DNA using a single-locus probe. The resulting pattern was not as discriminating as the DNA fingerprint – consisting of only two bands for each individual, one inherited from their mother and one from their father – but could be worked up to high levels of specificity by using several probes. Jeffreys accordingly dubbed this method 'DNA profiling'.

Until the point when Jeffreys was handed the swabs from the dead girls, no one in the world had taken a forensic specimen and attempted to do molecular genetics on it. Jeffreys – together with Peter Gill from the Home Office Forensic Science Service – had tried both DNA fingerprinting and profiling previously on blood and semen stains, but always under laboratory conditions. That the technology was potentially powerful and revolutionary, they knew. Gill had already been working on DNA (house sparrow, not human) before he read Alec Jeffreys' *Nature* article, and rushed straight over to the Leicester lab to learn how it worked. A quiet population geneticist who had come by accident into forensic science, he had seen the future and it was DNA. 'Conventional serology had several shortfalls: it was not particularly discriminating – statistics like one in several thousands even were not high enough – the enzymes needed to perform tests like PGM were not particularly stable, and there was no way of separating sperm cells from vaginal cells. This made solving rapes difficult. DNA could do this – because sperm cells have this coating which makes them very robust. We had worked out that you could separate the cells by first exploding the vaginal cells in a normal detergent mix, then centrifuging the sperm cells to the bottom and washing away the vaginal cells. The remaining sperm cells could be popped open by adding another reagent, which destroyed their coating, and there you are.'

This method had worked well under controlled conditions, but for the first time, Jeffreys was confronted with a real sample: 'I had no expectation of it working at all. And it was an odd experience – we were dealing with specimens from murder victims, young girls. That was really quite distressing. I found it hard. Suddenly this wasn't messing about with test tubes, this was real, serious life stuff. OK, we had been doing paternity and immigration cases, but that wasn't life and death: this was in a different league.'

The police gave Jeffreys semen samples found on both the murdered girls, as well as blood taken from the imprisoned seventeen-year-old boy. His brief was clear: to confirm the boy's guilt of Dawn Ashworth's murder, and prove that he had killed Lynda Mann too. After careful lab work, Jeffreys managed to extract enough DNA to perform the DNA profiling test, using single-locus probes. He started with Lynda Mann: to his great surprise, there was a mismatch. His first thought was that the procedure was faulty – but he reran the test and the result was the same. This must therefore mean, he thought, that there had been two murderers – since the boy had confessed to killing Dawn Ashworth. He phoned the police, who were understandably upset – and not altogether unsceptical.

Jeffreys ran the same tests on the sample collected from Dawn Ashworth's body. The results were identical: 'Then I thought: "Oh shit, there's something wrong with the science." It was clear that we had a match with the two victims and a mismatch with this guy who had confessed. There were two explanations: wrong guy or wrong technology. Obviously I thought it was the latter.'

He racked his brains: could a person have a blood profile and a semen profile that were completely different? Jeffreys couldn't see how. He kept doing more and more tests – and coming up with the same results. He called the police again. They asked for the samples to be sent off to the Home Office for double-checking. Peter Gill then tested all three samples using the more discriminating multi-locus probes, and came up with identical results.

By this stage everyone was confused. The police called a summit meeting in Jeffreys' tiny office in the corner of his lab. He explained his findings and his fears: but ironically, it was the Home Office scientists who backed his work, and pulled the nail out of the kitchen porter's coffin. You've got the wrong guy, they told the police.

Chief Superintendent David Baker of the Leicestershire Constabulary then took a brave step: he decided to trust the science and release the suspect on the eve of his hearing. 'We couldn't challenge it. How do you challenge brand new science? Nobody else in the bleeding world knew anything about it,' he said later. It was an historic decision: a suspected murderer had been freed as a result of DNA fingerprinting.

Despite his colleagues' continuing jitters, Baker went one step further: he tried to harness this brand new science to help him catch the real culprit. In January 1987, he ordered that all local men of the relevant age, who could not produce a verifiable alibi, should be rounded up and asked to give blood samples, in an attempt either to catch the killer, or somehow to flush him out of the woodwork.

Jeffreys heard about it on the local radio. 'It was an

act of faith the like of which I have never seen before or since. My first reaction was horror: he had come to this conclusion without talking to me at all. I thought: "Oh my God, who's going to be going around testing all these samples?"'

To the Leicester lab's relief, the Forensic Science Service was given that job, and over the following months, they were deluged with blood and saliva samples, collected by subcontracted doctors, operating out of mobile blooding stations. They first ran the simple ABO and PGM tests, and only sent the samples of A 1+ secretors to the government lab at Aldermaston for DNA profiling. The police tried to track down thousands of men who had had some reason to be in the villages at the relevant times, and when they had safely delivered them to the doctors' needles, they concentrated their energies on the 10 per cent who didn't come forward. Some had refused out of fear of needles, others because they believed the tests infringed their civil liberties. All of these men had their alibis double- and triple-checked.

This mass 'blooding', as it came to be called, attracted considerable publicity. Camera crews from the United States, Australia, Brazil and across Europe crammed into the mobile units night after night. But the labs failed to match any of the 4,500 blood samples they had been sent to the semen found on the bodies of the two murdered girls. The police started to lose heart – maybe the science was rubbish after all? Maybe they had released the murderer after all?

On 1 August 1987, a year and a day after Dawn Ashworth's murder, and six months into the DNA profiling experiment, a group of bakery workers were having a drink at the Clarendon pub in Leicester. The conversation turned to the murders. A young man called Ian Kelly mentioned to the manageress of another bakery that one of his colleagues, Colin Pitchfork, had persuaded him take the blood test for him. Pitchfork had told him that *he* had already taken it for someone else, who was worried about his prior history of sexual offences. Another bakery worker at the pub said, 'That's odd. Colin asked me to do it too. Offered me 200 quid to take the blood test. He's just scared of coppers. A weird bloke, that Colin.' The bakery manageress was perturbed by the pub chatter, but she didn't act on it immediately.

Four days later, in a separate case, Alec Jeffreys testified for the prosecution in Flint Crown Court, where Robert Melias stood accused of unlawful intercourse with a fourteen-year-old mentally retarded girl. DNA fingerprinting tests performed by the Home Office showed that the baby she had recently given birth to was his. Jeffreys explained how it all worked, and Melias acquired the dubious distinction of being the first person to be successfully prosecuted in a case using DNA evidence.

In Leicester, six weeks after the conversation in the pub, the bakery manageress finally called a policeman friend of hers and related what she had heard. He at once contacted the murder task force. They were cautiously excited. They looked up Colin Pitchfork in their files: he had a history of indecent exposure, and had at one point been an out-patient at Carlton Hayes psychiatric hospital. He had been interviewed, but given a low-priority classification: he had only moved to the area after Lynda Mann's murder, and that night, he had been baby-sitting his three-month-old son, while his wife went to evening class.

The police went straight round to Ian Kelly's house with a warrant for his arrest on suspicion of perverting the course of justice. Kelly was mortified, and immediately told them everything: how Colin Pitchfork had pleaded and cajoled him into doing it, how he had stuck a passport picture of Ian in his passport and driven him to the blooding station. 'But I never thought he had done it,' Kelly said.

That evening, Saturday 19 September 1987, the police knocked on Colin Pitchfork's door. When it was answered by a thick-set redhead with uneven teeth, the police immediately confronted him with the words he must have been dreading for nearly four years: 'From inquiries we have made, we believe you are responsible for the murder of Dawn Ashworth on the 31st July 1986 . . . I am arresting you on suspicion of that murder. I must inform you that you don't have to say anything, but that anything you say may be taken down and given in evidence against you. Do you understand?'

Pitchfork was calm, almost as if he had been waiting for this moment. At the police station, he confessed to everything. He had exposed himself to over a thousand girls, and murdered these two because 'they asked for it'. His baby had been asleep in the back of the car while he was in the field strangling Lynda Mann. The police took a phial of his blood and sent it straight to Aldermaston. It was the 4,583rd sample to be taken. This time there was a perfect match.

On 22 January 1988, Colin Pitchfork was given a double life sentence for the murders, ten years for each of the rapes, and a further three for conspiracy to pervert the course of justice (Ian Kelly was found innocent). DNA profiling had saved an innocent man from spending the rest of his life in prison – and brought a killer to justice.

Alec Jeffreys was delighted, and more than anything by the fact that Pitchfork was eventually tracked down by a marriage between science and police work. 'That was important. The union kept the police happy, and showed that DNA can't do anything by itself.'

His technology was licensed to a British firm, Cellmark Diagnostics, an affiliate of Imperial Chemical Industries (ICI), which took DNA fingerprinting and profiling across the Atlantic when they opened a branch in Germantown, Maryland, in 1987. There, they came into competition with an American firm called Lifecodes, which was using a similar technique, derived from the work of the molecular geneticist Thomas Caskey, who had been hot on the heels of Jeffreys when his discovery was announced in *Nature*. Caskey's system was licensed as the 'DNA-Print test'.

The two labs competed with each other for the increasingly sought-after – and lucrative – genetic testing business.

Slowly at first, like a shy debutante in her coming-out season, DNA took to the courtroom. In the UK, the US and across the world, it became increasingly the science of first resort, in cases where physical evidence was available, most commonly rapes. The serologists worked hand-in-hand with population geneticists to develop a statistical standard for the probability of a given DNA profile in the population as a whole. First, they collected profiles from random, unrelated individuals of a particular ethnic group – it had already been proven that there was significant genetic variation between the groups; at any given locus, the genotypes of two random Caucasians are generally more similar than those of an African and a Caucasian, for example. Then, the different groups were weighted according to their occurrence in the population as a whole. Finally, what is known as a 'random match probability' was calculated: the chance that a randomly selected individual from a population would have an identical profile at the DNA markers tested. It was that number – for DNA profiling, typically one in tens or hundreds of millions – that was the key to the power of forensic DNA.

The era of forensic DNA had begun. By the end of the decade, DNA fingerprinting and profiling were sweeping happily around the world, heralded by many forensic scientists and lawyers as 'the greatest advance in crime-fighting technology since fingerprints', and 'a prosecutor's dream'. Police, lawyers and judges grappled with the unfamiliar technology and complicated terminology, trying to familiarize themselves with words like allele, locus, and restriction fragment length polymorphism, and more than that, to learn how they worked. Many found it overwhelming. As a US Supreme Court judge noted, 'the evidence was highly technical, incapable of observation, and required the jury to either accept or reject the scientist's contention that it can be done'. Nevertheless, he upheld the verdict of the first US rape case in which DNA was introduced. At the same time, private biotechnology companies raced to the patent offices in a bid to license their procedures, and sell proprietary materials and reagents to as many crime laboratories as possible.

It was becoming increasingly obvious, however, that the technology was only of use when there was a significant amount of biological evidence available. For DNA profiling analysis – using single-locus probes – on minisatellites, a drop or two of blood was required. There was often enough sperm collected in rape kits for it to be profiled, but in more than 75 per cent of murder investigations in which there was any biological evidence, DNA testing was impossible; the samples of blood, hair or skin collected from the crime scene were either too small or too degraded.

9

Paul Frediani's future had been decided in ten hours in a closed jury room, at the end of which he had been sent to prison. It had come as a shock – even during the trial he had not let himself entertain the thought that he would be found guilty. But here he was, locked up for twenty-four hours a day in the segregation wing of Vacaville prison, undergoing psychological evaluation in order to determine his 'destination prison', the place he would serve the balance of his sentence. And then there was the murder: would they try to pin that on him? His attorney had warned him, as soon as they heard that he would be a suspect, to make sure he knew where he was on 22 August, and with whom. But no one had ever come to talk to him about it, though he was sure that they had come to the apartment complex secretly, to watch him, ask questions. But they had never approached him directly and no one had been to talk to Andrea. Surely, if they had something concrete, some physical evidence, he would have heard about it?

He did not have too much time to ponder. His case was up for appeal. Using his half-share of Andrea's townhouse, he was able to make bail again, and on 6 February 1986, he returned to civilian life, with month-old twin sons. Andrea had let her small town-house, and rented a ramshackle cottage in the hills of Burlingame, only a couple of miles from Helena Greenwood's old Atherton home. He didn't have a job, but twice a week, he headed up to Golden Gate University, where he was working on his MBA. There was no way of forgetting about the case; every time Paul drove south down El Camino, the long, straight road running from the city of San Francisco into the increasingly developed computer and biotechnology heartland centred around Palo Alto and San Jose, he would pass Walnut Avenue. If the traffic was bad enough, and he was heading south, he could have caught a glimpse of the white picket fence.

The wheels of the appeal were already in motion, and Frediani's court-appointed attorney assured him that the chances of overturning the verdict were strong. It had been an unusual case, made so primarily by the absence of the victim. The jury had pondered the intangibles: why had Helena Greenwood not been present to give her testimony in person? Had Frediani really confessed, or was Detective Chaput lying? Was Andrea's alibi just a desperate attempt to save the man she loved from incarceration, or were the couple really out house-hunting that Sunday morning in April? In the end, it was Frediani himself who had tipped the scales of justice; the jury had not been impressed by his testimony, they told Murray afterwards. He was the one who sounded like a liar.

The appeals lawyer did a thorough job preparing

his brief. He cited numerous reasons why the verdict should be reversed, most of which stemmed from the mysterious incongruities between Steve Chaput's and Joe Farmer's accounts of their interview with Frediani at Belmont police station the previous April. 'The defence showed that not only had key evidence [Farmer's report] been withheld under dubious circumstances,' the argument ran, 'but Officer Farmer's report suggested that Officer Chaput either misled the jury in testifying about the order of specific questions and actual responses, or his recollection and report were inaccurate . . . [Farmer's report] supported appellant's version that his so-called "confession" had been taken out of context, and was nothing more than a relatively innocuous statement that he had probably done some things he could not recall because he had a few heavy drinking bouts with friends.'

The attorney argued that indeed the entire interview with Frediani had been in violation of his Sixth Amendment right to have his attorney present. Under American law, once a suspect has a lawyer, there can be no interviews about that case outside the lawyer's presence. Since Frediani had already hired Collins for the indecent exposure charge, and since Farmer and Chaput questioned him about that as well as about the sexual assault, he should have been there. Thus his 'confession' – if indeed he was confessing to having assaulted Helena Greenwood – should not have been admissible as evidence. That Collins had not picked this up at trial was an unforgivable slip, and a denial of Frediani's right to effective counsel.

Apart from the fingerprint, the statement made under dubious conditions at the police station was the only evidence pointing towards Frediani's guilt. Would the jury have been able to convict him on the basis of a single fingerprint found on a teapot outside the house?

The appellate lawyer also singled out Martin Murray for criticism. His attack on Andrea for her failure to come forward with her alibi at the preliminary hearing amounted to 'prejudicial misconduct', while his reference to Frediani's 'perversion' was irrelevant.[1] 'Assuming this is not a witch trial to burn appellant if he was "perverted", one is hard pressed to find a valid reason for Mr Murray to make such a statement,' the attorney wrote. '. . . Mr Murray seemed intent upon creating an atmosphere of passion and prejudice against the appellant by injecting his own unsupported opinions of sexuality into the trial, clearly a prohibited tactic.'

The brief infuriated Martin Murray. Not only had Frediani, he believed, murdered his chief witness in an attempt to escape justice, but now they were trying

1. The court reporter had made a mistake in transcribing one of Murray's objections. When he had said, 'It's well established perverted sexuality has no relationship to normal sexual ability,' she had instead written '. . . relationship to homosexuality'. This mistranscription later became a key point in the appeal – and one which continues to madden Murray.

to claim that Murray was the cause of an injustice. He responded with a measured denial of all the claims; the case had been fair, and even if a mistake had been made in not submitting a copy of Farmer's statement to Collins before the trial, it was inadvertent and corrected immediately it became known. Further, the questioning of Andrea had been entirely proper, coming as it did in response to 'very strange behaviour for a woman who was planning to marry defendant, was pregnant with his twins, hoped to buy a house with him and who had deeded him half her property so that he could make bail.'

The behaviour would have seemed even stranger had the judge known that on 24 May 1986 – only three months after Frediani's release on bail pending his appeal – Andrea had marched down to Burlingame police station complaining that Paul had thrown her across the room. He had been tense since he had come home from prison, she said, and was acting increasingly erratically. That morning, she was getting ready for work when he woke up. She told him that she would be home a little later than usual, as she wanted to go to a movie or have a drink after work. This apparently enraged Frediani – he accused her of having an affair, and tried to prevent her from leaving the house. When she asked him to move his car, which was blocking hers in, he refused and told her to walk to work. When she asked again, he reportedly threw her on the bed, then grabbed her hair and pulled her on to the floor.

'Frediani picked [Goodhart] up and threw her into mirror/bureau,' the report continued. 'He pulled up her dress, and said that she was fat and ugly as he poked her in the stomach. Frediani then said that their children were not his, but someone else's because they did not have his blood type. This proved that she was seeing other men. [Goodhart] denied this.'

Andrea escaped into the bathroom. Paul followed. As she was looking in the mirror, he jammed her head into it three times, apparently saying that he had to bang it into her head that he hated her, because she hated him. He pushed her back into the laundry basket, then picked her up with both hands around her neck and started to throttle her.

'Stop, stop,' she gasped. 'I can't breathe.' He let her go, and as she was touching up her make-up – Andrea still worked at the cosmetics counter at Macy's – he repeatedly told her he hated her. When she went into the kitchen to get a Coke, he grabbed the can out of her hand and threw it into the sink. 'You're a whore,' he spat.

She allegedly countered that she had been to his office the previous night, after he had left home for a meeting with some old colleagues, but he hadn't been there. She accused him of seeing someone else.

'I'm going to kill you,' he said, according to Andrea's report to the police that evening. Then he apparently changed tone.

'He complained that Goodhart was not being affectionate, and had left him alone on the couch last night,' the report continued. 'Goodhart said that Frediani was the one not being affectionate, and that she had stopped being affectionate because of his violence. Frediani apologized, and asked Goodhart to promise that neither would cheat on the other.'

Frediani moved his car and Andrea escaped to work. That evening, she went into the police station to give her detailed and dramatic report. She didn't want to press charges, she said, but she wanted Paul to know that the incident had been documented in case she decided to leave him. If that happened, there was no way he was going to keep the boys. A policeman knocked on the door a couple of days later, to tell Paul that Andrea had filed a report about a domestic violence incident. He was not asked any questions, nor given a chance to relate his version of what had happened.

Andrea did not know that the police were keeping a watching brief on Frediani. Martin Murray had made sure that all the patrol officers at Atherton and Burlingame stations had seen his mug shot, knew where he lived and the licence number of his white BMW. If, as Murray believed, Frediani had some sort of sexual compulsion, then it would only be a matter of time before he acted on it, violating the terms of his bail and giving Murray the excuse to throw him right back into prison.

But what Frediani did next was totally unanticipated. A former colleague of his, Nick Koronias, saw him at the Central Park bookstore on Fourth Avenue in San Mateo. He knew why Frediani had disappeared from his job so suddenly, and was curious to find out what he was up to. He decided to play private investigator and follow him. Keeping his distance, Koronias shadowed him along the highway. Frediani turned off at Foster City and, to Nick Koronias' surprise, parked on Lincoln City Drive, opposite his old office building. Looking around and behind him, Frediani went up to the front door of the Lincoln Properties building and started to rattle it.

At this point, Koronias decided that it was time for a real policeman to take over, so he hurried off to call 911. 'There's something funny going on,' he told the dispatcher. 'I think you should send someone out to Lincoln Properties in Foster City right now.'

Detective Smith was there in minutes. Koronias pointed towards the entrance to the building. The doors, habitually locked by a magnetic key system, were open. Smith entered the lobby, where he was joined by three fellow officers. They secured the entrance. Smith was back on his walkie-talkie. 'Smith calling HQ. Request a K-9 unit at Lincoln Properties. Suspected break-in.'

Officer Miles arrived shortly afterwards with his police dog, Dux. Together, Smith, Miles and Dux started checking each floor of the building. As they climbed the stairs, Miles would shout out: 'San Mateo Police K-9, come out or we will send the dog in.' There was silence. The office doors were all locked, but using Nick Koronias' magnetic key, they carefully checked and secured each one. It was only when they reached the fifth floor that Dux began to get excited. He led his handler straight to the men's bathroom. All the cubicles were closed, and the room appeared to be empty. Dux, however, thought otherwise; he went directly to one of the rear stalls, and started scratching at its door. Miles kicked it open, then flattened himself back against the neighbouring door. While Dux barked at whatever was in the stall, Miles pulled out his service revolver, then jumped into the open doorway, feet apart, knees bent and arms outstretched in the classic shooter's pose, shouting, 'Hands up! Don't move or I'll shoot!'

There was Paul Frediani, sitting on the lavatory with his trousers down. His feet were off the floor, and his raised hands were cloaked in thick tan work gloves. Miles called Smith, and together they pushed Frediani face-first on to the tiles and searched him. Then they pulled up his jeans and took off his gloves, handcuffed him and marched him back to Foster City police station.

Once again, Frediani found himself sitting in a police interview room in the early hours of the morning. Once again he was read his rights. What, asked Detective Smith, had he been doing in his old office?

'I went to use the gym on the second floor,' Frediani replied.

'How did you get in?'

'The door was unlocked.'

'Can you tell me your movements from the point where you entered the building, please?'

'Well, before going to the gym, I went to the stairwell, and began running up and down the stairs. That's how I usually begin my workout. But on my way down from the sixth floor, I needed to use the bathroom, so I stopped on the fifth floor, and you found me before I got to the gym. I was only in the building for about ten minutes. I mean, that's all.'

On his report, Smith noted that, 'At the time he was apprehended, he was not breathing hard, nor was he perspiring.' Frediani repeated his story over and over. There was nothing concrete to disprove it. While Smith was taking his suspect to the station, two other officers had checked the building with Nick Koronias. They couldn't see that anything had been taken, though several of the computers were turned on. 'The suspect may have entered the building with the intent to commit a crime,' Smith wrote. 'However, at this time, we are unable to determine his intent.'

Frediani was charged with attempted burglary and released. The report was circulated among the local police stations, and a copy landed on Martin Murray's desk. 'What had he been doing there? I don't know. Was there a smoking gun, linking him to Helena Greenwood's murder? Maybe that was how he found her address? Or maybe he knew where they kept the money? Maybe he thought there would be a female employee in the building that he could rape? I don't know. What I do know is that he went there at night.

The dog finds him sitting in a bathroom stall wearing gloves with his feet up. I don't know how many people you know that use the bathroom facilities with their feet up. And why would someone need heavy gloves in the Bay area in May? I mean, we're not talking about Minnesota winters.'

Murray had had enough. He didn't want Frediani out on the streets for a minute longer. He prepared a motion to revoke his bail. 'Based on the defendant's activity while on bail, he has demonstrated that he poses a danger to the community,' Murray maintained, at the same time requesting the judge to issue a warrant for his arrest.

Not only was there the assault on Andrea and the strange attempted burglary, but Frediani had been spotted the month before, sitting in his car on the side of the road at 3.45 a.m., and two days after the burglary, while adjusting the chain of his bicycle at 11.15 p.m., he was hit in the face by a man wielding a tree branch, apparently unprovoked. 'He was always out at night, scouting around. A scary guy. You would think that while you're out on bail, waiting an appeal on a charge like this, you would be on your best behaviour,' Murray said. 'But the compulsiveness of this guy is such that he couldn't do that. Sex criminals are compulsive: they have the highest rate of recidivism of any class of criminal, except drug users – but it's the sex criminals you have to worry about, because there is no effective way to treat them.'

Judge Haverty agreed, and on 23 June, when

Frediani was picked up for prowling – he said he was looking for his cat, had seen a car, and hidden behind the bushes because he knew the police were following him – he was told that his bail had been revoked and that he was going back to prison. The police first accompanied him home, where the twins were asleep alone in the house – Andrea was at college, having left Paul in charge of them. He was sent back to Vacaville to await the results of his appeal.

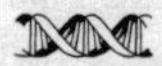

A month later, on 30 July 1986, the phone rang in Helena Greenwood's old office at Gen-Probe, now occupied by her successor as director of marketing, Lois Schmidt. The office manager, Gisela Koestner, was passing and picked it up. A man was on the other end of the line.

'I want to speak to Lois Schmidt,' he said.

'She's away from her desk at the moment, can I take a message?' Koestner asked.

'Tell her that this is the man who murdered and raped her predecessor.' There was half a minute's silence before he hung up.

Koestner went straight to the company president, John Bishop. He immediately called the police, who came over to take a statement. The caller had a mature, businesslike voice, Koestner told them, with no accent or peculiar dialect, as far as she could tell. He sounded calm, maybe in his thirties to forties, and appeared to make no attempt to disguise his voice. The police talked to Schmidt, who was clearly shaken. 'Do you know of anyone who has a grudge against you?' they asked her.

She couldn't think who it might be. They wrote up their report, and asked to be contacted if the mysterious caller got in touch again.

This wasn't enough for Lois Schmidt. She knew what had happened to Helena Greenwood, and that her murderer had never been caught. No job justified that kind of risk, she told Bishop, and handed in her resignation. He promised to ensure her security if she would stay on until they could find someone to take over.

He found the number of a firm of private investigators, headed by two veteran cops based up in Orange County. They came highly recommended: Bernie Esposito and Bill Tynes had together hunted down the 'Freeway Killer', after a gruesome spree which left twenty-two young men and boys dead. It was the culmination of a long career in law enforcement for the detective team, and they had had enough. In 1982, they left to form Tynes & Esposito. Four years later, John Bishop called them down to San Diego.

'We were hired initially to look into the death threats that had been received by Miss Schmidt,' Bernie Esposito recalls. Now working part-time for his firm, and spending the balance on the golf courses of America, he is well-built and tanned, and drives the latest model Mercedes sports car. 'We agreed to provide round-the-clock security for Miss Schmidt until she left the company. It wasn't going to be that long. I also agreed to ask around to see if I could find out where these threats were coming from.'

He spoke to most of the Gen-Probe staff, but none of them had any serious ideas. Industrial espionage was again mooted, but not found to have any legs. Esposito soon learned that Lois Schmidt's predecessor, Helena Greenwood, had been killed a year previously. 'I wondered whether there was anything about that particular position? I wasn't getting a lot of answers with the here-and-now, so I started looking for a possible tie-in with Helena Greenwood.'

He explained to John Bishop that they would be happy to investigate that aspect, for an additional fee. Bishop agreed. Although no one at Gen-Probe would admit it, they were feeling guilty about Helena Greenwood. In the excitement of launching their first products, seeing them gobbled up by a hungry marketplace, their first marketing director had been all but forgotten. After her death the previous year, Sydney Greenwood had met Bishop, Adams, Birndorf and the rest. They were full of enthusiasm for a fitting memorial for Helena. One of them suggested a library, and when Sydney offered to paint a portrait of his daughter to hang in it, they told him it was a terrific idea. He went back to England and painted it from memory. It took him a year – a year of pain and joy, when he would drift into memories of his only daughter, only to start back into the reality of her absence. When it was finished, he framed the picture, wrapped it up carefully and sent it to America. He heard nothing. A few months later, a large parcel arrived back on Sydney's doorstep with an 'excess postage due' stamp on it, and no explanation as to Gen-Probe's change of heart. He was shattered, and destroyed the portrait – he could not live with it.

It was the final straw for Sam Morishima too. Soon after plans for the Helena Greenwood library were scrapped, he resigned. The company she had loved and been so excited by had changed beyond recognition, had evolved into a sleek, successful brand leader. 'I felt dreadfully let down,' Sam recalls. 'I worked so hard for that company but the atmosphere had changed drastically. I keep trying to work out now, why didn't I go to Helena's funeral? And what I remember thinking was that Gen-Probe was Helena's baby and someone had to stay at home to watch the baby. And now they weren't going to hang Helena's picture in the library.'

They had, however, hired a private investigator to look into her death. Esposito arranged through a friend at the local Sheriff's office to have a meeting with Decker and Kelly. They went out to lunch and discussed the case. The San Diego detectives confided their suspicions about Frediani, and rued their lack of hard evidence. Afterwards, they took the PI on a tour of the crime scene, and when he offered to see if his home crime lab in Orange County would look for fingerprints using the new superglue method, they expressed enthusiasm. But the idea was soon immobilized by red tape.

Esposito persuaded Gen-Probe to pay for him and Bill Tynes to fly to San Francisco to check things out at that end. They tracked down his former roommate, Barbara Powell, spoke to his old friends Jim Thoren and Arthur Settlemeyer, found out about the traffic accident Frediani had been involved in north of Los Angeles a week before Helena Greenwood's murder – placing him at least in the right geographical half of California – but they too failed to find anything concrete to link him with the murder. They returned south with a strong suspicion that Frediani was their man. But he was in Vacaville prison at the time of the strange threatening phone call, in administrative segregation, 'Ad seg', without the use of a phone. He couldn't have made that call – and if he didn't, then who did?

Andrea went to visit Paul in prison each weekend, bringing the boys. With their father away, they had become the maypole around which she danced. She had to work hard to support them, but she vowed that she would do whatever she had to do to protect them, and that they would not suffer from their unorthodox start to life.

On 16 January 1987, the appeals court handed down its verdict. The tone of the decision was measured and lofty, in tune with its content. It agreed that Chaput's and Farmer's reports revealed inconsistencies, and that from Farmer's account, it was clear that 'I was really drunk when I did those things' referred to the indecent exposure charges. Murray's comments on perversion, moreover, were deemed 'inflammatory non sequiturs',[1] that were 'unprofessional and inconsistent with the office of public prosecutor . . . The failure of the defence counsel to strike the statement, seek an admonition from the court, or seek other sanctions indicates ineffective assistance of counsel,' the judgment ran.

'The totality of instances of misconduct, error and ineffective assistance of counsel lead us to the conclusion that reversal is required . . . When appellant's statement is either removed or placed in proper context, the impermissible attack on the sole alibi witness is removed and the improper comments and cross-examination by prosecutor are eliminated, it is reasonably probable that the appellant would achieve a more favourable result.'

Frediani read about his successful appeal in the newspaper in prison. Martin Murray immediately pledged to ensure that he would not escape what he was sure was his due punishment. Now that he knew Frediani's defence, Murray was sure he could get another conviction if the case was tried again. Steve Chaput had already been checking and double-checking Frediani's alibi, and it was looking leaky.

1. Again, the judgment depends on the mistranscription of 'normal sexual ability' as 'homosexuality'. This may, Murray believes, have made the crucial difference to the appeals court's decision to reverse.

Retrying a case was an expensive business, but Murray decided that if the first twelve people could find Frediani guilty, then the next twelve may well too. He decided to press ahead. The date for the second trial was set for 27 July 1987.

With his bail still revoked, Frediani spent the time waiting in jail. His new attorney, a short, rambunctious public defender called Edward Rojas, appeared optimistic. Andrea was still visiting with the boys, but with decreasing regularity. The already shaky foundations of their relationship were beginning to crumble. Despite what he had said at the first trial, Paul would not have counted Andrea as among the loves of his life. She had pushed for marriage, was continuing to do so, but as a way of papering over the fractures, he thought, rather than healing them. And he had been burned by the wedding ring before.

When he arrived at college, Paul Frediani was a relationship illiterate. He had never even kissed a girl, and in his first semester, he made few attempts to date – he was too shy to make that first move. By the end of the year, however, with the confidence of a fraternity brother, he was going bowling, taking women to the coffee shop or out for a walk, though little more. 'I left school for the summer break with my virginity intact – much to my chagrin,' he said. He shared a ride home for the holidays, and got a job working for his father's company, saving enough over the summer to pay for his yearly room and board expenses at college. But it was that first summer that he became smitten with a local girl called Mary Pat, and so as to keep seeing her, he took a year out from the University of Eastern New Mexico, and enrolled at his home-town college. By this time, he believed himself to be deeply in love. The relationship wasn't without its hitches – Mary Pat had been dating a friend of Paul's called Dave for the previous two years, and while he was away for the summer, Paul assumed they had broken up.

But when Dave got back, the trouble started. 'I go over to Dave's house the day he came home, as I looked forward to seeing him, hearing about Europe and telling him about how happy I was with my new and first girlfriend. He was happy to see me, but troubled. He said he was on his way to see Mary Pat – he had heard she had a new boyfriend. I was shocked and said, "I thought you two broke up." He said no, only that they could see other people over the summer. So after I mustered the courage, I said, "Dave, I know who she has been seeing, and that guy is me." He was totally dumbfounded. I for one was his friend [and] I was not known for dating anyone.'

Mary Pat started seeing both of them, then, in January, it became too much. 'I had taken her to see *The Way We Were*, and I could tell something was up. I asked her a couple of times, and she ended up telling me it was too much pressure, and she would stop seeing both of us. So there's Katie saying, "She's beautiful, Hubble, why don't you bring her when you come . . ." I cry over Lassie movies and obviously was fighting hard to cover the tears. I was crushed. I had adored her. The entire time, I had only kissed her and never touched her. We never had a cross word for each other. But in the end, I lost the girl I loved *and* one of my best friends.' He finished the semester at his local college, but pledged to return to New Mexico for his junior year.

He bought a '64 T-bird and started back in style. He was soon dating a girl at college, and in time, and after mutual professions of love, they lost their virginity to each other. 'After the first time, we got good at it. I was happy that I lost my virginity before my twentieth birthday. Barely,' he recalled. For the rest of the year, and through that summer, they were an item. But they argued, and broke up, and when he wasn't devastated, he realized he could not have really loved her. Instead, he embarked on his first wild phase: 'I started dating a lot and sleeping with many. I even discovered that popular girls in school were after me.' He felt he was making up for time lost at high school. 'I even dated Miss New Mexico.'

After graduating, he found a job as an accounts clerk for a company selling scientific instruments back east. He was working hard, most of his friends were married or engaged and he was single. Life wasn't half as exciting as it had promised to be, so one evening when his college ex-girlfriend called, 'I gave in and asked her to marry me.' A few months later, they were walking down the aisle of a pretty Catholic church in her home town in New Mexico. The frat brothers came to cheer him on, the Frediani family were in the front pew, and there was a terrific party after the ceremony. But the arguments continued, and the new marriage drifted towards the rocks.

Paul was promoted and transferred to the New Jersey branch of his company. 'I was quiet and unassuming, but I worked hard. I thought I would retire in New Jersey some day as an accounts payable supervisor. I guess I did not have much appreciation of myself, and surely not much foresight.' Months later, he was surprised to be offered a job in the head office in Chicago. He took it, but after a few months, he and his wife split up permanently. Paul buried himself in his job. He had few friends in Chicago, few distractions. He was sent to San Francisco one week on a training course to use the new software about to be installed in the Chicago office. It was his first time in California, and for the first time, he felt he belonged somewhere.

San Francisco was cosmopolitan, glamorous, full of energy and originality – so far from the conservative conformity of his roots. He spent the weekend roaming the city, climbing the hills and looking out over the Golden Gate bridge to Marin County to the north, and back across San Mateo and Belmont towards Palo Alto in the south. It was beautiful. He never wanted to leave. On the first day of his course, he found another reason to stay: he fell in love instantly with one of the accounts clerks from the local office, an olive-skinned, dark-haired girl called Cris. He sat down beside her and told her she had the most beautiful eyes he had ever seen. Immediately, he thought, 'Here is a girl I could marry' – but she rejected his tentative advances and tried to ignore him.

He was both disappointed and delighted – it was evidence at least that his heart was not dead, he was just very choosy. On Friday, standing in the lobby with his bags packed, Cris came up to Paul to say goodbye. She apologized for her coldness – said she had heard that he was married and that she had a boyfriend. She wasn't interested, in any case, in getting involved with someone who lived 2,000 miles away. But Paul was, in his own words, 'on fire'. His heart was beating like a drum machine and he could not but believe that she was feeling the same. When some colleagues came up, she vanished, and all he wanted to do was run after her and ask if she felt the magic too. On the plane, his colleague told him that Cris had confided in her boss that she was keen on Paul too. He wanted to open the emergency exit and parachute right out on to her desk. Impulsive, romantic, he immediately started thinking about quitting his job, moving to San Francisco, starting over again with Cris.

A week later, he drew in the courage to call her at work. They talked for forty-five minutes. He asked if he could call her that evening at home. They chatted for hours. And the next night and the next. After two weeks, she told him she was going to break up with her boyfriend; soon afterwards, Paul told her he loved her. 'We'd been talking on the phone for hours each night, and we really got to know each other really well, I thought. We talked more than other couples covered in a year. It was so right. I asked her to marry me, and she immediately said yes.' They planned to wed in December – and in October, her parents offered to bring him over to San Francisco for a few days so they could get to know him. Cris was waiting at the airport and she ran into his arms. It was the first time they had touched, first kiss, first hug. He met her parents, her best friends. They got on like pastrami and rye.

He came back for Thanksgiving and when she asked whether he would consider moving to San Francisco, instead of her coming to Chicago, he turned immediately to the jobs pages in the paper. He was offered a job, with a pay rise, at the first place he applied to, a small think tank in Palo Alto, only streets away from Syva, where Helena Greenwood was at that time making the sideways leap from research into marketing. He hired a trailer, packed everything he owned, and drove west. 'As I reached the top of the last grade to San Francisco, I could see all the lights and remember thinking, wow, this is something! I'm really here in the city I love, with the most wonderful woman I could ever imagine existed. Who knew the problems that lay ahead?'

The wedding was postponed until a bigger one could be planned, and at first he lived with Cris at her parents' house, in separate bedrooms. But it all started to go wrong; the parents were uncomfortable with Paul and Cris cuddling and kissing in front of them, they did not like the long hours he worked, and resented him playing softball on weekends instead of being home with the family. When Cris told her mother that they had slept together, the situation ignited.

Her mother collared Paul one morning and accused him of using her daughter. When he protested, she insisted that he must have psychological problems; why else would a son have moved away from his family? Paul finally lost his temper and started shouting back. He later called her 'the most evil person I have ever met. She claimed to be a witch and said she would put a spell on me and dance on my grave.' That night, when he got home from work, Paul found his bags on the front step.

It took some time to patch things up with Cris – they were apart for a while. One day, she called him up and said the only solution would be for them to go to Nevada that weekend and get married. Surprised but delighted, Paul agreed. Once the ring was on her finger, her parents were happier. Cris and Paul moved into a rented apartment. Her mother called a truce, while her father, an auto mechanic, helped Paul work on his car. Paul's parents flew out to meet the in-laws, and for a time, everyone was happy.

Then Cris's father got cancer. She went to see him every night after work and at weekends. But if she skipped an evening, her mother would tell her that it was killing her father. 'We ended up splitting mostly because she believed in her parents being first and foremost, and was tired of being pulled apart. I tried and tried to patch things up.' But she would not give up her daily family visits. 'After a couple of months of trying to get her back, I gave up.' Paul let their apartment go, and when he saw an advertisement in the local paper for a roommate in a nice complex in George Avenue in Belmont, he decided to go and have a look. The landlord, Jim Thoren, appeared to be the perfect antidote to a broken marriage – he was expansive, always on for a party, a guy's guy with a penchant for fast women. Paul decided it was just what he needed and moved in.

He was soon back on the wild side, partying with Jim and Art Settlemeyer five nights a week, going to clubs, drinking, picking up girls and sleeping little. 'Without really trying – my heart wasn't into it – I started sleeping with one or two new women a week.' It was a crazy time and the George Street complex was like a twenty-four-hour party. Jim Thoren's place was always at the centre of the action; it overlooked the main pool and on weekends, he, Art and Paul would mix cocktails and take them poolside. Paul was more reserved than Jim, but he was accepted by the party set and admired by women. He grew his hair long, a couple of inches over his collar, and laughed to think what his father would have said about it. He didn't care that much – he made little effort to stay in touch with his family back east.

He was working at Lincoln Properties by now, as financial controller. Somehow, he managed both the hard partying and hard work. He was earning well and enjoyed his job. Then Cris started calling. She told him she wanted to try again. They went to a marriage guidance counsellor, but Paul was not too sure. He had been seeing another girl whom he liked enough to forsake the one-night stands. She was called Kit, nineteen, a student at UC Davis, near Sacramento. They had, in Paul's own words, 'fantastic sex', and he was not sure he wanted to give her up for Cris.

Even seeing them both – weekdays with Cris, weekends with Kit – was regarded as abnormal behaviour by Jim Thoren, who wanted a comrade wolf, not a stay-at-home swan. Paul moved into a single-room apartment in the same complex and continued his double life. Things were going better and better with Cris – and he told himself he was going to break it off with Kit once the summer was over and she went back to college. But a week before term started, Cris found out about the other woman. That was it for her. She packed her bags and left. Paul never heard from her again.

'I felt horrible,' he remembered. 'I couldn't find the words to justify what I had done. If nothing else, I had too much respect for her to ask her to forgive me after that. I blew it and have regretted it ever since.

I promised I wouldn't make the same mistake again.' Weeks later, Kit dumped him.

It was not long before he met Andrea. There was the story of the cologne bottle in Macy's, Sunday brunches, house-hunting, the first arrest, pregnancy, the trial, and now there was prison and visits with the boys. Frediani could only hope – believe – that when the sexual assault case came back into court, for retrial, this time the jury would find him innocent. He would be granted another chance.

10

'Holy Shit!' Kary Mullis pulled his new silver Honda Civic off Highway 128 and scrabbled for a pencil and paper in the glove pocket in front of his sleeping girlfriend. It was a balmy spring evening in April 1983, the buckeyes were in flower, and he had been hit by the kind of flash of inspiration that is normally preceded by the adjective 'divine'. He had invented, he believed, a method to grow DNA.

Kary Mullis was always coming up with crazy schemes. As a kid, living in the small town of Hickory in rural South Carolina, he tortured cows by hanging slices of apple on the electric fence. By the time he was seven, in the early 1950s, his family had moved to the state capital, Columbia, and he had been given his first chemistry set, with predictable results. It was fun, a blast in both senses of the word. In his teens, he and his friends built rockets out of scrap metal, which they manned with parachute-wearing frogs and blasted a mile into space from the Mullis backyard.

He spent the summer following high school graduation working at a professional laboratory supplying chemicals to research institutions, and after his first year at the Georgia Institute of Technology, he started synthesizing discontinued chemical compounds for the same company in his friend's garage. He had already decided that he was going to be a famous scientist: there was no point in being merely another drone in a white coat and goggles. His intention was stiffened after his high-school girlfriend broke up with him a term into college. 'I remember being heartbroken about that and driving back from college thinking, "One of these days I'm going to be famous, and she'll regret it."'

Mullis stayed at Georgia Tech for as long as he could swing it, majoring jointly in chemistry and women, which still left enough time to go to lectures on anthropology, sociology, physics, maths and music. He was not the conventional archetype of the bespectacled scientist: he looked and acted more like a surfer dude than a lab rat – in his mid-fifties he still does, tanned and wiry with salt-stiffened hair – and believed in astrology (he is a Capricorn) and the nurturing powers of a couple of bottles of Californian red. In his early twenties, he married for the first time, had his first child, and moved to Berkeley, where he had been accepted at graduate school. It was the 1960s, and Berkeley was already cloaked in its radical-chic rags. For a boy from the conservative south, it was 'like being let out of jail'.

In Georgia, no one was 'synthesizing new molecular forms of psychedelics and saying, "What do these things do? How does it feel if you take this stuff and put it in your mouth?" In all the chemistry labs and biochemistry labs in Berkeley there was a little element of that going on; like when I first arrived there, they hadn't decided that these things were bad for you and that they were going to be illegal.' Inspired, Mullis came up with a 'cosmological theory' that he felt was 'a little more steady than the Big Bang'. He sent his idea off to *Nature*, in an article entitled 'The Cosmological Significance of Time Reversal', which to widespread incredulity was published. 'It was unprecedented, sort of, for a graduate student to publish in *Nature*,' Mullis recalls with a certain smidgen of pride. 'I did it because I didn't realize it was so unprecedented. I thought, You have an idea, you send it off to *Nature*.' Despite frequent absences from the lab – both physical and metaphysical – Kary Mullis completed his Ph.D., and in 1972, became Dr Mullis.

Still in his twenties, he divorced, and in time remarried. He went with his second wife to Kansas, and while she was at medical school, he took a sabbatical from science and tried writing fiction, eventually giving up because he could not 'figure out how anybody could ever be unhappy'. Instead, he succumbed once more to the lure of test tubes and beakers, working in a paediatric cardiology lab until he became fed up with, as he put it, slaughtering animals and 'ending each day with a bag full of rats' heads and other gross things'.

It was while he was buried in entrails that his second wife bolted. 'It was a well-documented phenomenon and it didn't hurt my feelings,' he wrote in his part-memoir, part-collection of essays, *Dancing*

Naked in the Mind Field. 'In fact, it was about three months before I realized that she had left.' Instead of mourning, he filled their house with electrical equipment and embarked on a series of bizarre experiments, which culminated in turning himself into an electrical conductor. By running an electrical current through an electrode pinching each wrist, and consciously manipulating his heart rate by looking at pictures of naked women, he could control the resistance of his skin and switch on and off a lamp across the street, to the awe of a pretty nursing student.

Back in Berkeley with his soon-to-be third wife, Cynthia, Kary Mullis was managing The Buttercup Bakery, when an old Berkeley compatriot of his, Tom White, walked in to offer him a job at Cetus Corporation, based in Emeryville, California. Like the whale it was named after, Cetus was destined to make a big splash in the scientific world. It had been started eight years previously by a triumvirate of young men: a biochemist, a physician, and a Nobel laureate physicist turned molecular biologist, who quickly snapped up those brilliant scientists who were willing to sell their brains for a hefty salary. Cetus was the first biotechnology company to recombine – manipulate – DNA to develop vaccines or therapeutic medicines. It was cutting-edge technology, blurring the line between academia and industry. And like Syva, which Helena Greenwood joined the same year, it was a stimulating place in which to work. Mullis was back in his element. 'It was really fun to learn how to synthesize DNA,' he recalled. 'It was just organic synthesis, pure and simple. No rats. And it was the heyday of biotechnology. There were all kinds of bold ideas floating around all the time about what we were going to make, and there was absolutely no restraint in terms of imagination . . .'

Despite periodic improbable flights of fancy, Mullis was good at his job, and soon found himself in charge of the laboratory dedicated to making oligonucleotides. An oligonucleotide is a short string of synthetically manufactured DNA which, under the right conditions and with the right chemical primers, will act as a probe and bind to a complementary sequence of nucleotide bases in single-strand DNA. It was a probe of this kind that Alec Jeffreys devised to look for his RFLPs, and that Gen-Probe was named after. By 1983, this process of manufacturing DNA had become highly automated, in part thanks to Mullis' work in introducing and writing computer programs that took over much of the manual labour, and he was having problems occupying his seven technicians.

'Laboratory machines, which we loaded and watched, were making almost more oligonucleotides than we had room for in the freezer and certainly more than the molecular biologists – who seemed to be working even more slowly and tediously than we had previously suspected – could use in their experiments. Consequently, in my laboratory at Cetus, there was a fair amount of time available to think and to putter.'

He was thinking while he puttered on that warm, moonlit night in the late spring of 1983, the creamy clusters of buckeye flowers arching over the road. He was looking for some easy way to read a random letter in the sequence of DNA – whether it was an A, C, G or T. This would be of immeasurable aid in all branches of genetics – particularly in medical diagnostics. A group at Cetus, led by Henry Erlich, was trying to find a method of detecting sickle-cell anaemia, an often-fatal inherited disease which causes blood cells to collapse in the absence of oxygen. By this time, they knew that the condition was caused by the mutation of just one base – among the 3 billion in the human genome. If that base could be easily identified, then isolated, an unborn child's susceptibility to the disease could be detected. The main problem was that the individual bases, nucleotides, are tiny – even now, no microscope is powerful enough to see them – and thus difficult to pinpoint.

Mullis' aim was to design a series of chemical reactions that would, in essence, highlight and then magnify a stretch of DNA until it could be easily read chemically. It was not a far-fetched idea, owing to DNA's self-replicating mechanism. The oligonucleotides he was manufacturing were already being used to stick to a longer strand of DNA containing complementary sequences. However, this matching process was not completely accurate. It might locate a thousand different places that were similar to the one he was searching for – in addition to the correct gene. He needed to make it zero in on the target alone.

'Suddenly I knew how to do it,' he recounts. 'If I could locate a thousand sequences out of billions with one short piece of DNA, I could use another short piece to narrow the search. This one would be designed to bind to a sequence just down the chain from the first sequence I had found. It would scan over the thousand possibilities out of the first search to find just the one I wanted.' He stopped the Honda to think about it, but even immobile, the idea made sense.

He pulled back on to the road. 'It took about a mile or two to realize that what you could do for one base between two oligos, you could also just back 'em up and make as big a piece as you wanted.' The first stretch of DNA would self-duplicate, producing a chain double the length and with exactly the same base sequence repeated twice. He recalled writing computer programs, and the immense power of iteration, and he realized that if you were to run the chemical reaction again, the length would double – and so on in an exponential fashion. 'That is when I stopped the car again and said Holy Shit . . .' He worked out that if he repeated the reaction ten times, he would have more than a thousand copies of this piece of DNA; twenty cycles would make a million; and a billion, trillion and zillion wouldn't be far off. And all would contain the same sequence repeated over and over again – in a much larger piece of DNA that would be far easier to see. He would find the proverbial needle in the haystack by making the needles outnumber the hay.

'I had just solved the two major problems in DNA chemistry. Abundance and distinction. And I had done it in one stroke . . . This simple sequence would make as many copies as I wanted of any DNA sequence I chose, and everybody on earth who cared about DNA would want to use it.' By the time Mullis and his still-asleep girlfriend had reached his cabin on the edge of the giant redwood forests, he was convinced that he was going to get a Nobel prize. His only doubt centred on the beauty and simplicity of the method: if it indeed worked, then why hadn't anybody thought of it before?

Back at Cetus on Monday morning, Mullis made a beeline for the library. But nothing relevant to DNA amplification showed up in the recent literature. For the next few weeks, he described his idea to everyone he could collar. No one had heard of it being tried; no one could see why it shouldn't work – yet no one took it particularly seriously either. Mullis, after all, was the man who had allegedly been spotted in Aspen skiing down the centre of an icy road through fast two-way traffic, convinced that, as he had had a vision that he would die by crashing his head against a redwood tree, he was safe wherever there were no redwoods. As his then colleague Henry Erlich said, 'Kary Mullis is a very creative guy, but . . .'

It took months for Mullis to jump from the creative to experimental stage. First, he presented the concept of PCR to his colleagues at a Cetus seminar in August. Nobody was interested. 'Most of the people left the room before I was done,' he recalls. Nevertheless, the following month, he primed his test tubes. The success of the process rested on the power of a natural cellular enzyme called polymerase to catalyse the formation and repair of DNA. What Mullis hoped to do was to start and stop a polymerase's action at given points along a strand of DNA using the synthetic probes. He added the enzyme and some appropriate oligonucleotides to a piece of human DNA, heated it to denature it – split the strands – and cooled it off. Nothing happened.

Over the next few months he tried again and again. He switched from using human DNA to plasmid, a simple, double-stranded circular DNA molecule found in a variety of bacterial species. Then, on 16 December 1983, a few days after his girlfriend had abandoned him, he got his first positive result. He placed the DNA in a test tube with a mixture of primers, enzymes and other reagents, and subjected it to repeated heating and cooling cycles. The plasmid 'grew'. The technique he called the Polymerase Chain Reaction (PCR) worked. 'It meant I was going to be famous,' he said. He had discovered a way to mimic nature's way of copying DNA – in a test tube and to order.

He returned to human DNA, using the region of the beta-globin gene containing the sickle-cell mutation that Erlich's group had been working on.

By June 1984, he was sure he was getting some sort of amplification, but it was nowhere near ready for practical or commercial use. He prepared a poster explaining his PCR work to display at that year's Cetus scientific meeting in Monterey. Nobody looked at it. Mullis was still suffering from his girlfriend's defection and had been acting in an increasingly erratic manner, and his more level-headed colleagues were getting annoyed by his histrionics and disinclined to take anything he did or said seriously.

The powers-that-were at Cetus were sceptical about PCR. They realized that it would be important if it worked, but at that point none of the top scientists believed it would. Still, they conceded that it was worth looking into a bit more, and so it was decided to pull Kary out of the synthesis lab, and put him to work full-time on PCR. He would have a year to prove it was viable.

This is where the two stories of how PCR developed from conception to the marketplace diverge. As Mullis tells it, he and his assistant, Fred Faloona, continued to experiment, until the process was obviously, and patently, viable. It was only at this point that Cetus finally woke up to what they had – a technology that would prove to be among the most important and powerful of the late twentieth and twenty-first centuries. Then, everyone wanted a piece of it and rushed to stake their claim in the history of the invention process.

Erlich's crowd have a different version. Mullis, they

say, never managed to make PCR work on human DNA. It was to that problem that the sickle-cell group applied themselves in the late summer of 1984. Although Mullis and Faloona were part of the team, most of the work switched to Erlich's lab because, according to Henry Erlich, 'By now it had become a genetics project and not a chemistry project, and Kary was primarily a chemist.'

Their approach was slightly different: 'Kary was thinking about PCR as a way to produce DNA – but what I thought was, if you could amplify a gene in a genome where it is, say, one in a billion, then it could be used in an analytic way.' What Erlich needed to know was whether PCR could be made to work on a complex template – a piece of DNA that contained more than just a pure gene. After five months of experimentation, they developed procedures which enabled them to amplify beta-globin – a protein – a couple of thousand-fold. 'But when we analysed what we had produced in the test tube, only about 1 per cent was beta-globin. It wasn't highly specific, therefore, but nonetheless it was sufficient to enable us to do prenatal diagnoses of sickle-cell anaemia, so we were very encouraged.'

The emphasis changed – from 'Why hasn't anybody thought of this before?' to 'They must be about to come up with their own PCR.' The Cetus method needed to be patented, and that required external scientific validation, in the form of publication. A plan was hatched: the first patent application for

PCR would be filed in March 1985, followed by a presentation to the American Society for Human Genetics annual meeting and almost simultaneous publication. Since there were essentially two components to the PCR discovery, Kary Mullis' 'pure' concept, and the Erlich team's 'applied' technology, it was decided to write two papers.

According to Mullis, the Cetus establishment – Henry Erlich and his cohorts – purposely rushed their article into print before he felt PCR was ready for worldwide scientific scrutiny. He was furious, and to this day, maintains that Cetus effectively 'stole' his process, and tried to steal the glory associated with it.

The other version of history maintains that Kary Mullis was not at all keen to publish, but instead wanted to keep PCR a trade secret, and sell tubes of reagents, into which the DNA would be put. This was not practical (it would have been relatively simple for Cetus' competitors to come up with their own product by reverse-engineering). His colleagues began to suspect that it was more a matter of procrastination, especially as the summer progressed, and Kary had still not written his paper. The applied team, meanwhile, submitted theirs to *Science* – the premier American scientific publication – and it was duly accepted, and on 20 December 1985, published under the title, 'Enzymatic Amplification of Beta-Globin Genomic Sequences and Restriction Site Analysis for Diagnosis of Sickle Cell Anaemia'. The paper concluded with a conscious echo of Watson's and Crick's famous 1953 concluding understatement to their *Nature* article. 'The ability of the PCR procedure to amplify a target DNA segment in genomic DNA raises the possibility that its use may extend beyond that of prenatal diagnosis to other areas of molecular biology.'

Mullis finally completed his paper and in December 1985, submitted it to *Nature*. It was rejected. He resubmitted it to *Science*. It was rejected. Mullis blamed Erlich and his group for scuppering his chances and stealing his credit by prepublishing their article thus, to the world in general, relegating his role in the creation of PCR to that of a collaborator. It was not until mid-1986 that he finally managed to establish his credentials as the first author of PCR, when he presented a talk to a scientific symposium at Cold Spring Harbour Laboratory, headed then by James Watson, who was of course no stranger to revolutionary papers on DNA. (According to Mullis, Cetus even tried to block this talk.)

What is beyond debate is that PCR caused an explosion of excitement in the world of molecular biology, with ripples quickly lapping into all fields of science. In June 1986, when Henry Erlich and his group introduced another DNA polymerase, called *Taq* polymerase, into the reaction, Kary Mullis' concept was brought into pure and elegant reality. 'I sometimes refer to this as the revolution within the revolution,' says Erlich. The new polymerase – an enzyme isolated from bacteria found in the geysers and hot springs of Yellowstone Park – was heat stable, allowing the reaction to be performed at far higher temperatures, which vastly increased the specificity, from 1 to 95 per cent. The efficiency was also improved, eventually allowing the process to become automated.

In 1989, *Science* named Taq polymerase its first 'Molecule of the Year' – PCR was truly on the map. Kary Mullis had fulfilled his ambition of becoming a famous scientist. His ex-girlfriend from high school, now a molecular biologist in Atlanta, started to use PCR in her research into diarrhoea. It was only when she met someone from Cetus that she found out that Kary Mullis had invented it. 'Kary Mullis? He used to be my boyfriend in high school,' she said. She gave the Cetus employee her number to pass on to Kary.

When he called, she invited him down to Atlanta to give a lecture. 'She picked me up from the airport,' Mullis recounts, with unconcealed enjoyment, 'and I thought, finally, she will see me for what I am. But on the way back, we stopped at a bar, and she told me that she was gay. It was funny realizing that all my frustration with her in high school wasn't because I was ugly: she just didn't like guys.' If he'd known that at the time, would he still have had the impetus to invent PCR? A chuckle, 'I think so, somehow.'

Inevitably, Mullis and Cetus eventually parted ways, Mullis with a $10,000 bonus in his pocket – the paltriness of which still makes him fume – after Cetus sold the patent rights of PCR to Hoffman La Roche for 300 million dollars. A decade after the illuminating

April drive to Mendocino, and only months before his fiftieth birthday, Kary Mullis received an early-morning phone call at his beachfront apartment in La Jolla, only two miles from Del Mar, where Helena Greenwood was murdered. 'Congratulations, Dr Mullis,' the caller said, 'I am pleased to be able to announce to you that you have been awarded the Nobel prize.'

The world's media heard at the same time, and immediately deluged him with calls. It was a newsworthy event beyond the normal: rarely had the Nobel been awarded to an industry – as opposed to academic – scientist, and, even more unusually, for the discovery of a single experimental technique. But the power and widespread utility of PCR demanded global recognition. Mullis ducked out of the house with a friend to go for his habitual morning surf. 'When we came out of the water [a] camera crew was waiting . . . They didn't know me, and they were asking everyone who came out of the water if he was Kary Mullis. Andy Dizon admitted to being me. They asked him how it felt to win the Nobel prize. He proclaimed that it was like a dream coming true. They asked him what he would be doing the rest of the day, and he turned to me and said, "Wow! I just remembered *this* is Kary Mullis."'

The Nobel, says Mullis, is proof that PCR is his and his alone: if Erlich had indeed been behind it, then surely he would have shared in the prize. Indeed, there are many scientists who protest that Mullis should not have been the sole recipient of science's most prestigious prize. They continue to maintain that Henry Erlich's work in making PCR into what is probably one of the most useful – and widely used – biochemical tools, the genetic equivalent of a photocopying machine, has been under-credited. But Mullis emphatically disagrees: 'Henry Erlich? He was just the lucky person in the lab down the corridor who got to use PCR to amplify stuff.'

It was to this lab that a forensic scientist called Ed Blake came for help one day in the summer of 1986. Blake was one of the country's foremost serologists, a pioneer in blood and enzyme work. But in the case of *Pennsylvania v. Pestinikas*, he faced a particularly taxing problem. A man in his nineties had been found dead in a nursing home. He looked as if he had been in Auschwitz rather than a private institution: a skeleton covered by loose skin. His room was dilapidated and cold. The state decided to prosecute the owners of the home under an obscure law, whereby a person in a position of custodial responsibility over someone who is legally incapable of looking after themselves is held to be criminally liable if those duties are not exercised correctly.

The prosecution's case rested on autopsy findings which strongly indicated that the old man had been starved. The defence attorney acting on behalf of the owners of the home, the Pestinikases, naturally requested an independent autopsy. That is when the fun started. The second pathologist – with the original one in attendance – reopened the body. To his considerable surprise, he found not only that some of the organs and tissues were in the wrong places, but there was a discarded rag. The original pathologist immediately disclaimed responsibility for such shoddy work, suggesting that the body had been tampered with some time after his autopsy. His bizarre claim was made feasible by the fact that the Pestinikases had the opportunity – they owned the funeral home, as well as the nursing home.

The prosecutor's theory was that the Pestinikases had swapped the old man's tissues with those of another of their dead clients, to cover up evidence that they had starved him. He asked Ed Blake to determine whether or not the tissues from the first autopsy came from the same person as the tissues from the second autopsy. It was an interesting case, and a difficult one too: the formaldehyde used to preserve the body made conventional enzyme analysis impossible.

Blake had read with great interest Alec Jeffreys' and Peter Gill's article 'Forensic Application of DNA "Fingerprints"' in *Nature* the previous December, in which they 'envisaged that DNA fingerprinting will revolutionize forensic biology'. He was also up to date on the progress of PCR, due to the fortunate coincidence of renting lab space in Cetus Corp's headquarters in Emeryville. He decided to ask Henry

Erlich whether he thought that DNA fingerprinting could be used on the poor old man's tissues.

Erlich was happy to help. He had already been working to develop a system similar to Jeffreys', using RFLP to help solve paternity disputes, and was eager to test it in the forensic field. However, once he had extracted the DNA from the tissues, he found that it was highly degraded; the chains were too short for DNA fingerprinting. He suggested they try, for the first time, to use PCR to amplify the DNA they had, sufficiently to be able to type it and see how it compared to the reference sample. It was completely new ground for both of them: up to that point, Erlich had only used PCR on beta-globin, which would be of little use to the present problem, as every human shares virtually the same beta-globin sequence.

He turned to another of his favourite genes, HLA (Human Leukocyte Antigen) DQ alpha. This was known to be highly polymorphic – varying significantly from person to person. At the time, they knew of seven different variants – or alleles – at the locus HLA DQα1. Working together, Blake and Erlich succeeded in developing a testing procedure. First, the sample would be amplified using PCR, then exposed to a nylon test strip, on to which allele-specific probes had been added at designated spots. If the sample contained a particular allele, its probe would change colour, producing a visible spot on the strip. It worked. The tests were not as discriminating as Jeffreys' DNA fingerprinting and profiling, but far more sensitive, allowing the analysis of smaller and older samples. (In time, a kit for performing this DQα – and later, polymarker tests, which used similar PCR-based technology on six different loci simultaneously – was developed by Cetus, and marketed worldwide.)

Blake and Erlich ran the samples from the dead man and his disputed organs. The results matched: there was a strong likelihood that the tissues taken from the first and from the second autopsies came from the same man. The chances of them coming from two random individuals were, they estimated, around one in fifty to one in 100. In 1986, that was a good result.

Blake was delighted. He recounts the case details with relish. Not only had they solved an awkward forensic challenge, but, he realized, he had been shown the key to the future, and he was the first forensic scientist to make a copy. The irony of this case was that, while Blake had been hired by the prosecution, the results of his analysis benefited the defence: the Pestinikases might have starved the old man, but there was no evidence to suggest they had switched around his body parts. It didn't reflect very well, however, on the work of the original pathologist.

In the event – and despite Ed Blake's findings – the Pestinikases were found guilty based on a sliver of evidence. The ambulance attendant who had come to the home in response to the Pestinikases' call had noticed a glass of orange juice on the night stand next to the dead man's body. The glass was glistening with condensation, which he thought odd: why would it look as though it came straight from the fridge if the guy had been dead some time? Blake suggested to the prosecutor that, when the Pestinikases found the man dead, they had brought him a glass of orange juice to make it look as if they were conscientious custodians. The jury agreed with the theory and the Pestinikas nursing home was closed for ever.

Ed Blake's life was also never the same. 'Going from the protein/enzyme approach to the DNA approach – particularly with PCR – changed everything. The sensitivity of PCR took the same evidence that was a nightmare with conventional technology, and made it the best evidence that you could possibly have.'

11

29 July 1987. It was the end of a sultry San Francisco July, but when Paul Frediani took his seat in the Redwood City courtroom on the first day of the second trial, he looked less of the summer beach bum of two years before, and more like a seasoned old lag. His skin had already taken on the putty colour and consistency that prison confers, and time never really takes away. It must have seemed eerily familiar when Martin Murray stood up, walked towards the jury box and began: 'Imagine the horror of a woman alone in bed at night, sensing something in a room and awakening to the sight of a man near her bedroom door with a flashlight in one hand and a gun in the other . . .'

The jury, hearing for the first time the events of April 1984, was attentive. Murray's litany of evidence, delivered with fervour, sounded as impressive as it had twenty-two months earlier. They paid equal attention to Edward Rojas, as he delivered his opening statement. To veterans of the first trial, there were few surprises, until near the end: 'You'll be told by a witness that on April 5th 1984 . . . two days before this incident, Mr Frediani underwent eye surgery . . .'

Murray's case followed a familiar pattern: first Roger Franklin, a widower now for two years but with wounds still raw, still having to answer painful questions, and still in the present tense:

'What is your wife's educational background?'

'She has a Ph.D. in chemistry . . . She is basically involved in research.'

Thomas Christopher, recounting the events on the night of the assault: 'She was seated on a couch against the right wall as you come in . . . She was answering questions. Helena was a very strong woman . . . She is a, you know, a woman that is able to, you know, she's very strong.'

Neither were in court to hear Martin Murray's secretary act the part of the third Helena Greenwood in a rerun of her preliminary hearing testimony. The expert witnesses dealt with the fingerprint and the serological analysis of the sperm found on the bed linen in fairly sharp order. This was the best science available to the courtroom: forensic DNA was still a year away. At the same time, in England, Leicester police were 'blooding' every young man they could find in order to track down the Enderby murderer; on the east coast of America, Cellmark and Lifecodes were preparing to open their doors to their first forensic customers; while Ed Blake was hard at work in his laboratory near Berkeley developing markers for use in PCR-based DNA typing.

Twenty miles south of him, Murray called Chaput to the stand. To avoid the problems thrown up by the first trial, he wanted to forestall awkward questions about the interview. Chaput said he hadn't written down the exact words that had been spoken as he assumed the interview was being recorded. 'It wasn't until we finished that I asked Detective Farmer if I could take the tape and he said it wasn't turned on. And I asked why. He said because, you know, Frediani wouldn't talk if it were on.'

Murray rested. Rojas opened the defence with Feng Liu, the diminutive Chinese lady, this time supplied with a professional translator. She repeated her story of the black man who had shouted at her dog on the night of the assault.

Rojas called Andrea Goodhart to the stand. This was always going to be a tricky testimony: in finding Frediani guilty in the first trial, the jury had implicitly failed to believe Andrea's alibi, that she had been with him the night of the assault, and that they had visited 90 Walnut while house-hunting after brunch the next morning. She stood in the witness box and raised her hand as the clerk swore her in:

'Do you solemnly swear that the testimony you will give in the matter now at issue before this court shall be the truth, the whole truth, and nothing but the truth, so help you God?'

'I do.'

'Do you know this man, David Paul Frediani?'

'Yes, I do . . . He and I have lived together. We have children. We are common-law spouses.'

'How long has that relationship been going on?'

'As far as us living together, from about June of '84. I met him in January of '84.'

Rojas took her back to the night of 6 February 1985, when Frediani had been arrested for the indecent exposure charge, and taken to the station for questioning. Detective Farmer and Officer Halleran had turned up at the apartment he and Andrea shared.

'And in there you are reported or quoted as having said that you met Mr Frediani in June of 1984. Is that a correct statement?' Rojas asked. He was forestalling one of Murray's possible lines of attack, highlighting the inconsistencies between that version of the time frame of their relationship, in which they had not met by the date of the assault on Helena Greenwood, and the version which had them meeting five months earlier.

'No. I may have been quoted as saying that, but that is not what I said . . . The officers that came to the house that we lived in asked how long I had been *living* there and I told them since June.'

Murray raised his eyebrows.

The defence attorney began a new tack: Frediani's eye surgery. 'Do you recall specifically that particular April 5th 1984 operation?'

'I don't recall the operation because I wasn't there, but I recall the fact that it had occurred . . . He was happy and relieved and the pupil was completely dilated . . . He had to sleep with a patch on. I am sure we celebrated the fact that he wasn't going to lose the eye after all, that it was going to be all right and when it healed, he'd be able to see perfectly. He wouldn't have to wear glasses or contacts . . . We probably had dinner together, either made dinner or gone out to dinner . . . I would venture to say that we stayed at home because Paul couldn't drive at night. With this operation you can't see light properly . . . The doctor explained to Paul not to drive at night because it would be painful with your pupil completely open . . . It would be like looking at the sun.'

'What was wrong with his eyesight?'

'He couldn't see 20:20.'

At the time of the first trial, Andrea explained, she hadn't put two and two together and realized that Paul was being accused of assaulting Helena Greenwood on the same weekend of the operation, clearly an impossibility, since he couldn't drive at night.

Murray rose for his cross-examination. He disliked Andrea Goodhart almost as much as he abhorred her lover. And this time he was forewarned about the alibi and had no reason to hold back: she was not pregnant. He asked which film they went to see on their first date. Andrea said she couldn't remember.

'This was your first date. You don't remember what movie you saw on your first date?' He made it sound like she had forgotten her first child's birthday.

'No.'

'So you met him in January, first date was the middle of January, and by March you decided that you wanted to live with him and buy a house together?'

'Yes.'

His eyebrows were back in orbit.

Murray then spat out questions seemingly at random. How many houses had they looked at that day? (Three or four.) Was Frediani circumcised? (Yes.) The eye surgery. Her work. The date she moved in with him. When she moved out, then in again. 'Was the reason that you moved back in with him that you felt it would look better to the jury if you were back with him at that time?'

'Objection, Your Honour, irrelevant and argumentative.'

'Sustained.'

What was the house like in Middlefield that they were looking for when they happened upon 90 Walnut? (Don't remember.) Did she work at Macy's that Sunday? (Can't remember.)

Rojas recalled Chaput. It was back to Helena's description of her assailant: 'Did she tell you anything about the eyes?'

'She described them, as I recall, as being dark, on the dark side, and she was only able to see a little bit of the area around the eyes.'

'Did she mention anything particular about one eye or the other?'

'No.'

'Did she tell you that she noticed any redness in one eye or the other?'

'No.'

Out of the presence of the jury, Rojas reported that he was having problems persuading one of his witnesses, a Dr Simon, of the need to testify. He was refusing point blank to come to court without a subpoena. The subpoena was issued and served on 31 July. The doctor called back. 'He stated to me flatly that he would not be here at one o'clock on today's date, 3 August, because it was impossible for him since he had patients to care for . . . I pointed out to him that the subpoena itself says that failure to appear as required was a contempt of court. He indicated to me that he would take his chance with that. I then explained to him what the seriousness of the charge against Mr Frediani was and why his testimony was required. And the upshot of the conversation ended by him saying, "I will try my best to do something about my schedule, and if I can be there, I will be there. If I can't I won't."'

Monday came, and Dr Simon sent a message: 'I will not be there . . . I guess I will explain to the judge why it was I wasn't there when they bring me in in cuffs.' He informed the clerk that he would be in his office.

'Waiting arrest or what?' Rojas asked.

'Yes,' the clerk replied.

'I guess that's an invitation to dance we probably shouldn't pass up.' Rojas asked the judge to issue a bench arrest and a policeman was promptly dispatched to bring the recalcitrant doctor to court.

While they were waiting, Murray jumped into the breach and called Officer Patrick Halleran as a rebuttal witness. Halleran was the policeman who had turned up on Andrea Goodhart's doorstep at half past one in the morning to ask questions about her boyfriend, at that time in the jailhouse trying to explain how a fourteen-year-old girl could have mistaken a natural bodily function for masturbation.

'She stated that she had met Mr Frediani in June of 1984,' Halleran said, flipping through a small notebook, '. . . had been dating him since that time and had moved in with him in November of 1984.'

He had taken notes while he was talking to her, he said. 'Written in my hand it says, "Known June '84, dating until November '84, moved in."'

He had gone over his notes with her after the interview.

As Halleran stepped down, a man swept into the courtroom. He was either a doctor, or auditioning for a starring part in a hospital drama. He was dressed in full operating kit – green scrubs, hat, mask around his neck. Before even being sworn in, he turned to the judge. 'The manner of my coming here I think needs to be brought to your attention.' The judge said that could wait.

Rojas started his questioning. Frediani, 'appears familiar', the doctor said. Referring to his notes, on 19 January 1984, 'I did an operation which is called a radial caratotomy. It's a surgery which reduced the nearsightedness and myopia in the eye.' At the time, it was a new procedure, revolutionary and complex. That was on Frediani's right eye. Two months later, he repeated the operation on the left eye. It didn't work: there was an area of perforation and the wound leaked. So on 5 April 1984, Frediani came in for repeat surgery. Dr Simon cut the cornea of his left eye, and when he had finished, sent his patient away wearing a patch, with instructions to return the following day.

On Friday 6 April, he was back for a follow-up appointment. 'It consisted of removing the patch, examining the operated eye, placing eye drops in the eye and instructing the patient his limitations,' he explained, '. . . not to touch or press the eye or allow anything to come in contact with the eye that would cause pressure on the eye . . . At that time I place a drop in the eye to dilate the eye . . . Some people will have their eye dilated for seventy-two to ninety-six hours with the type of medication that I use. Other people, their eye will be dilated for twenty-four hours or less.'

'Would it be fair to say that moderate to bright lights would perhaps cause some discomfort?' Rojas asked.

'Yes . . . I provide [my patients] with sunglasses – darkened glasses – at the time of the visit and tell them if they are experiencing light sensitivity to wear their sunglasses.'

'Would headlights at night be an irritant to somebody that had a dilated eye?'

'Could be, yes . . . My patients wear a metal eye shield at night following the surgery who are approximately one week post-op. They are instructed to wear the shield at night so that they don't inadvertently place their fingers or hands in their eye or roll over on the corner of a pillow.'

Murray took over. 'Do you advise your patients, and did you advise Mr Frediani, that he should not drive a motor vehicle at night?'

'No.'

'Would it be terribly painful for an average individual to turn on, say, an overhead light in the bedroom after say, seventy or twenty-four, or thirty-six hours after having your eye dilated?'

'The answer again is a quantum based upon the individual. Some people, following the surgery, after having their eye dilated, are exquisitely light sensitive to the point if they walked into this courtroom in that situation they might shield their eyes with their hands even while wearing dark glasses. On the other hand, there are people who work outside in the daylight and actually not be bothered with it at all.'

Once the doctor was finished – still protesting his forced appearance – Rojas called his client, the defendant David Paul Frediani, to the stand. Even with the jailhouse pallor, Frediani was a good-looking man in a well-cut suit. Rojas took him through the events of three years before, the brunch, the teapot, house-hunting: he also thought they had seen three or four houses after 90 Walnut. Frediani didn't falter. The arrest and interview: he had never, as far as he recalled, told Farmer that he didn't want it to be taped.

Was he still in a relationship with Andrea?

'Yes.'

'Doing well?'

'Very much so.'

The eye operation had been extremely painful, he said. 'They give you painkillers, but I did not take any because, for one thing, I drove home after the operation, but all I had was the local that they put in the eye. But that wears off, you know, you want to be home in bed, and it takes about an hour and a half to wear off.' He had driven to the follow-up appointment the next day wearing sunglasses, and the day after that, Saturday 7 April, 'I just remember being in a very good mood. I mean, I was going to have perfect vision. That's the only sensation or specifics that I can remember.'

It was a relief, especially after the debacle of the initial operation on his left eye. That time the doctor had made two incisions, and 'He made the third one and immediately stopped half-way into it, immediately put a door through it and forceps on the eyeball. I said, what is going on? It took a couple of minutes and he was irrigating it and I knew something was up and he said, "Paul, I don't want to tell you this, Paul, but I punctured your eyeball" . . . I was very much concerned.'

'How long after you had surgery on April 5th 1984 was it before you drove a motor car at night?'

'It was quite a while. The vision at night is really bad. The lights show up as nothing but a big, huge star. It is like looking into wax paper and especially with the eye dilated, I am very light sensitive and bright headlights would be excruciating pain and I avoided that.'

Murray stood in a courtroom to face Frediani for the third time in as many years. That Sunday, when they were out house-hunting, how had they found the houses to look at?

'The only source that you mentioned in the previous proceeding was a *Sunday Chronicle* that had a list of open houses; isn't that correct?'

'Yes, that's correct.'

Murray picked up a blue sheet of plastic from his table and approached Frediani with it in his hand. 'I'd like to have marked for identification a microfilmed copy of the *Sunday Examiner Chronicle* for April 8th 1984.' He showed it to Frediani. 'Did you specifically testify previously that there was a portion that listed open houses for that day?'

'Well, that's generally the source we use. I can't say for certain that was the source we used that day, but this was the kind of reference sheet we used.'

Murray was not going to let his prey take any more backward steps. He picked up a transcript from the first trial and made Frediani read out: 'Like I said we generally got the *Sunday Chronicle*,' he read. 'It had this section we open up, and it's got this huge set of addresses in various areas that specifically say what are open.'

Then Murray showed him the sheet of microfilm of the *Sunday Chronicle* of 8 April 1984. There were no houses listed in the Menlo Park area.

'I take it you picked out a particular home because you drove all the way to Menlo Park to look at it; is this right?'

'Yeah, I believe we had an appointment or something like that; it was something brought us to that attention.' Frediani was beginning to sound less articulate.

'So you did look at a house in the Middlefield Road area?'

'That's correct.'

But he could not remember exactly where it was. Murray pointed towards a map he had pinned to the wall and started firing questions again: How long did it take to get to the brunch place from home? (About half an hour.) What time did they arrive? (About 10 to 10.30.)

'Whenever it first opens up. It's like a buffet breakfast and we generally like to get food when it's fresh . . . you walk in the door and they give you a table and you usually don't even sit down. You go to the buffet.' They were probably there about an hour, he reckoned.

On redirect, Rojas asked his client whether he wore cologne in his groin area – he said not. He rested his case.

Murray called the manager of Jan's restaurant in Portola, where Frediani and Andrea had allegedly had brunch before house-hunting the morning after the assault. He elicited the information that brunch is served from ten on Saturday mornings. Back on the stand, Chaput said that he had driven from Jan's restaurant to 90 Walnut as fast as he could one Sunday without breaking the law, and that it had taken twenty minutes. The records clerk at Macy's in Hillsdale confirmed that Andrea had checked in for work at 11.59 a.m. on Sunday 8 April. She had started working for Macy's the previous month, and on her list of emergency contacts, she had not mentioned Paul Frediani – despite having supposedly moved in with him at around the same time. Another blow to the alleged time frame of their relationship.

Murray's building blocks were in place, and when he stood to deliver his closing statement, all he had to do was smooth out the cement. He ran through the evidence, poured scorn on Frediani and his alibi, the mother of his children, and finished up with some oratory on the power of the justice system.

It was a hard act for the diminutive Rojas to follow. He made a couple of digs at Murray's case, then carefully went through the holes. Helena Greenwood had stated that her assailant was coloured, to some degree: his client was clearly white. The assailant asked for money: Frediani was earning a decent salary. And then there was the eye surgery; would someone who has just undergone a risky procedure risk his eyesight and go out without a patch to break into someone's house?

On the morning of Wednesday, 5 August 1987, Judge Bible instructed the jury of their responsibilities and sent them off to deliberate. They did not know that on the same day, in a courtroom on the other side of the Atlantic Ocean, a British jury was listening to a bearded geneticist called Alec Jeffreys explain for the first time in a courtroom how DNA fingerprinting could be used to tie a rapist to his victim. The California jury did not have this science in their armoury, but nevertheless, it took them less than four hours this time to come to a decision: just as in the trial two years earlier, they found David Paul Frediani guilty of burglary, forced oral copulation and of using a firearm in the commission of a crime. That evening he was back in prison, facing a minimum balance of two more years of incarceration. If he was good and avoided trouble, Frediani could expect to be out before his thirty-fifth birthday.

Detective David Decker had not been able to go to San Francisco for the second trial. He was still convinced Frediani had killed Helena Greenwood, still looking for something – an eye-witness, a fingerprint, a credit card receipt – anything that would place him in Del Mar on the day of the crime. It was time, thought Decker, to pay his prime suspect a visit. On 16 September 1987, two years and a month after the start of their investigation, Decker and his partner, Charlie Kelly, made the trip up to California State prison, Vacaville, about twenty miles north-west of Sacramento, to see if they could get anything out of him in person.

It was the first time Decker had seen the man

he believed to be responsible for murdering Helena Greenwood. Frediani was dressed in the regulation prison blues, a V-necked T-shirt and baggy cotton trousers. He entered the small interview room with a swagger, a confidence born out of having done time, lived with the tough guys. Vacaville is a medium-security prison – none of the inmates are in for long stretches, so the atmosphere is more mellow than at San Quentin, or Folsom. But it is still prison. Many of the prisoners are violent offenders.

The San Diego detectives were polite, addressed him as Mr Frediani. They explained they were investigating Helena Greenwood's death, and asked where Frediani was at the time. 'At home,' he replied. 'I was on leave from work, so I hung out by the pool, played tennis with my friend Charlie, went for bike rides. I am sure I spoke to Andrea on the phone at least once during the day, because we always did.'

He had picked up his car from the body shop that morning, he recalled, and pulled up in the car port just as his roommate, Barbara, was coming down to get into her car. She was dressed up, and heading to meet friends for happy hour. 'Your poor car, what happened?' she asked. He hadn't told her about the crash the previous week; she was shocked at the state of his BMW, Frediani told the detectives.

The crash, Decker said. Where were you headed for when you crashed? Frediani explained that the previous week he had decided to take a break before the trial. He wasn't working, and Andrea had suggested he get away before the pressure really started to build up. He had initially thought of going to Lake Tahoe – he had been there several times before with Arthur Settlemeyer and the guys – but had changed his mind once he got on the road and headed south towards Los Angeles instead. 'Did you tell anyone you were going to Los Angeles?' Decker asked. 'No, it was a spur of the moment decision,' Frediani replied. He was nearing the city, when he saw the high peaks of the Magic Mountain 'Big One' roller coaster, and decided to pull off the I5 freeway. 'I thought, "I've never ridden a roller coaster before, what the heck,"' he said. But as he was swinging off, a car heading in the opposite direction failed to obey a stop sign and ploughed straight into him.

The highway patrol turned up, questioned them both. Frediani was angry, he told Decker. He was proud of his car, and now his trip was ruined. Plus, the man who had crashed into him spoke no English and had no insurance. The car was a near-write-off, steam pussing from the radiator – and who was going to pay? He managed to get it towed to a garage to patch it up, and the next day, limped slowly back to Belmont. 'I took it to the auto body shop a block from the apartment, who said they would do the best they could, then picked it up on August 22nd. I particularly remember that day, because my attorney warned me you guys would want to know my movements after he told me that Ms Greenwood was dead, so I made a point of remembering them.'

Had he been heading down to San Diego? Decker asked. (No.) Had he ever been to San Diego? (No.) Did he know Helena Greenwood's address? (No.) He didn't even know she was living in San Diego, only that she had moved to southern California, but that was a big area.

'He was confident,' Decker said. 'We walked away thinking that we had definitely been able to talk to the murderer, but that he had been able to cover his tracks, had had plenty of time to come up with a story, and to stick to it. We weren't able to break his story, but I remained convinced that he was our prime suspect.' Back in San Diego, he was forced to admit that the investigation was faltering. He carefully collated his notes and reports, and filed them in a cabinet with the other unsolved crimes; the cold cases.

Frediani could only walk away from that meeting as far as his cell, to wait to hear from his attorney about how the new appeal was going. He had high hopes again – much of what had persuaded the appellate court to overturn his first conviction had been duplicated in the second trial. All he needed was another bit of good luck. In the meantime, he was adapting to life in Vacaville. He had a decent cellmate, an old-timer who knew the ropes and, by giving Frediani his patronage, had assured his safety. Besides, most of the other inmates were up for parole in the next couple of years, and none of them wanted to jeopardize their chances of an early release. So he kept to himself, tried hard not to annoy his fellow inmates, and like them, willed time to pass.

In the United Kingdom and America and across the world, the first tide of DNA testing was beginning to reach its high-water mark. Following the successes of the Enderby murder case, the Melias rape and the Pestinikas civil conviction for criminal liability through PCR-based tests, the media had grabbed this forensic cash-cow by its teats and was milking it for all it was worth. It was portrayed as a revolution, powerful and infallible. Defence attorneys, on the whole, just lay back and submitted when presented with DNA evidence incriminating their client to the exclusion of millions or billions of people. These were figures they felt incapable of challenging: before the advent of forensic DNA, juries were habitually convicting defendants on serological evidence placing them within a hundred or so people who could have committed the crime. This was exponentially more damning.

There were numerous high-profile successes. In England, Alec Jeffreys was asked to use his methods to determine whether the body of a dead Brazilian rancher was Josef Mengele, the Nazi doctor widely known as the 'Angel of Death', who infamously used sets of twins in his eugenicist experiments to determine the relative importance of nature and nurture. After the end of the Second World War, Mengele had allegedly fled to Brazil, where it was rumoured he bought a ranch and lived the rest of his life out of the grasp of Western justice.

Committed Nazi hunters had never given up the chase, however, and in 1985, declared that Mengele had been hiding under the identity of a rancher, Wolfgang Gerhardt. Gerhardt had died six years previously, in a swimming accident, and was buried in the cemetery of Knossos Signora du Rosario in the small town of Embu. The body was exhumed in 1985 and subjected to minute investigation by forensic scientists – odontologists compared the body's teeth to Mengele's dental records, while forensic anthropologists attempted to reconstruct the skeleton and compare it with known photographs of the Nazi doctor. After months of work, the team declared themselves satisfied beyond reasonable doubt that Gerhardt and Mengele were one and the same.

But the Israeli authorities were not completely convinced: they wanted to be 100 per cent certain that one of their chief figures of hate was indeed dead and about to be reburied. By the late 1980s the technology was in place. DNA testing was in the news, and in 1988, the Israelis suggested to the German government that it be used to provide definitive proof of Mengele's identity. The Germans were only too eager to put this unsavoury episode firmly to sleep, so they turned to the inventor of DNA fingerprinting, Alec Jeffreys. He in turn enlisted the help of Dr Erika Hagelburg, an expert in extracting DNA from bones. This is not an easy task, even with fresh bones. Jeffreys knew from the outset that DNA profiling was not an option – there just wouldn't be enough material for that – and so they would have to use a PCR-based technique.

By 1988, it was already almost impossible to imagine a life before PCR. It had been just three years since the first articles were published, but already the technique was finding its way into the laboratories of scientists in an astonishing range of disciplines. Even Kary Mullis cannot have realized how basic, how fundamental the process he had invented would become. 'I can't keep up with the things people are doing with PCR,' he wrote in his autobiography. 'What will happen to it? It's like asking what stories people will write with a new software program. PCR is the word processor of biochemistry.'

It had also become the new wonder-tool of forensics, able to analyse microscopic samples of DNA, from urine, nail-clippings, even the trace of saliva on the back of a postage stamp. Where it paled in comparison with the RFLP-based techniques used in DNA profiling, however, was that most of the markers used were considerably less variable than minisatellites – and the minisatellites themselves were too long to be amplified by PCR. Given a choice – and a substantial amount of DNA evidence – most forensic scientists would still have plumped first for the discriminatory power of DNA profiling. But in most criminal cases, they didn't have that choice; the DNA was inevitably too scarce, too old, too degraded.

By the time Dr Hagelburg had finished grinding up Gerhardt's femur in her laboratory in Oxford and carefully extracting the DNA, Jeffreys was ready in Leicester with a newly developed set of probes and primers to isolate a range of variable loci using PCR. He also had blood samples provided by Mengele's wife and son. These he analysed, deriving alleles from both at the identical set of loci. By comparing them, he could instantly see which of the son's alleles were the same as his mother's. If the Brazilian rancher was indeed Mengele, then the son's DNA should match his in every other case.

It was hard work; the DNA from the bones was highly degraded and a result was by no means a sure thing. However, after several months, Jeffreys had a profile for the skeleton. Every single one of young Mengele's alleles that had not matched his mother found a match in the profile of the dead rancher. The probability that they could have been inherited by chance – if the skeleton was someone other than Mengele – was put at less than one in 18,000. Jeffreys had determined to a 99.994 per cent degree of certainty that the Angel of Death and the Brazilian rancher were the same person. The Israelis were delighted, and Josef Mengele was officially struck off Simon Wiesenthal's list of fugitive Nazis.

In California, Ed Blake was increasingly being sought after by law enforcement agencies, keen to use the new technology on their cases. After Pestinikas, he had retreated to his laboratory, to work on developing additional markers for use in PCR-based DNA typing. The first ones, created with Henry Erlich in his lab down the corridor from Kary Mullis' at Cetus, were not managing to come up with statistics anywhere like those generated by DNA profiling analysis. But the new ones were looking good – and the more independent loci that he could test for each case, the more discriminating the results would be.

In the late 1980s, he worked on a double rape case in Menlo Park, not far from Atherton. A suspect was arrested, positively identified by one of the victims and locked up in jail. He consistently protested his innocence, and when he eventually persuaded his attorney to push for DNA tests, Ed Blake was contacted. 'I do the testing and it eliminates the suspect. It was a total shock to the prosecution. Then the shit hits the fan,' he says with a chuckle. 'It just didn't make sense given the clarity of the eye-witness ID. Everything stops while they reconsider what to do. The lead detective comes to talk to me about my work, how confident I was in the results, and I say, "Totally."'

The prosecuting attorney was severely affected by Blake's news. She was shaken by the idea that a man, who science said could not have done the crime, had spent much of the past year in prison, was weeks away from trial and a possible rape conviction. She consulted with a local high-flyer, Martin Murray, fresh from the second Frediani trial. DNA had come along too late for him in that case, but he had quickly caught on to the new technology, and he was a convert. Murray recommended that they release the initial suspect – the first time in the United States where a case against someone had been dropped as a result of PCR testing.

A year later, a man was caught in the act of raping a woman in a park not far from San Mateo. His name was Armando Quintanilla and he had no choice but to admit to the sexual assault. Across the county border, the lead detective on the Menlo Park double rape wondered whether Quintanilla might not be their man too. He started investigating Quintanilla. He took a sample of his blood and sent it to Blake for testing. It fitted: Quintanilla was among the 5 per cent or so of people who could not be excluded from having raped the two women. The detective started to hunt back through the evidence – there was another semen stain on the back of the victim's shoe, which again did not exclude Quintanilla. And then the *coup de grâce*: a fingerprint had been lifted from the outside of the first victim's car. It had not matched the original suspect, and had been thought to be less than vital. But when it was compared to Quintanilla's, it matched. The wrong man had nearly been sent to prison for a crime he had nothing to do with. DNA testing had proved his innocence, and together with compelling and familiar fingerprint evidence, led to Martin Murray's successful prosecution of Armando Quintanilla for serial rape.

It was headline-grabbers like Quintanilla and the

Mengele identification that impressed not only the public, but the legal community too. The DNA revolution was in full flow in the forensic community; there was a rush to court with more successful prosecutions than before, and most importantly, perhaps, early DNA tests led to the exclusion of thousands of prime suspects before their cases came to court. This meant more work for the labs performing the tests. There was still only a handful of them with the expertise and technology to achieve results – the market leaders, Lifecodes and Cellmark, had more work than technicians trained to carry it out, and thus had little incentive to subject the evolving technology to rigorous validation procedures. The FBI, in a bid to catch up, had fast-tracked a programme to develop its own procedure for DNA typing, which it planned to offer to crime labs across the world. But there was plenty of business knocking at the commercial labs' doors, and there were compelling commercial incentives for each lab to keep its products and processes secret. They neither published nor presented their methods for peer review; the results of tests were not standardized or replicated publicly. In reality, they could not be, since each lab was using its own set of primers and reagents, producing incompatible results which precluded comparison. And the legal process was so obviously overwhelmed by the magic of DNA that it did not raise the necessary objections to force the labs to go through the costly and time-consuming checking and revalidation process.

12

It was Groundhog Day in the California Appeals Court. Frediani's case for reversal was submitted. The prosecution countered. The court overturned his conviction. Same arguments, same conclusion.

'I was upset. It was a blow,' said Martin Murray. 'I thought we had tied him up pretty tight that time, but once again, the court saw fit to reverse.' Twelve years later, and now in the top hierarchy of the San Mateo District Attorney's office, the implied injustice of this decision still threatens to burst the seams of his tasteful dove grey shirt. 'In my entire career I've only had two cases reversed, and these were both of them.' He had to decide whether to go for a third trial. It was the end of January 1989; Frediani had spent more than three years in prison, on and off.

Paul Frediani's lawyer suggested to his client that they investigate the possibility of a plea bargain, to avoid another trial and the year or so of waiting in jail, not to mention the possible outcome. Frediani gave the go-ahead, but Murray was less keen. He wanted to try Frediani for a third time; the case had become personal, he did not think the reversals were justified, and he did not want to let him get away with the assault – as well as the murder. But he could not afford to let it turn into a vendetta; he had to weigh up the odds of a conviction against what he had to lose by going ahead with another expensive procedure. His instinct was to forge ahead: two juries had been convinced of Frediani's guilt, the chances were good that a third would be too. And now he had a new weapon: DNA. The successful resolution of the Quintanilla case had impressed him profoundly. This time he would test the sperm stains on the pillowcase taken from Helena Greenwood's house, and if they matched Frediani's DNA profile, there would be no way he could continue to protest his innocence.

On 14 April 1989, Murray filed a motion which would require Frediani to submit blood samples for DNA testing. The judge concurred and issued a formal order. Frediani's lawyer called a meeting. His client, he said, wanted to deal. Murray thought hard. 'The vagaries of trial and appeal had been well demonstrated in this case by then. If we went to another trial, there's always that crap shoot: you have twelve members of the community and if one of them doesn't agree, you don't have a conviction. And then the roll of dice with the appellate court again. But if he were willing to accept some kind of deal, yes he'd be out sooner, but he would have the conviction on his record and, in the end, I thought that would be worth it to avoid the uncertainties.'

On 18 May 1989, David Paul Frediani changed his plea from 'not guilty' to 'no contest' to the burglary and sexual assault. It is essentially an admission of guilt, and carries a criminal record, but unlike a straight guilty plea, it cannot be used against the defendant in a subsequent civil action based on the same facts. So it was sort of: I'm not going to say I did it, but I'll weather the punishment anyway. In return, the gun use allegation was dropped: six years total, reduced to three for good behaviour, and he was almost walking through the prison gates before the ink had dried. And before any DNA testing had been performed.

'I thought then that a person who was innocent, as he had proclaimed through two trials, would certainly want to see the results of DNA testing before going to trial,' Murray said. 'The fact that he avoided the DNA testing by pleading spoke volumes.' That was not how Frediani saw it. That he would be on the state register as a sexual offender, with a standing order to report to his parole officer at regular intervals, did not worry him. All he cared about was that on 12 July 1989, he would be a free man, free to eat what he wanted and when he wanted, go to bed in the afternoon and get up before midnight, ride his bike for miles and miles without anyone asking where he was headed. He would be able to see his sons, complete his MBA before his time limit expired; it was a new world out there and he wanted to enjoy it, criminal record or not. Before he could leave, however, he had to submit to a blood test after all: a new law had been enacted just the previous year, which made it compulsory for convicted sexual offenders to provide blood samples to the Department of Justice. These would not be tested at the time, but retained for possible future DNA analysis.

The day came. He raced through the formalities, signing forms, changing into his outside clothes. Paul's sister Donna – good, sensible, loyal Donna – was waiting for him outside the prison gates. She drove him to a residential hotel above a restaurant south of San Francisco, where she had found him a room, spent a couple of days with him to make sure he was up on his feet again, gave him $700 and told him to call her if he needed her. It was a bizarre role reversal: he had always been the big brother, strong and faintly superior; she the little sister, gritting her teeth through back pain, looking up to handsome Paul. They had never been particularly close and this was always going to be an awkward reunion, shaded with gratitude and shame, and a sense that deep down, under her practicality and sisterly kindness, Donna must be angry about the anguish Paul had caused their parents.

In the last year, Andrea had met someone else, who was now living with her. She had stopped bringing the twins to visit the prison – she said she didn't want them questioning why Daddy was in 'the big house', not at home with them. Paul didn't mind about the break-up of the relationship – here was a chance for him to start afresh. He contacted none of his old friends, revisited none of his old haunts. He grabbed the first job he could where they asked no questions about what he had been doing for the past three and a half years – driving a delivery truck. The pay was around $900 a month, barely enough to cover his rent and the $250 a month he had agreed to pay Andrea to help support the boys. As long as he kept paying, she told him, he could see them whenever he wanted.

He was living like a Spartan – getting up at 4.30 a.m. to cycle the twelve miles to work, driving through his lunch hour so he could finish early, in order to bike back to his room, shower, eat a can of tuna, then catch the 5.30 p.m. bus to Golden Gate University, where he was racing to finish his MBA in time. He'd get the 10 p.m. bus home, fall in bed at 11.30, and it never seemed like any time before his alarm was buzzing before dawn. On weekends, he would bike over to Andrea's house and take the boys to the park. He started building them a tree house in their garden, like the one his father had built him when he was a boy.

He was exhausted but exhilarated. No amount of hard work could dampen the joys of being free. While he enjoyed the routine of truck driving, his aim was always to get back into a suit-and-tie job. He answered an ad in the paper for an accountant, and one morning in September, got up extra-early, so he could fit in an interview on his rounds. He picked up the truck, whizzed around his appointments, then stopped by his room to pick up his suit and drove into the city in time for his meeting. He was vague when asked what he had been up to over the past few years – he did not mention his stint at the state's pleasure – and delighted when he was offered a job at MSAS Cargo. Pay was double what he was getting for driving a truck, and, most importantly, he was back in finance. He bought an old Chevy at an auction the month before he turned thirty-five, and he was set to go.

'I put out of my mind the 30–34 years and truly felt like I was twenty-nine. I would think of movies I had just seen – and realize that was not the previous year, but five years ago. It happened all the time. I felt like I was starting my life all over again from the beginning, just like after graduating from college. I had my new dream job; I was still going to night school twice a week; I was driven to catch up.'

Paul threw himself into his work. He was first into the office in the morning, last out at night, except when he had evening classes at Golden Gate. On his second day – against his expectations, even his wishes – he 'saw Eileen and fell in love'.

'It was the most intense passion of my life,' he later said. 'There was nothing I could do about it. The first time I spoke to her I felt my face turning red and thought my heart was going to explode. I became totally aroused. The funny thing is, she was so plain and ordinary to look at, but I could only see how beautiful she was. Every time I passed her, I got aroused. We started having coffee together in the mornings and talked incessantly about everything. She was smart and witty. We thought alike, liked and disliked the same things. I finally plucked up the courage to ask her out for a drink, but she refused.

She said she didn't want to date a co-worker, and besides, she made a better friend than girlfriend.'

What began as a friendship nevertheless progressed into a relationship after Christmas, when Paul drew her a card and composed a poem inside it. Three months later, he went to live with Eileen and her thirteen-year-old daughter in their Redwood City apartment. He had told her early on that he had been in prison, and she had apparently accepted it with understanding. Nineteen-ninety was, in Paul's words, 'a fantastic year . . . We drove to work together, saw each other all day – I never tired of being with her, which was a new experience for me. My kids came over every weekend, and all five of us did things as a family. Her daughter and I became buddies and she told me how happy she was I came into her mother's life, and that her mother had never been happier, or easier to live with.' That summer, Paul completed his MBA and to commemorate his graduation, Eileen framed his diploma and gave him a ring, engraved with 'I will always love you'.

'I wanted to marry her so bad,' he recalls. 'But she had a real hang-up about marriage, so I never asked. She warned me it would take years, and I decided to be patient. Over the course of the year her appearance changed. She started growing her hair longer, growing her nails, wore more make-up and better clothes. I didn't notice the change myself. I always thought of her as beautiful. But looking back at pictures, the difference is absolutely astonishing. I'm shocked I didn't notice, plus, I believe with all my conviction, that the same would apply if she had gone the other way . . . I'd love her the same if she was 300 pounds. I could sit in a room with her with nothing to do and still be so content. She was my soul mate.'

The following year, they took the boys to stay with Paul's parents on the East Coast. They went swimming and fishing in the same fishing hole that Paul's father had taken him to when he was a boy. Everyone got on well; his parents liked Eileen immensely, adored the twins, and for the first time, he felt they treated him like he was an adult. Paul was truly happy.

Even the constant attention of the police could not spoil his enjoyment of life. 'For the first years after I got out, I was constantly on guard; they were always on my tail.' He reported monthly to his parole officer, who had warned him, when they first met, that if he was caught doing anything even remotely suspicious, he would be back in prison faster than he could unknot his silk tie. He was determined not to give them that pleasure.

Four hundred and fifty miles south of San Francisco, a small blonde woman in her early forties heard Frediani's name for the first time. It was 1992, and Laura Heilig had just joined the San Diego Sheriff's homicide squad. She was a junior member of a large team hunting a serial killer; over the last few years more than twenty women – prostitutes and hitch-hikers – had been murdered, and their bodies dumped on the side of the road. One of the investigation leaders was Detective David Decker. They were talking late one evening when he told her about Helena Greenwood. It was a case that had never left him, he said; he knew who her killer was, but he hadn't been able to pin him down.

When, a few months later, Laura Heilig was given the assignment to review all the old cases in the Sheriff's Department filing cabinets, to separate the open from the closed, the rapes and assaults from the homicides, she recognized Helena Greenwood's name and read the file with interest. 'It was intriguing, of course,' she says, 'because of the victim being a scientist and the likely suspect having probably travelled down here to kill her. But I didn't have time to look into it in detail. I logged it in my memory bank, assigned it to the appropriate drawer, and then I was transferred back to fresh homicides and had nothing to do with it for many years.'

It was the children who showed the first signs of blotting on Frediani's happiness. Eileen's daughter had turned fifteen and was becoming increasingly difficult and belligerent, particularly towards him. His boys were also starting to reject Eileen; he was sure Andrea had turned them against her. It was then, according to Paul, that the arguments started. They would last for days; periods of silence and coldness, followed by accusations and recriminations. Eileen remembers his ugly temper, and also his emotional, romantic side. 'He has two personalities,' she said, 'just like a Jekyll and Hyde. He even looked different when he was in a rage, his nostrils flaring, these wild eyes, this rage . . .'

'I can say without a doubt that I never caused an argument,' Paul recalls now. 'But I always made them worse. We would be having a shouting match and an hour later, I would be pleading for forgiveness. I grabbed her arm a couple of times to turn her towards me in a violent fashion, which only made it worse, and caused me to beg harder for forgiveness. I should never have touched her like that: I am truly ashamed. I was just so exasperated. I couldn't anticipate what would set her off.'

'He once flew off because I did not butter the toast properly,' Eileen claimed recently. 'He started throwing everything. I was scared to death of him.'

'I know I was pretty uptight back then,' he says. 'With parole, my secret at work, my kids, my work pressures . . . But the main thing was I loved her so much, and when she walked out on me, I had no faith in the future.' Two years after their relationship began, Eileen suggested they try living apart for a while. It was effectively over.

Andrea was continuing to cause trouble with the twins. They would be out when he went around to pick them up for a pre-arranged date, and it was becoming harder and harder to get hold of them. The phone was never answered. 'Then one day in spring

1996, she said I couldn't see them any more. Just like that. I asked why. And she said they were afraid of me. That was rubbish – we always had a great time together. I said, if they tell me that, then I will believe it. A day later, they rang up and one of them says, "I don't want you to be my Daddy any more." Boy, I was blown away by that. But I didn't think it was serious. Every day I expected them to call me, but they never did.'

It was another blow, just when he thought his life was beginning to come together. At work he was rapidly climbing the corporate ladder, he started dating again, bought a '93 black Lexus Coupe. He felt, he said, that he had mellowed into his old self. Parole and prison had become a distant memory. The murder investigation had slipped out of his mind; eleven years had passed since Helena Greenwood's death, and after the visit from the detectives two years later, while he was still in Vacaville, he had heard nothing more about it.

13

DNA was like a handful of picture cards in a game of real-life poker: whoever held the DNA evidence was bound to win, and all too often, the opposition quietly folded before the bidding began. It took a few years before the defence won a hand.

On 5 February 1987, Vilma Ponce was turned into a human pin-cushion after a man broke into her Bronx apartment and stabbed her more than sixty times. Her common-law husband, Jeffrey Otero, came home from work to find her lying in a dried lake of blood, and their two-year-old daughter, Natasha, dead in the bathroom. He thought he had seen a man rushing away down the corridor, and after giving a description to the police, they soon arrested Jose Castro, a janitor in a neighbouring building.

Castro denied any involvement, but when the police searched his apartment, they found a watch with a spot of dried blood on it. Apart from the somewhat shaky identification by Otero, it was their only piece of evidence, and they sent it off to Lifecodes, to see whether the blood on the watch matched that of Vilma or Natasha.

At Lifecodes, they managed to extract 0.5 μg of DNA from the bloodstain, enough to perform DNA profiling at three loci, as well as to determine the sex of the donor. On 22 July 1987, Lifecodes delivered their report to the DA: 'The DNA-Print pattern from the blood of Ponce matches that of the watch with three DNA probes. The frequency of these patterns in the general public is 1:189,200,000.' And that appeared to be that.

The defence attorney was not so certain. He was a conscientious sort, and having not previously worked on a case where DNA typing was involved, he was wary of throwing in his cards before checking his hand. He decided to enlist the help of two defence lawyers, Barry Scheck and Peter Neufeld. Former public defenders turned professor (Scheck) and private attorney (Neufeld), they had been bitten by the DNA bug early on in its inception and, keen to find out more, had attended a conference on forensic DNA typing at the Cold Spring Harbour Laboratories on Long Island the previous year. There, they had heard not only about the miraculous power of the new technology, but also the potential problems. They had been particularly impressed by Eric Lander, the director of genetic research at MIT, who had challenged Michael Baird of Lifecodes about his presentation. Baird had shown an X-ray DNA print (autoradiograph) with two lanes which didn't quite match. He called them a match anyway, claiming that one lane had run faster than the other – a phenomenon known as band-shifting – but he hadn't run internal controls to back this up. In academic or medical diagnostic genetics – Eric Lander's home patch – this would have been unacceptable.

As soon as they became involved in the Castro case, Neufeld called Lander, who agreed to help. The first step was to get him on the stand at the Frye hearing to determine the acceptability of the scientific evidence. (In American courts at that time – and in some jurisdictions to this day – where new or contested scientific evidence is involved, the contestants have to go through a Frye hearing, named after the 1923 case, *US v. Frye*, in which a Washington DC court ruled against the admissibility of lie detector evidence in a murder case because the technology had not been accepted in the relevant scientific community. The ruling stated that: 'Just when a scientific principle or discovery crosses the line between experimental and demonstrable stages is difficult to define. Somewhere in the twilight zone the evidential force of the principle must be recognized, and while courts will go a long way in admitting expert testimony deduced from a well-recognized scientific principle or discovery, the thing from which the deduction is made must be sufficiently established to have gained general acceptance in the particular field to which it belongs.') In the Castro case, the defence was attempting to get the DNA-Print evidence excluded: without it, the prosecution case would crumble.

The Frye hearing in *New York v. Castro* lasted fifteen weeks. Lander, the world-famous geneticist, was lined up against Michael Baird, one of the original forensic

DNA scientists. Lander spent a total of six days on the stand, and in addition prepared a fifty-page report criticizing Lifecodes' results, which he said were 'so far below reasonable scientific practice in molecular biology as to be appalling'. The lanes on the autorad were dark with non-specific background, he claimed, the quality of data was poor, and Lifecodes had not even followed their own procedures in interpreting it. In contrast to Baird's estimated odds of a random probability match of nearly 200 million to one, Lander arrived at a figure of one in twenty-four.

It was overwhelming for the prosecution's scientific witnesses, Richard Roberts and Carl Dobkin. They convened an out-of-court meeting with Lander and his fellow defence expert witness, to review the scientific evidence, after which the four scientists issued an unprecedented joint statement declaring that, 'the DNA data in this case are not scientifically reliable enough to support the assertion that the samples . . . do or do not match. If these data were submitted to a peer-reviewed journal in support of a conclusion, they would not be accepted.' They put the blame on the adversarial nature of the legal system and its inability to deal effectively with complex science. They concluded by urging the adoption of universal standards in the forensic use of DNA testing.

The Frye hearing was turned on its head. The prosecution, however, decided to press on with the proceedings, rather than admit defeat and withdraw the DNA evidence based on the advice of its own scientific experts. The hearing resumed, with the former prosecution witnesses now testifying for the defence. Unsurprisingly, the court ruled that the bulk of the DNA evidence was inadmissible. In his decision, Judge Gerald Sheindlin of the New York Supreme Court wrote: 'The testing laboratory failed in several major respects to use the generally accepted scientific techniques and experiments for obtaining reliable results, within a reasonable degree of scientific certainty.' He suggested that attorneys who had defended people convicted on the basis of DNA typing review the transcripts to see whether they had grounds for appeal.

The only person in the defence team who did not celebrate the result was the defendant, Jose Castro, who, shortly after the successful Frye hearing decided to confess to the crime in return for a reduced sentence.

The Castro case marked a watershed in forensic DNA. Until that point, any DNA evidence had simply been waved through the trial process, with little more than a cursory check of the expert's credentials. What could a defence lawyer do? The technology was cutting-edge, complicated and had been greeted with such fanfare by the scientific community and media alike that they saw little room for manoeuvre. But what was rarely taken into account – until Eric Lander and Co. brought it into the full glare of public scrutiny – was that molecular biology as practised in universities, and forensic serology as practised in crime labs, are different disciplines. One is dealing with fresh, liquid blood, analysed under controlled laboratory conditions and subjected to stringent peer review; the other uses the same techniques, adapted only slightly for use on dried blood samples, which might have been handled by different people, come into contact with microbes and other unknown samples found on streets or in carpets and exposed to environmental insults – heat, humidity, light and temperature. Yet despite the added complications, the results were subject to fewer controls. DNA analysis may have been rightly hailed as the wonder-tool of medical diagnostics, but what was good for the ivory towers did not necessarily work on the murky streets.

The media turned its fickle face in response to the Castro case. *Nature* reported 'DNA fingerprinting on trial'; *Science* went further with their headline 'Fight Erupts over DNA Fingerprinting', while in a long *New Scientist* exposé, published in March 1990, William Thompson and Simon Ford asked, 'Is DNA fingerprinting ready for the courts?' Their conclusion was, 'not yet'. This kind of questioning publicity prompted defence lawyers to start hiring independent experts to check the results of prosecution DNA tests on their clients. In many cases, they found that the claims could not be substantiated. In the five months following the Castro Frye hearing, prosecutors in California, Pennsylvania, Massachusetts, Arizona and Louisiana chose to withdraw DNA evidence rather than present it at trial. In November 1989, the Minnesota Supreme

Court ruled that tests performed by Cellmark Diagnostics failed to meet minimum standards for the scientific validation of its laboratory protocol. Cellmark, additionally, had refused to disclose information needed for independent evaluation of its tests and had failed to publish data of its procedures in peer-reviewed scientific journals.

William Thompson, a genial law professor with a psychological bent based at the University of California in Irvine – midway between Los Angeles and San Diego – was not remotely surprised by the Castro case and resulting brouhaha. He had been looking into forensic DNA – its plus points and potential pitfalls – ever since reading Alec Jeffreys' first *Nature* paper in 1985. At the time, he was studying jury decision-making, examining how they assess scientific and mathematical evidence, particularly in connection with blood and protein typing. 'The statistics I was dealing with then were typically in the range of 1:50 or 1:100, which seemed to be convincing enough for people to convict on, as long as the other evidence was reasonably strong. Then along came Jeffreys with his amazing new technology and suddenly he was quoting figures like 1 in 30 billion. I thought, "Wow. This is incredibly powerful, but how are juries going to understand it?" I got out the articles and tried to read them. They made absolutely no sense to me. I will never forget the opening sentence of the first one: "Hypervariable 'minisatellite' regions in human DNA" . . . I mean . . .' He trotted off downstairs to see a British molecular biologist called Simon Ford. Ford talked and walked him through the technology, until Bill Thompson felt comfortable in the company of multi-locus probes, alleles and Southern blotting.

'It quickly became apparent that this was really exciting. But it was not simple. I saw immediately that the issue was not only juries having trouble understanding it, but lawyers too.' Thompson and Ford decided to write an article for lawyers explaining the new technology. Deep into their research, they were invited to a conference of forensic scientists in San Diego, to talk about what they had learned. First, Ford outlined the molecular biology. Then it was Thompson's turn to approach the lectern. 'I said something along the lines of, "This looks very promising, but for it to be used in court, we have to pass the Frye standard." I outlined the possible weaknesses, as I saw them: validation of the statistics, standards for matches, all the things that seemed pretty apparent to us. I thought I had given a nice talk about what would have to be done, when this woman from the Orange County crime lab stood up and said, "This kind of talk is dangerous. You shouldn't be saying these kinds of things in public. Defence lawyers might find out about this and use it. We've all got to work together here, and if you have concerns, you can talk to us privately, but you shouldn't write an article about this." It was the first time that I had come into contact with forensic scientists and my first inkling that there was something different about them as a race. Here was I, a young assistant professor at the university, thinking that I was doing something helpful, and suddenly I was being denounced on the grounds that I was dangerous. Of course, it was an exciting thing for me that I might be dangerous . . .'

As the time came for the article to go to *Trial* magazine, Thompson became increasingly aware that forensic science was a minefield of politics, the scientists resistant to any publicity that even suggested that the technology was anything but definitive, infallible, unquestionable. Cellmark even threatened to withdraw its advertising in an attempt to prevent publication. 'I couldn't understand it. The article was, on the whole, very positive, along the lines of: DNA testing, promising technique, may need additional validation. So why were they so resistant? My theory is that the scientists saw this as a tool that was going to improve their professional status, increase their budgets; they were using techniques to do something wonderful that couldn't have been done before, and they felt protective over it.'

Thompson's and Ford's take on DNA typing duly appeared in *Trial* in late 1988. The following year, an expanded paper was published in the *Virginia Law Review*, at around the same time as the Castro case reached its surprising denouement. 'I looked at the evidence in the Castro case,' Thompson says. 'And it was pretty typical of the evidence that was coming along at that time. The RFLP test wasn't very sensitive, and they were often dealing with inadequate material, which weakened the results, led to band-shifting and so on. In many cases, there had to be an element of interpretation to make sense of the results; realigning the bands, recalibrating the machines, reading faint smudges as bands and discounting others as artefacts.

'We quickly became anathema to prosecutors and forensic scientists and beloved by the defence bar. We were deluged with phone calls from defence lawyers, whose clients had been incriminated by DNA evidence and didn't know what to do about it. They wanted to talk to us, pay us money and get us into the courtroom. They would send us lab work and ask if we could see any problems with it. In the early days, there were lots of problems. For instance, there was no matching standard for RFLP – how close did the bands have to be to be called a match? Three per cent? Five per cent? What troubled me most – and still does – is that the testing was never done in a blind manner, as is standard throughout the scientific community. Whenever you have to deal with data that has potential ambiguities, requiring subjective judgment by an expert, the expert should do it blind. But the forensic scientists always know exactly which samples come from the suspect, which from the victim.'

Thompson tells a story about an academic colleague of his, an authority on the mating of finches, who was using DNA typing – both RFLP and PCR – to test finch paternity. When he asked her whether she did it blind, she looked indignant. 'Of course we do,' she said. 'We couldn't get National Science Foundation funding if it wasn't blind. We couldn't get published in peer-reviewed journals if it wasn't blind. You have to understand,' she told him, 'my work is extremely important: it has to do with the entire evolutionary history of the finch.'

In the forensic world, the people who are doing the interpretation are, in most cases, considered part of the prosecution team; they meet with the detectives, they know the particulars of the case, often they have strong expectations of what they are going to see. Thompson pulls out a case he worked on to show some notes, scribbled in the margin by a DNA analyst from one of the well-known labs: 'Suspect known Crip gang member. Keeps skating on charges, never serves time. This robbery he gets hit in head with bar stool, left blood trail. Detective wants to connect this guy to scene using DNA. Death penalty case.' He tells of another case where a forensic analyst defended the positive scoring of an ambiguous band by stating, 'I must be right, they found the victim's purse in [the defendant's] apartment.'

'I am a psychologist,' Thompson says. 'My research is on how people make judgments. And if I know one thing it is: what you expect to see and want to see influences what you do see, when you are looking at something ambiguous.' He has files and files of examples in which dodgy DNA results were called as matches, initially with RFLP-based DNA profiling, but later with PCR-based testing and the new-generation STR testing. Among the most shocking cases are those where laboratory error came into play. In one rape case, the lab had mixed up the suspect's and the victim's samples, resulting in the 'suspect's' DNA being found on the victim's panties, in vaginal extract taken in the rape kit, on the bed clothes. Purely by chance, the defence attorney asked Thompson to look at the lab report, and he immediately sniffed trouble. Why, he asked the lab, was there no sign of the victim's DNA in any extract? Oh that, they replied, must have left it in the centrifuge too long, thus killing the vaginal cells. The idea that the samples might have been inadvertently switched had not occurred to them. 'Why not?' Thompson asks. 'Because they thought he was the guilty party and they were seeing what they expected to see.' In this case, the suspect was immediately released – but had Thompson not happened to look over the lab results, he might have been serving a thirty-year prison sentence. 'The jury would have heard the experts talking about a DNA match to the exclusion of, say, 300 billion people, and despite the suspect's protestations of innocence, despite in many cases him having a concrete alibi, they would have convicted. The scientific evidence is that powerful.'

He estimates that in one case in every three or four that he looks at he sees some sort of problem. Not all point to the suspect's innocence, necessarily, only to the possibility of it. They create doubt – in some cases, reasonable doubt. Ambiguous results have a powerful effect on the calculation of probability statistics, as in the Castro case, and this is something that is rarely taken into account in the testimony of expert witnesses. Thompson has found himself spending more and more time helping in cases, and less on his academic work. 'At first, I was driven by disappointment and anger. We would write things and people would ignore it. Challenging the admissibility of the technology seemed to be the only mechanism to encourage the labs to do what I thought they should do . . . It's fun too,' he added after a pause.

But he strongly rejects any implication that he is anti-DNA. Far from it, he says. 'Don't get me wrong. DNA has revolutionized forensic serology, which has gone from being a little backwater to the premier, major evidence there is. More than that, I think DNA testing will change the way society works in important ways; it has the potential to control and reduce crime dramatically. It is a very important new tool that has the power to be very beneficial – it has already been very beneficial. What I don't think people realize, however, is that it also has the potential for misuse – they don't recognize how often it can be problematic, subject to misinterpretation, and how hard it is to deal with the cases where somebody is incriminated falsely through bad DNA evidence. We have to be very careful.'

In the early 1990s, the defence backlash against DNA testing picked up steam. Barry Scheck and

Peter Neufeld, acting under the aegis of the National Association of Criminal Defence Lawyers, set up a DNA task force. They lashed out against sloppy lab work and junk science, and while there was no way they were ever going to be able to repudiate DNA testing, they at least raised attorney and public awareness of its shortcomings. If it wasn't a bulldozer out on the sloping playing field, it was at least a team of energetic and determined workers, armed with shovels and wheelbarrows, attempting to create a semblance of level.

Over the following five years, the US National Academy of Science commissioned first one, and then a follow-up report into forensic DNA. Their aim was to devise a series of protocols and procedures which would banish uncertainty and the need for often lengthy and costly Frye hearings. The battles fought in the committee rooms were every bit as fiercely contested as those in the courthouses. The results of both the 1992 and 1996 reports, recommending standardization, mandatory accreditation and proficiency testing for DNA labs, and an overseeing committee of experts, were criticized by prosecutors and the defence bar, each protesting bias against their side. The subject of most controversy was what was seen as a botched compromise over how to measure the statistical probability of matching DNA samples. The battle continued.

The skirmishes over validity, however, did little to check the stream of convictions based on DNA, which by 1990 were becoming increasingly common in courtrooms across America and the world. The objections being raised were little more than tiny clouds on a distant horizon. It would ultimately be the success of DNA which shook the criminal justice system most profoundly.

Long before Barry Scheck and Peter Neufeld became involved in the Castro case, they realized that there was something rotten in the criminal justice system. They had long suspected it: that based on bad evidence, the wrong people were being convicted for crimes they did not commit, serving long stretches in jail, possibly even being put to death: innocent people, men and women with parents and children.

They had met in the mid-1970s, two young men with missions. Scheck had grown up on the meaner streets of Brooklyn, where his father, a former tap dancer turned celebrity manager, guided his son through the shady world of the nightclub circuit. Barry was formidably bright; he excelled as an undergraduate at Yale and later at UC Berkeley law schools despite riding every left-leaning bandwagon that passed his door, and on graduating, spurned the offers of cushy jobs at slick law firms with offices on the upper floors of Wall Street skyscrapers in favour of the Bronx Legal Aid Society. Operating out of dingy offices only blocks from Yankee Stadium, in the homeland of the underprivileged, underpaid and unemployed of New York City, fervent young lawyers, working all hours for a pittance, practised street justice. It was there that he met Peter Neufeld.

Neufeld's background was resolutely middle-class liberal intelligentsia. From an early age he was organizing schoolboy revolts against what he regarded as moral outrages: from the Pledge of Allegiance to the Vietnam War. It took a mere sniff of injustice to get him on his soap box and shouting. For him, Bronx Legal Aid was due payment on account to society before the fees started rolling in, and the pair soon hooked up as a formidable team. Both their friendship and working partnership survived their departure from the legal aid – Scheck to academia at the Cardozo School of Law in Yeshiva University, on the lower reaches of Manhattan's Fifth Avenue, and Neufeld to private practice.

In early 1988, Gary Dotson had become the first wrongfully convicted man to be exonerated on the basis of DNA evidence. After serving the best part of twelve years in prison for a rape he did not commit – and could not possibly have committed, according to the testimony of a handful of witnesses – his innocence had been proved by PCR-based tests performed by Ed Blake. It was the signal that Scheck and Neufeld had been waiting for, their call to delve among the growing population wallowing in the American penal system in search of innocence. Scheck organized a forum on DNA testing at Cardozo Law School, at which he called for defence lawyers to contact him with cases of wrongful conviction. The idea was to use the brain power at his disposal – his third-year students, keen for practical experience – to work free of charge on cases where it appeared that DNA could be used to reverse a conviction. He and Peter Neufeld would provide the legal presence and experience to back up the students' ground work. They called it the Innocence Project.

To their surprise, the first problem was lack of cases. Defence lawyers were hardly knocking at their door, racked with guilt and desperate to expose the cases they had failed to win. And there was a prevailing ignorance about how DNA could be used, and an unwillingness to shake the bedrock of the legal institution. 'We always knew that there had to be innocent people in jail and that their innocence could be proved through DNA,' says Scheck. 'But people didn't realize then – and still don't – how amazingly powerful the technology is. Prosecutors, defence lawyers, forensic scientists, let alone the prisoners and their families don't know that you can get DNA from the shaft of a hair. They don't know that this cup you're drinking from will have saliva on it, from which DNA can be extracted. They don't know you can get it from the sweat off the headband of a hat. They don't know you can gender-type a bloodstain. They don't think of these things, so they don't see all the different ways that you can prove somebody innocent.'

It was in 1992, at the same time as San Diego detective Laura Heilig was reading about Helena

Greenwood's murder for the first time, and Paul Frediani was settling into life as a free man, that the Innocence Project came formally to life. Scheck and Neufeld had been involved in some way in the majority of the ten or so successful post-conviction exonerations that had been effected using DNA to date. They were discussing the phenomenon on TV on the *Phil Donahue Show*, when Scheck turned spontaneously to the camera and urged anyone who believed that they – or a family member – had been wrongfully convicted of a crime, to write to the Innocence Project at Cardozo Law School.

The dam had been unplugged, and soon hundreds of letters were arriving each month, overflowing from the informal in-tray behind the project's door. Their return addresses were prisons around the country; their authors, desperate men serving life sentences or waiting for death. 'Dear Innocence Project,' a typical letter would read. 'In 1989, I was convicted of a crime I did not commit . . .' There would follow a familiar story of how someone, once ensnared by the justice system, can be sucked into its deep throat.

A process soon evolved out of the chaos of the early days of the Innocence Project: an early weeding-out of cases that were clearly unsuitable, with follow-up letters to those which promised to have physical evidence available for DNA testing. The cases that were accepted were shared out between the students participating in that year's clinical programme. The selected students were typically committed as well as hard-working. Far from being a practical component to their academic degree, it began to take over many of their lives, as they became more and more obsessed with the cases of the prisoners they were trying to help. As they got to know their subjects, so their stories became real, and the students became enmeshed in the drama of lives wasted in prison, families decimated, crushed dreams.

Most of the cases dated back to the 1980s and earlier, to a time before DNA testing. The students soon discovered that in the large majority of cases there was no evidence; it had been either lost or thrown away, along with the keys to their clients' cells. At that point, the Innocence Project would be forced to close the case and move on. Even when the evidence is tracked down, the struggle has barely begun. The local prosecutor has to be persuaded to release the evidence for testing. Sometimes they agreed immediately – more frequently, at least in the early days, they did not.

'Any decent person recoils at the horror of an innocent person being put in jail for the rest of his or her life, or facing execution,' says Barry Scheck. 'And that's what we're talking about in these cases: the worst nightmare one can imagine. And yet there is resistance to doing the tests, there's resistance to letting them go once the results come in, that at times just absolutely astonishes me and frankly drives me nuts. Why? Each case is different, but I think that, in some instances, there is an institutional inability to admit a mistake for whatever it is. I can't understand it in some cases because the prosecutor that we're dealing with was not the prosecutor at the time of trial. And yet . . . they don't want to admit that the system can make these kinds of horrible, horrible errors.'

Prison years are long years. For many Innocence Project clients, they pass only with the aid of hope. After the initial injection of promise following their acceptance by the project, the prisoner would get used to an initial contact from his assigned student at the beginning of the academic year, then only brief – negative – progress reports until it was time for a new intake, a new student, a new beginning to the process.

In the cramped cubicles on the eleventh floor of an undistinguished building in lower Manhattan, the Innocence Project began to reap the rewards of persistence as first one, then a trickle of exonerations turned into a steady flow. Each was greeted with tremendous fanfare by the staff and students working on the project. Cheers, even tears each time. As Scheck freely admits, 'You become entwined in people's lives, personally involved. Over the last few years, we have met interesting and impressive people, with extraordinary stories to tell.'

With each wrongful conviction came not only a human drama, but another example of failure in the system. Each man had been given his day in court and in every instance, a supposedly fair and unbiased jury of their peers had found him guilty. In some cases, the key factor had been mistaken eye-witness identification; in others, false – often coerced – confessions or police corruption, inadequate legal representation, prosecutorial misconduct or what Barry Scheck has termed 'junk science': inaccurate microscopic comparison of hair, fingerprints, fibres or bite marks.

The experience of Innocence Project clients also points to racist juries, the use of jailhouse snitches as witnesses and the presentation of serological results which appear to include the defendant as factors leading to wrongful convictions. It all adds up to a terrifying picture of a system that does not work. 'You must remember, however, that DNA is not the magic bullet,' says Jane Siegel Greene, who for many years was the executive director of the project. 'It is not going to fix the criminal justice system, but what it does do is open this window on what is wrong with the system. It allows us to show with complete certainty that these people are truly innocent and that is incredibly powerful and important.'

Of the people who know about and write to the Innocence Project, the vast majority are immediately excluded from help because their case did not involve physical evidence – it was perhaps a shooting or burglary. Of the small residue, three-quarters have to be let down at a later date when it is found that the physical evidence that did exist has been lost or destroyed. Of the rest – the 25 per cent of the original tiny sample – nearly two-thirds have been proven innocent. By the beginning of April 2002, that number stood at 104 – 104 people who had spent an average of a decade in prison for a crime they did not commit.

'Think about the rest of them,' urges Scheck, 'the great majority of cases in which there was no physical evidence in the first place, no DNA to test. They were convicted on the same grounds, the same mistaken eye-witness identifications, the same junk science and prosecutorial misconduct. What recourse do they have?

'I don't know how many innocent people there are in our jails, and jails across the world, but it must be a great number. A horrendously great number.'

And innocence in itself is not always enough. To this day, in many states, there is no automatic constitutional imperative to release a prisoner based on the wrong outcome of a trial: faulty procedure is grounds for reversal, but not a faulty verdict. As the Chief Justice of the Supreme Court of the United States, William Renquist, wrote, 'A claim of actual innocence is not itself a constitutional claim.' Merely proving you are innocent after conviction is not enough to guarantee release.

For every case in which the criminal justice systems of the world have been proven – primarily through the agency of DNA – to be too eager to convict the innocent, there are multiple examples of guilty people slipping through their nets and escaping punishment.

The Innocence Project is Scheck's and Neufeld's baby, their mission, but it is not their bread and butter.

Both take on private cases, and frequently work together. When the call came in 1994, asking if they wanted to join Johnnie Cochrane and Robert Shapiro on the O. J. Simpson defence 'dream team', with special responsibility to fight the DNA evidence that had been amassed against the former football star charged with the murder of his ex-wife, Nicole Brown Simpson, and her friend Ronald Goldman, it was a challenge they could not pass up.

From the start, it was clear that DNA was going to play a major role in the trial; its making or breaking. Pre-O. J., few people had even heard of DNA; the trial changed all that; to this day, in the US at least, its three initials are inextricably linked to Simpson's two. Even a couple of weeks before the trial, an article in *Nature*, hardly the most sensationalist of publications, began by commenting on the new-found interest in DNA. 'The US public, usually indifferent to matters scientific, has suddenly become obsessed with DNA,' wrote Eric Lander, the MIT professor who had made such a fuss about forensic DNA during the Castro case, and Bruce Budowle, the FBI's chief DNA expert. 'Nightly newscasts routinely refer to the polymerase chain reaction (PCR) and even the tabloids offer commentary on restriction fragment length polymorphisms (RFLPs). The new-found fascination with nucleic acids does not stem from recent breakthroughs in genetic screening for breast cancer susceptibility or progress in gene therapy – developments which will indeed affect the lives of millions.

Rather, it focuses on the murder case against the former US football star, O. J. Simpson.'

Once the trial started, the world watched transfixed as week after week, month after month, some eminent DNA expert or another sat on the witness stand, exploring the intimate details of a tiny molecule in microscopic detail. Eyes glazed, minds wandered, but the television sets stayed on. The advance publicity from the prosecution camp was that DNA would win them the case. There were no eye-witnesses, O. J. had never officially confessed – though the handwritten note he left before taking off on his Bronco adventure was certainly construed by some as an admission of sorts – the evidence was primarily circumstantial. It rested on the infamous 'trail of blood'.

After months of investigation, the prosecution forces – police and attorneys – had amassed what appeared to be the strongest DNA evidence against a single defendant ever seen. Over fifty blood samples had been tested at three different laboratories. The results appeared to be overwhelming. At the crime scene, Nicole Brown Simpson's townhouse, apart from puddles of the two victims' blood, police found five drops of blood on the walkway and three stains near the back gate. After testing, all revealed profiles consistent with O. J. Simpson's. The famous blood-soaked right-hand glove found at Simpson's Rockingham estate contained a mixture of DNA profiles; both of the victims' plus one which was consistent with O. J.'s. A dark navy sock collected from Simpson's bedroom the following afternoon was tested months later and found to have a bloodstain containing DNA with a profile consistent with Nicole Brown Simpson's, and other minute DNA material consistent with O. J.'s. Blood samples collected on two separate occasions from O. J.'s Bronco jeep – from the carpet, steering wheel and console – contained DNA profiles which were consistent with both the victims' and O. J. Simpson's.

For Marcia Clark and her team, for most of the media reporters and commentators and a majority of the watching public, that was incontrovertible evidence of O. J. Simpson's guilt. A hero had fallen, plunged from the pinnacles of success and fame to the dungeons of criminality. But Scheck and Neufeld had other ideas. They gathered around them a mini-team of DNA experts and advisors – Ed Blake from up in Richmond, California, Bill Thompson from Irvine, Henry Lee, chief criminalist for the state of Connecticut, Nobel laureate and surfing hero Kary Mullis – and prepared to fight. After examining the evidence, they found numerous flaws in the prosecution's version of events, numerous factors that did not add up – which pointed, conversely, to a police frame-up. It was enough to shake the juices of moral outrage in any committed defence attorney, and to stir their desire for a courtroom fight.

Certainly the defence did a more than effective job in deconstructing the prosecution's seemingly air-tight case, exposing the potential shortcomings of forensic DNA evidence. It was a step away from the Innocence Project and its reliance on the power of DNA – and back to Castro. The timing could have been better – shortly before the trial began, in the same *Nature* article, Lander and Budowle had announced that the 'DNA fingerprinting dispute [had been] laid to rest'. Former opponents across courtroom floors, they were now satisfied, they said, with the guidelines and standards introduced after the second National Research Council study. Both Scheck and Neufeld had been on a number of committees involved in pushing for these standards. Now they were fighting from the opposing corner.

They did it with their customary élan. Their defence was a model of effective, creative – same might say pugnacious – advocacy, part oratorical brilliance, part dogged endurance, hammering away at the prosecution witnesses until they seemed to crumble, picking at their evidence until it appeared worthless. The defendant, they said, had cut himself at home that evening, perhaps while fetching his mobile phone from the jeep, which accounted for the presence of his blood in the house, on the driveway and in the car. The blood drops found at the crime scene and on the Rockingham glove were contaminated with Simpson's DNA at the LAPD laboratory by criminalist Colin Yamauchi, who admitted on the stand that he had spilled some of Simpson's blood from a reference phial while working in the evidence room, and shortly afterwards, handled the glove and the swatches containing blood from the crime scene drops. The laboratory sloppiness – regular practice in the LAPD lab according to a recent, year-long study – was augmented by police misconduct, Scheck intimated.

In support of their theory, a significant amount of the reference blood drawn from Simpson the day after the murders was later found to be unaccounted for, while there were indications that the phials containing the reference samples drawn from Nicole Simpson and Ronald Goldman were contaminated with O. J.'s DNA. Dr John Gerdes, testifying for the defence, claimed that extra alleles consistent with O. J.'s profile appeared when the supposed pure samples of the victims' blood was typed at all three labs, suggesting that the samples had been contaminated at an early stage. The defence further contended that the swatches used to collect blood from the crime scene were switched the day after collection. The original swatches had been sealed and stored in a truck until the end of the day, when they were returned to the LAPD lab and left to dry in test tubes overnight. The next morning, criminalist Andrea Mazzola packaged the dried swatches in paper bindles, which she initialled. However, when defence experts examined the bindles, they found that none of them bore Mazzola's initials, and further, that it appeared that some of them exhibited wet transfer stains – the sort of stains that would arise when paper came into contact with wet swatches. This, the defence alleged, indicated that one of the detectives had taken blood from Simpson's reference tube, created his own swatches, and swapped them with those collected from the crime scene. Lead detective Philip Vanatter had kept Simpson's reference sample in an unsealed tube in his truck for several hours, contrary to accepted practice, and then driven across town to the crime scene before handing it over to criminalist Dennis Fung. ('But why,' cried the prosecution, 'if the detectives believed O. J. was guilty, would they have needed to plant his blood at the scene?')

The blood on the sock, furthermore, a large, crusty stain matching Nicole's DNA, was not discovered until several months after the crime, before which, three people had failed to notice it. This, according to Dr Lee, bore all the hallmarks of having been planted when the sock was lying flat on the ground, not on someone's foot. As for the bloody glove – that was tainted evidence: it had been picked up by Detective Mark Fuhrman, who was comprehensively depicted as a racist in court. And the back gate: a photograph taken the day after the crime showed no sign of the bloodstain – collected two weeks after – prompting Barry Scheck's famous question: 'Where is it, Mr Fung?'

This was the defence argument in a nutshell. At the trial, it went on for weeks and months. Experts arguing over minutiae that was often the province of a scarce handful of specialists around the world. Rewatching sections of the trial, reading transcripts of the intense examination and cross-examination of key witnesses, it becomes possible to understand how the jury could choose to discount the DNA evidence. Much of it was a mess – and every single spot in that famous trail of blood had a conceivable alternative explanation for its presence. Whether, taken as a whole, those explanations could be construed as reasonable – or whether without the skill of lawyers like Scheck and Neufeld and their scientific team, they would have surfaced at all – is academic. The defence won, and Scheck and Neufeld undoubtedly contributed significantly to the defeat of DNA.

In the end, their much-anticipated scientific trump card, Kary Mullis, was not even called to the stand. In the decade since his flash of inspiration, PCR had made Mullis rich and famous. As well as the Nobel, he had won the even more lucrative Japan prize – both of which now sit, garlanded in twinkling red fairy lights, in the otherwise tasteful Newport Beach apartment he shares with his artist fourth wife, Nancy. These days, he is invited around the world to talk about whatever he wants, and occasionally asked to testify in high-profile court cases. At the Simpson trial, he was planning to testify about the need for blind testing of DNA samples, and the problems related to using PCR – the technology he had invented – in the forensic arena. But advance publicity focusing on his unabashed enjoyment of LSD and alcohol persuaded the defence lawyers that it might not be a good idea.

To some who know Scheck and Neufeld well, and respect their crusading work, particularly with the Innocence Project, the O. J. case was a confusing episode, a blot on an otherwise clean moral history. They who had spoken out loudly and bravely about a corrupt criminal justice system had, in the eyes of many, twisted the system to obtain an unjust verdict. To others, however, the provision of a strong defence for Simpson was not only ethical, but the noble thing to do, upholding the tenets of the traditional adversarial system. What was undeniable was that the trial had been a setback for courtroom DNA. Police forces and forensic laboratories around the world were forced to tighten up their techniques and procedures for collecting and preserving samples. Even Innocence Project clients like Herman Atkins, exonerated after serving twelve years in the hardest prisons in California, cannot find excuses for what the O. J. case said about the criminal justice system. 'O. J. had the money to purchase these kinds of guys and they did what they had to do. What they showed is that the law can work for you and against you, depending on how much money you have. If I'd had those guys working for me from day one, I would never have gone to prison. It's appalling; in all honesty it's an act of treason to the very justice system that we've been taught to believe in and support. This is not justice in any shape or thought. It is always the poor who find themselves victim of the justice system here in America, and it just happens that the face of the poor is usually black or Hispanic.'

To Scheck and Neufeld's supporters, it was a relief when they returned to the East Coast and their list of indigent clients. 'Maybe at some psychological level,' Henry Erlich suggests, 'the Innocence Project is their way of trying to compensate for the cases like O. J. that they have been involved in?'

Scheck and Neufeld would say that O. J. was the other end of a system riven with faults which need to be exposed. And their mission is having practical effect: not only are there 104 more innocent people walking around America thanks to DNA, but a growing number of states are instituting innocence protection legislation – giving convicted prisoners the right to DNA testing, ensuring physical evidence is kept at least for the duration of their sentence, and providing appropriate compensation for the wrongly convicted.

14

Every day, Laura Heilig drives an hour and a half from her home in the hills to a modern office building in a nondescript northern suburb of San Diego, wedged between two busy freeways. The County Sheriff's Department headquarters looks as if it is deep undercover. But for the handful of white transit vans, parked in spaces clearly marked 'Evidence Vehicle', you would never guess it was the nerve centre for investigations into all sorts of grisly crimes. Nor would you point to Laura Heilig and say, 'There goes an ace homicide detective.'

She takes the lift to the second floor, walks down the middle of a long room, institutional grey, truncated cubicles like rooms for dwarfs on either side. Hers is towards the end on the right. Pictures of smiling blond grandchildren are propped on her desk, alongside a framed quote from the Bible. And opposite the family pictures, pinned to a large corkboard just a chair swivel away, are an array of faded photographs, and colour photocopies of photographs, that are almost as familiar. They are of women, mainly, and some children, smiling for the school photographer. They have one thing in common: they all died violent deaths. One girl was a prostitute, found dumped beside the freeway, another the heir to a Midwest publishing empire, who came to visit her uncle and aunt in San Diego in 1975, and was stabbed and bludgeoned to death as she lay on the sofa one evening. On the left side of the board, half-way up, is Helena Greenwood, sitting on a flat stone in the sun, knees up, arms braced by her side, wearing shorts and a vest. Her face is turned away from the camera. It looks as if she is catching her breath after a summer walk. She is relaxed, appears carefree. It is the photograph of her that Laura Heilig likes to keep in her mind: she has seen so many others, of a crumpled body, a bruised cadaver on a shining metal autopsy table, cut open, peeled back.

Helena Greenwood and her fellow long-dead victims of violent crime are Laura Heilig's daily companions. She knows their birthdays, their eye colours, the names of their brothers and sisters, fathers and children. What she does not know is who killed them. Yet. It is not just her job to find out, it is her mission. She wants to track down these murderers for the sake of the victims' families, to bring them some degree of peace to muffle the lasting agony of loss.

She remembers reading the Helena Greenwood file back in 1992, while sorting through the piles of old cases. It was one of her first jobs on the homicide squad, a routine task for a junior detective. Then, after a few weeks in a small room, she was back in the world of the newly dead, working fresh homicide. She enjoyed her work, being part of a team, solving riddles, but it was not what she would have imagined herself doing thirty years previously.

She was seventeen and pregnant when she married her first love, and willingly sacrificed her high school diploma to follow him up from San Diego to Los Angeles. While he went to film school, she supported the family, running a print shop from a Beverly Hills basement and looking after first one, then two children. They split up soon after he graduated, and Laura took the kids and moved back down to San Diego. She was desperate for money and worked where she could – as an ambulance attendant, a nursing aid in a convalescent hospital, a waitress. She married again over the years, a couple of times, but not for keeps.

She was digging ditches for a construction company when she suddenly woke up one morning in 1982 and thought, 'Boy, I'm thirty-one, and my body's not going to hold out digging ditches for another twenty years.' She had two children to care for, and they were living from day to day. Her sister suggested she think about working at the Sheriff's Department – she had a friend, a woman who was a deputy sheriff and enjoyed it. Laura talked to her, and it sounded enticing, the benefits, stability, paid vacations, a retirement plan, health insurance – nothing she had ever known before.

After four months at the police academy, she worked the County jails for four years, before being transferred on to patrol duty in the eastern reaches of San Diego County. Before too many summers had passed, she was a detective in the central investigations division, hunting murderers. It was towards the end of the 1990s that the Sheriff's official archive team was formed: three experienced detectives, all seasoned and unshockable veterans of the homicide squad. But instead of picking their way through fresh blood and flies, their concerns became the cold cases, and their beat a large warehouse full of half-forgotten files of unsolved murders.

Laura Heilig was newly remarried when the new team was formed. She and her fourth husband, a great bear of a biker, with grey moustaches as wide as his Harley's handlebars, were building a house in the eastern hills far from the city, and retirement was already more than a dream. Her plan was to work a few more years in the relatively refined world of the long-departed, before taking early retirement, exchanging the burden of daily contact with death for more prosaic worries, like whether the rain had come at the right time for the avocado crop. The archive unit, with its close-knit team, relatively regular hours and emphasis on desk-work, seemed to be a good place for her last years on the force. Her fellow detectives, Victor Caloca and Curt Goldberg, were friends as well as colleagues, the job promised the satisfaction of a successfully completed cryptic crossword. They shared out the murder files between them, and started the painstaking task of sifting through the pages of police reports, witness statements, brown paper bags of evidence, looking to see if there was anything that had been missed first time round, any evidence that new scientific techniques could now make sense of.

It was April 1998 when she picked up the Greenwood file for the second time. She recalled reading it before, and Dave Decker talking about it. Back in those days, the office had been stretched. The crime rate was higher, and they didn't have the money or resources to go into individual cases in depth. Decker had told her that he hadn't been allowed to spend much time up in San Francisco investigating the case. But he was fairly certain he knew who the killer was: David Paul Frediani, who had sexually assaulted Helena Greenwood the year before, and killed her to prevent her testifying at trial. He was their man all right, but the evidence had not been there to book him.

Laura read Decker's detailed report, the coroner's conclusions, examined the crime scene investigator's diagrams. She was relieved to find that the physical evidence taken at the time of the autopsy – fingernail clippings and scrapings – was sitting, apparently untouched, in the vast property warehouse. She sorted through them, relogged and barcoded the individual elements, and decided it would be worth seeing if there was anything there, any tiny bits of DNA that might provide a clue to the murderer's identification. She wasn't overly hopeful; the unit had had several cases recently where they had hoped to find DNA pointing to a killer, but nothing turned up but the victim's own. This was more than likely in strangulations, where victims had scratched themselves while trying to prise their attacker's hands away. She could see scratches on Helena Greenwood's neck in the autopsy photographs; the chances were that they were self-inflicted too. Still, it was worth a try. It was their only real hope. This was not the kind of case where she could have gone out and recontacted witnesses years later, who maybe had had a reason to lie for the suspect at the time, but whose circumstances had changed sufficiently for them now to tell the truth. In this case, the people who had been interviewed were basic, upright individuals. Physical evidence was the only option and that meant DNA.

She looked carefully at the fingernail clippings and scrapings, fragments of keratin and dirt stored in see-through plastic boxes labelled 'left' and 'right'. She could see nothing else, but that didn't mean that invisible clues were not there, microscopic double helixes displaying the identity of Helena Greenwood's killer. In January 1999, the clippings and scrapings were packaged carefully. They were sent, along with seven strands of Helena's hair, complete with root – to use as reference samples for her DNA – to the Serological Institute (Seri), a private DNA lab which shares a building with Ed Blake's Forensic Science Associates in Richmond, California. To get there, the courier's van would have had to pass within a mile of Helena Greenwood's old home in Atherton, and cross the Bay Bridge to Berkeley, where she and Roger had lived for their first year in California.

Months passed before Laura heard back from Seri. She was in no particular hurry, the case had been sitting unsolved for fourteen years, and a little longer was not going to make any difference. She knew that the cold cases get pushed to the back of the lab's freezer, to make space for fresh blood samples. It was September when she picked up a phone call from Mary Buglio, a criminalist in the serology department of the Sheriff's crime lab. 'Good news on the Greenwood case,' Mary told her. 'Gary Harmor at Seri found foreign DNA on the fingernails.'

Laura was elated. It was a hit at last – so many of her cases were turning into dead ends, their files returned to the archives still open. She told Vic and Curt, reported to their sergeant, Tom Bennett, then started the ball rolling on the next stage. 'I called up the California Department of Justice DNA lab. I was hoping that they would have a sample from Frediani on file. As a registered sex offender, they would these days for sure, but when he was released from prison in 1989, it was still the early days of DNA, and I worried that they might not have started collecting them yet.'

She needn't have. The DOJ had the sample, taken almost exactly a decade earlier, on 12 July 1989, the day Frediani was released from Vacaville. It had been stored for the last decade in a freezer in their lab in Berkeley. They would send it to a certified laboratory on receipt of written instructions, they told her. She asked for it to be sent to Seri, just a couple of miles north of Berkeley. The DOJ refused: Seri had not yet been accredited; it was against their rules. 'We said, "Then send it to us and we will send it to Seri," but they said they couldn't do that, as our lab wasn't accredited either. Now, of course, I'm so glad we didn't touch it. Instead, we said, "OK, then send it to Cellmark Diagnostics," which they agreed to do. It was then that the case really started humming.

'Because I hadn't been that optimistic about finding anything before, I hadn't really gotten to know Helena, the way I normally know my victims. I didn't want to get too excited about it at this stage, but I started quietly trying to find out what I could about Helena.'

David Paul Frediani was unaware of the activity at the San Diego Sheriff's Department. He was in the southern suburbs of San Francisco, working, keeping fit and making friends, slowly. Since the break-up with Eileen, he had dated a couple of women, most recently Maria, to whom he had become particularly attached. 'She is a socialite, beautiful. It started well, but one day she just cooled off. I didn't know why at the time. We had been away for the weekend, had a wonderful time. She had told my friend Diane that she really liked me. Then suddenly she wouldn't return my calls. It was only later, when I bumped into her at a charity auction, that she told me. She had found out that I had been in prison – it was pure coincidence, a friend of hers was the court reporter at my trial and recognized my name. What was stupid was that Maria was the first person I hadn't told about it up front. I just thought that, at last, it was behind me, that I wouldn't have to carry that albatross for the rest of my life.'

He was living in a studio apartment in Burlingame, just one large room, but in a nice complex, well located. On weekends, he went jet-skiing, played softball in the park, watched videos. He hadn't looked up his old friends, or revisited his pre-prison life. Jim Thoren once saw him on the other side of the street, and could have sworn – probably did – that his old drinking and 'howlin'' partner had seen him too, but cut him dead on purpose. Paul never returned to the bar and nightclub circuit; these days he preferred quiet restaurants and small gatherings at people's houses. He spent a lot of time with Dave Rangwirtz, his closest friend at work, and his wife Beverley and two children. Or with Kathy Clark, a chiropractor with the figure of a long-jumper, whom Paul had met when he consulted her for back problems. They went out often, just as friends – Kathy would take Paul to parties or they would go for a drink after work, and he would consult her about his love life. 'We were like brother and sister. Sometimes, Kathy would come over late at night if she had had an argument with her boyfriend. She would be in her pyjamas, and we would watch videos. Our favourite was *A French Kiss.* We must have watched it forty times.'

Work at MSAS Cargo had been going well – after seven years, he was regarded as conscientious and efficient, with a flair for figures. If he was thought by some of his colleagues to be 'pretty reserved, a little bit aloof' and not, in the words of his supervisor, Ralph Arellano, 'Mr Personality', it was nothing that was going to harm his steady climb in the ranks. 'I lived and breathed that company,' he said. 'They were unaware of it, but they had given me the break of a lifetime and I would have done anything to repay them for that. I worked on the basis that every dime the company spent was coming out of my own pocket, and if there was a way I could save them money I would find it.' In 1996, the company sent him and a colleague on a tour of their South American affiliates, and it was when he got back that the trouble started. His story is that a fellow worker – 'I thought she was a friend' – called Melinda Tan, desperate for his job, checked out his criminal record on a whim and, triumphant with her discoveries, took them to the management. Paul was called in to explain. It was a sticky moment; he had clearly lied on his application form. 'What else could I do?' he asked them. 'I wanted the job so badly.' The whole prison business had been a big mistake, it was firmly in the past, would in no way affect his performance. After consultation, the board decided that he would be allowed to stay.

But shortly afterwards, Melinda Tan told another colleague of hers that Paul had been bragging that he had slept with this woman. He hadn't, and denied ever saying he had, but Tan swore that he had told her about it. A couple of Paul's close friends at the company, Dave Rangwirtz and others, went to remonstrate with the woman. Paul had never mentioned anything about her to them, they said. It wasn't in his nature to brag. Couldn't she see that it was Melinda up to dirty tricks? The mini-scandal would have died away, had Tan not then turned to the president, with a formal complaint about Paul threatening her. The compound damage was enough to persuade the company to let him go, though his immediate boss emphasized that it was with regret. Tan stepped straight into his old shoes.

Paul was devastated. 'I was a wreck when I lost the job. It had been everything to me. I worked long hours, made friends of my colleagues. I couldn't imagine what I was going to do next.' Still, it was not long before he had picked himself up again, and by 1999, he was working as a financial analyst for the telecommunications colossus Pacific Bell on a hefty salary. Life was once again looking up.

'It was good for us that Frediani knew nothing about our investigations,' said Laura Heilig. 'If the DOJ hadn't had a sample, we would have had to contact him with a warrant for the blood. Who knows, that might have got the wind up him and he might have taken off. Plus, it would have given him time to get an alibi together. So this was all happening behind the scenes.'

The sample from the fingernail scrapings was at a lab in California; Frediani's reference sample across the country at Cellmark in Maryland; Laura Heilig and

Mary Buglio sat it out at the Sheriff's Department in San Diego, waiting for news.

On 9 November 1999, the call from Cellmark came through to Mary Buglio. She contacted Laura's sergeant, told him what she had learned, and said she was coming over to talk to Laura in person. 'I wanted to play a joke on her,' Mary recalls. She is a warm, elegant lady in her mid-forties, with an Indira streak of white in her thick brown hair. She started as a criminalist 'long before the O. J. case made it fashionable', married a document examiner from the lab a few doors down and clearly lives her job. She and Laura got on well. 'Laura's sergeant wanted to be in on it, and Vic and Curt, so they were all there when I walked in and said, "Laura, I have some news about Frediani's sample." I was trying to appear disappointed. She was looking at me, as if thinking the worst.'

'Oh my God, what happened?' Laura asked.

Mary couldn't maintain the charade: 'It's a match!' The two women hugged each other and danced around the room.

Laura Heilig called the District Attorney's office to set up a meeting. She and Vic and their sergeant took their places at a round table in one of the conference rooms on the fourth floor of the Vista courthouse building, base of the north county division of the San Diego DA's Department. A committee of lawyers filed in to fill the rest of the seats. 'We have a case to present to you,' Laura began. 'In 1985, Helena

Greenwood was strangled to death at her home in Del Mar . . .' She briefly outlined the events of 1985 and her investigations, up to the point when Cellmark rang. 'At present, the probability of a random match has been calculated at around one in 1,800. The labs have indicated that they can now run more tests, which should produce better numbers.' The committee of attorneys gave the go-ahead for further tests, and assigned a deputy district attorney to the case. Her name was Valerie Summers and, coincidentally perhaps, she was a striking, dark-haired woman in her late thirties, not dissimilar in age and colouring to Helena Greenwood. She also carried with her a reputation as a merciless trial lawyer.

For the initial analysis, both labs had done the PCR-based DQα1 and Polymarker tests, initially developed by Henry Erlich and Ed Blake over a decade before. 'I was 99 per cent sure it was him,' says Laura Heilig. She is cautious by nature, not a person to throw herself around any corner – except, perhaps, matrimonial – without knowing what's waiting for her. 'But we needed that extra certainty – you don't know how many times we've got all excited about a result, and then the further tests come back and it's not the guy you think it is. RFLP was not an option, the sample was far too small for that. But I had heard about this new technology, STRs. I don't think we had used them before – certainly we weren't using them here in 1998, so they must have come on-line in 1999, around the same time as we were sending out the Greenwood evidence. I knew they could give results on really tiny samples. It was just perfect timing, really lucky for us. We called up the labs and told them to get going on the STRs.'

Short Tandem Repeats were the new standard in the forensic community. Where DNA profiling using RFLP had given specificity, and the early PCR-based tests sensitivity and speed, STRs promised to combine the best of both. They consist of natural base pair repetitions in certain highly variable regions of a chromosome – similar though shorter in length to Alec Jeffreys' original 'stutters'. Their power in the forensic field comes from the ability to amplify the samples using PCR, then send in multiple probes, which analyse several loci simultaneously. Again, it was the same probe technology that was the core of Gen-Probe's technology, and which Helena Greenwood's old company was now employing in the diagnosis of an ever-greater number of infectious diseases – from HIV to tuberculosis.

By the mid-1990s, technology had been developed which made it possible to look at four loci simultaneously – good, but not good enough: match probabilities were too low. By 1996, a six-locus STR system had been introduced and used in combination with the amelogenin test, which determines sex. Getting better; match probability down to one in 50 million.

The big manufacturers – companies like Perkin-Elmer and Promega – were working on this new technology under conditions of complete secrecy. The DNA tests were performed in closed boxes – miniature automated labs. The samples were put in little plastic tubes, along with a host of anonymous chemicals supplied by the manufacturer in their own tubes, and the lid closed. A computer did the rest; amplification of DNA in one machine, slicing up and searching for probes in another, an analysis of the results in a third. The laboratory technician had no need to understand what goes on inside the box, any more than you need to know the difference between a carburettor and a big end in order to drive your children to school. The system is more easily standardized and validated if it cannot be tampered with, or adjusted by, forensic lab technicians. This is how the companies that make the machines and the cocktail of chemical reagents justify the cloak concealing the exact workings of their commercial interests. It makes it almost impossible for juries to question the validity of the results.

By the mid-1990s, it was already clear that the next step – politically – was towards national and international criminal DNA databases. For these to be of use on a global scale, the systems used would have to be highly specific, and able to transcend national boundaries. The race was on to develop technology for the world to use. With the increasing reliance on DNA evidence, the company that was first to produce a system acceptable to law enforcement agencies across the globe would be sitting on a money-spinner. Their aim was to tap into the lucrative database business.

The idea behind criminal databases is that samples, normally from buccal (mouth) scrapes or hair roots, are taken from every person suspected or convicted of a criminal offence, and the resulting profile stored on a computer in the form of a digital code. Originally if a suspect was found to be innocent, or an inquiry not pursued, their profile was removed from the database. When the police come across physical evidence at a crime scene, it is analysed, then punched into the computer in search of a match. That was the premise on which the first national databases were set up in the UK (1997) and US (1998). Hailed as an efficient short-cut to justice by the law enforcers, they were greeted with howls of outrage by civil rights activists, who claimed they were the first big step on a moving escalator to a Brave and-not-necessarily-fair New World.

Police investigating a burglary in Bolton, Lancashire, found a spot of blood by a broken window at the crime scene. It was analysed using the six accepted STR loci, and entered into the UK national criminal database. Ping, a hit: Raymond Easton, a forty-nine-year-old former builder from Swindon in Wiltshire, with a previous caution for domestic violence. The profile was calculated to have a match probability of one in 37 million: less than two people out of the 60-odd million population of Britain, but the only one on the database. Greater Manchester Police confidently drove the few hundred miles south to Swindon and knocked on Mr Easton's door. His daughter, Zena, answered. 'You can see my dad,' she told them, 'but forgive him if he doesn't get up.' Raymond Easton was suffering from advanced Parkinson's disease, couldn't drive and had trouble dressing himself.

If he could have leaped out of his chair with surprise at the police allegations, Raymond Easton would have – there was absolutely no way he could make it the several hundred miles up to Bolton, he told them, and besides, Zena had been home that day with a chest infection. Nevertheless, the police took a blood sample and sent it off to the Forensic Science Service for analysis. Several months later, in August 1999, the results came through: the new sample similarly matched the profile of the blood found at the crime scene for all six loci. Despite the obvious physical barriers, despite his alibi, Raymond Easton was charged with burglary on the basis of DNA evidence alone, and ordered to appear before the Bolton Magistrate's Court. Only a one in 37 million chance of having caught the wrong guy seemed to the police a safe bet.

The problem is that Raymond Easton's chance of being innocent was not one in 37 million – but only one in thirty-seven. This strange effect is to do with DNA testing and databases. The six loci combined have 37 million permutations, but there is nothing to stop two people happening to have the same profile at these loci. In the UK population of around

60 million, there are likely to be two such people. If you have a database of a million people, there is thus a one in thirty-seven (1:37) chance of any person finding their DNA profile double in the database.

The police appeared unwilling to address the practical difficulties of the case. When the FSS suggested that additional analysis was performed on the DNA, using the newly minted ten-loci STR kit, the police initially refused. Easton's guilt had been proven, they said, no argument about it. Only after pressure from the defendant's lawyer were the samples sent back to the laboratory bench – and Raymond Easton duly excluded as a result; his DNA profile matched none of the additional four loci. Charges were officially dropped against Easton in November 1999, although he was never notified of this in person, nor did he receive an apology or explanation.

Still, it had the required effect on the FSS. They immediately recommended the adoption of the upgraded, expanded STR system, utilizing ten loci plus amelogenin. The probability of a random match between two unrelated people fell to approximately one in 100,000,000,000,000. Statisticians worked out complicated formulae to allow for the effects of laboratory contamination, software inaccuracies, sloppy technicians, all of which were aimed at making the process perfect.

Peter Gill of the FSS, who was deeply involved in the development of the database, maintains that DNA evidence is 'always reliable'. Gill is a modest man. Habitually dressed in faded black jeans and dark jerseys, he is typically English in his inability to brag. Where the US forensic scientists are full of their successes, Gill has to be prompted into mentioning cases he was involved in. His pride, it soon transpires, is reserved for his country: 'The UK has always been at the forefront of forensic DNA research,' he states quietly, 'and we still are.' As head of the DNA research department of the major forensic body in the country where it all began, Gill has played a major role in the scientific advances, and earned a name for himself in the process. It was to Peter Gill that the Russians turned when they were looking for a definitive identification of the nine skeletons exhumed from a shallow forest grave near Ekaterinburg in Siberia and believed to be the family of the last Tsar. After using traditional forensic techniques, Russian scientists were fairly certain that the skeletons were those of Tsar Nicholas II, his wife, three of their five children and their entourage, but without DNA they couldn't be sure. As their labs did not have the latest technology, they sent one of their top DNA scientists, Pavel Ivanov, to England with a package of bones.

A monumental task, scientifically and politically controversial, it was probably the most complex of any forensic DNA typing examination yet conducted. Over a period of a year and a half, working at full steam in a small hut in the car park of the old FSS research centre near Aldermaston, Gill and Ivanov successfully employed STRs on the highly degraded nucleic material, and mitochondrial DNA analysis[1] on bone and hair material, to identify the Tsar, his wife and three of his daughters. The world's media were present when Peter Gill announced their results: they were 98.5 per cent certain that the bones belonged to the Romanov family.

Later, he performed more DNA tests on tissue samples of a woman who had claimed to be the youngest of the Tsar's children, Grand Duchess Anastasia. Anna Anderson, as she was most widely known, was the most plausible of the handful of men and women who insisted they had escaped the massacre. Since the time that she first crawled out of a canal in Berlin, nineteen months after the murder of the royal family, until her death in Virginia, USA, in February 1984, Anna Anderson had managed to persuade many people that she was Anastasia, including living relatives of the last Tsar, who had known the royal daughters in childhood. Once more, Gill found himself on a raised dais, reporting his results to an avid media. Using STRs again he had compared the DNA profile of Anderson's tissue with the DNA profiles of the bones of the presumed Tsar and Empress, and a blood sample donated by Prince Philip, a cousin of the Empress Alexandra, and determined that 'if you

1. Mitochondrial – mtDNA – unlike nuclear DNA, is inherited exclusively from the mother, 'passing from generation to generation unchanging, like a time machine', in Gill's words. So both sons and daughters inherit their mother's mtDNA, though the sons cannot pass it along to their children.

accept that these samples came from Anna Anderson, then Anna Anderson could not be related to Tsar Nicholas or Empress Alexandra'.

'These days I'm more involved in looking into the future, what's next, working on the database,' he says. His cubby hole of an office, in an anonymous light industrial park not far from Birmingham airport, sits almost directly on top of the basement freezers storing the million-plus samples from convicted UK criminals. A computer near by contains the database of their analysed profiles. He strenuously denies that there is any possibility of mistakes or misconduct in his laboratories, yet he still urges caution: 'DNA evidence must always be looked at in the context of the evidence that has to be analysed. It is an aid, not a substitute for police work.'

The UK database has undoubtedly had its successes – hundreds, probably thousands of perpetrators have been caught through finding their DNA at the scene and later matching it on the database. Stephen Snowdon, for example, who was arrested for stealing a bottle of whisky at a supermarket. When a sample of his DNA was taken and fed into a computer, it immediately linked him to the rape, years earlier, of a woman whose car had broken down. He was tried on the basis of the DNA match, found guilty and sentenced to twelve years.

The British government is gung-ho about the crime-solving possibilities of DNA databases and aims to increase five-fold the size of the national database within the next decade, partly through new legislation which has made it legal to leave on the base all the samples taken from suspects who were later proven to be innocent. According to an angry editorial in the *New Scientist* protesting against this, 'In effect, the sample – containing the very blueprint that makes you the person you are – will have become the property of the state. The authorities didn't need your consent to take it. They won't need your consent to keep it.' Even Alec Jeffreys, architect of DNA fingerprinting, thinks this is a step too far. 'It's discriminating, inconsistent with privacy laws and an example of ad hoc sloppy thinking,' he maintains. He believes that either the samples should be destroyed after a profile has been taken, and all profiles of innocent people removed from the database – or, more controversially, it should be more inclusive, containing everyone's DNA, collected at birth and filed with an independent agency.

The FBI's database, CODIS (Combined DNA Index System), is planned to be many times larger than the UK's, and in consequence, finds it necessary to use thirteen STR markers. In 1999, driven by the possibility of major cost and time savings, the FBI lab stopped using the first three PCR-based tests, DQα1, polymarker and D1S80; the following year they dropped all RFLP tests, in favour of the multiplex STRs. They currently hold over a million samples, and the database is growing daily by the thousands.

The San Diego Sheriff's Department had never submitted the profile of the DNA found beneath Helena Greenwood's fingernails to CODIS. They wanted first to check out the guilt of their prime suspect before throwing their options open to a computer. (They would not have found Frediani's DNA profile on CODIS, as his blood had been taken years before the system was up and running, and simply stored, unanalysed, in the freezer.) Cellmark had run the STRs at the same time as their initial tests. Laura had a fax of their results on her desk, so that in the second week of December 1999, when Gary Harmor rang through from Seri with his results, she could compare them instantaneously. Harmor's voice betrayed little emotion, and he read the results out as if he were reciting a train timetable. To Laura, however, the sequence of numbers was as exciting as a lottery jackpot. She put down the phone and punched the air. The statistics this time were conclusive. 'We got him,' she told Vic. 'Let's go.'

She was at work early the following morning, eager to start planning the next step. She telephoned Valerie Summers at the DA's office who, despite being mid-trial, was delighted with the news. She assured Laura that she would get an arrest warrant issued. Laura then logged on to a computer program for law enforcement officers called Autotrack, on which she found Frediani's current address, his driving licence number and car registration records. There he was still in Burlingame, with a big black Lexus. She then called

Chaput. The Atherton policeman was happy, very, very happy, he kept telling her; he could not believe that she had managed to get Frediani at last.

'When Laura called me from San Diego with the good news, it felt terrific, it felt great,' agreed Chaput, sitting in his bailiff's chair in San Mateo courthouse, where he now works, having been recently laid off by Atherton PD. He wanted to know how he could help. She asked him if he had kept any of the details from the old case, and perhaps a photograph of Frediani? Did he know whether the physical evidence – the semen-stained pillowcase and sheet – was still in storage? Chaput said he had kept the entire file and would send copies down straight away, but that the linen had been thrown away some time after Frediani's imprisonment. She asked him, if he had time, if perhaps he could drive by Frediani's apartment building, to check his name was on the mailbox, and the Lexus in his parking space. Chaput called back the next morning: 'He's there,' he told her. 'I saw the car.'

On the morning of Monday 13 December 1999, the arrest warrant was sitting on Laura's desk when Chaput's file arrived, along with a recent photograph of Frediani from his driving licence. She was surprised by what she saw: a sober-looking man in a suit and tie and serious expression. She and Vic had plane tickets booked for San Francisco the next day. She came into work early again: before leaving for the airport, she wanted to telephone Helena's father. 'I found Mr Greenwood's number and called him in

England. I told him, basically, that we had found Helena's murderer. It was an emotional conversation.'

Sydney Greenwood was eighty-seven years old when Laura Heilig's call came through. It was a complete surprise: he thought the world had long forgotten about the hunt for his daughter's killer. He had not. He was living in the studiedly quaint southern seaside town of Lymington, not far from the New Forest, and only miles from Sway, where Helena had grown up and been buried. He had been alone for fourteen and a half years – since 1985, when he had lost both his wife and only child. He had no remaining family. Where many would have given up and quietly succumbed to misery, self-pity and eventually death, Sydney Greenwood could not. He had retired from full-time teaching in the 1980s, but continued to paint, finding comfort in untamed nature, in the sea, the bare beauty of the South Downs. His exhibitions were well attended, his paintings popular. He was a respected man, visited occasionally by a dwindling group of old friends and former students.

Sydney Greenwood had stayed in touch with his former son-in-law. The year after Helena's death, Sydney had gone to visit Roger in northern California. The two men went for long, silent walks together in Marin County, striding across the green hills as if they could exorcize their pain through exercise. But it didn't work, each was wrapped up so tightly in a second skin of sadness. Sydney returned to the UK; Roger had to move on, build a life, if not repair his heart. After Helena's death, Roger had wanted nothing other than to drop out completely and see no one. He told Sydney that he 'could not face humankind', and planned to sail alone around the world.

In early 1999, just as Laura Heilig was packaging up Helena's fingernails to send them off for analysis, Roger Franklin discovered he had pancreatic cancer. It was already too advanced for much hope. He tried to fight it, but five months later, he died. He never knew that the case into his first wife's death had been reopened: he did not live to see anyone tried for her murder.

Cancer was eating Sydney Greenwood too, slowly consuming his prostate. For the last few years of the 1990s, he was in and out of hospital and nursing homes, preparing for, then recovering from, chemotherapy. Each time he came home a little weaker, but he was determined to look after himself. Even when the pain was at its worst, he would dress carefully, brush his hair, and when it was warm, sit in his garden under the weeping cherry. He was not going to give up.

'When that wonderful Detective Heilig called me in December to tell me that they were going to arrest a man for Helena's murder, I was so relieved, so pleased that at last it was going to be over. She told me that I must come out for the trial, but my doctors would never have allowed it. I don't think I could have made it. But I want to live to see the outcome,' he told me in the summer of 2000, his voice weak but clear. 'This case has haunted me for too long – now I am determined to stay around until the end.'

15

In the half-light before dawn on Wednesday 15 December 1999, four cars slipped into the garage beneath an apartment building in Burlingame. They parked strategically – one by each exit, the remaining two either side of the lift. Inside, seven detectives from both ends of California settled down to watch. To wait. It was an icy morning; their breath steamed up the windows until they were forced to let in the cold winter air. In the car nearest the lift, Laura Heilig burrowed into her leather jacket and wished she had brought along some coffee. Every twenty minutes or so, she would light up a cigarette, smoke it furiously, stab it out. She wasn't a big smoker, but she needed to be doing something. She found some sunflower seeds in the door pocket, ate a few, then got out of the car. She checked on Vic in his car, Steve Chaput, the original investigating officer in the sexual assault case, the other local detectives, walked over to the lift, looked to see whether it was on its way down, went back to her car. When was he going to come out? The first hour passed. Seven o'clock; the minutes continued to crawl past.

The vigil had started the previous evening. She, Vic and an investigator from the DA's office had flown up to San Francisco and gone directly to the Burlingame police station with a warrant for Frediani's arrest. The local detectives were only too delighted to help. They remembered Frediani: Brad Floyd had been his parole officer for many years, knew him well. 'He's a strange guy,' he told Laura, 'very cold.' Chaput joined them at the station. They decided to go directly to Frediani's building, to try to catch him coming home from work. But his Lexus was not there. They waited. By eleven o'clock he had not returned and they called it a night.

'We'll have patrol check the garage periodically,' the Burlingame police assured Laura, 'and call you as soon as they see the car.' She gave them the number of her hotel, only a few blocks across the freeway from Frediani's apartment, then went to her room to try to sleep.

The call came in at 5 a.m. 'The vehicle's there.' Laura was up, the forces regrouped and drove together into the garage before six. There was still no sign of Frediani. She got out of her car again and walked around, got back in. People were coming out of the lift at fairly regular intervals. Each time she heard a sound, saw the doors begin to part, she would stiffen, ready. But it was never him, just another dark-suited commuter on his way to a routine day at work.

Then shortly after eight, the doors opened. A tall, dark-haired man was walking towards the black Lexus. Laura's radio crackled. It was Chaput, he recognized Frediani from the sexual assault investigations and trials: 'Here he comes.' She got out of her car, quietly. Car doors were opening all around, people emerging like creatures from a swamp, converging on their prey. When she felt he had no escape, Laura called out: 'Mr Frediani?' He looked around, his head held high, stared at her down fifteen inches.

'Yes,' he replied.

'I'm Detective Heilig from the Sheriff's Department. We have a warrant for your arrest.' She did not say which sheriff's department – she wanted to see his reaction first.

'For what?'

'I'll tell you in a minute.' She didn't want him to run or start to fight. The plan was to surprise him, catch him off guard. That was why they hadn't just knocked on the door of his apartment; he could have turned violent, he might have had a gun, or a knife.

'Place your hands behind your back.'

She snapped on the handcuffs.

'What is this about?' he asked again.

'You're under arrest for the murder of Doctor Helena Greenwood.'

Frediani said nothing. Laura watched the colour drain from his face. 'His eyes got weird,' she recalled later. 'He was creepy. He just said nothing, absolutely nothing. You'd think that if you were innocent it would be "What the . . . ?" or "What are you talking about?". But he said nothing. We waited. I bet we were there five minutes, just standing, saying nothing, before the patrol car came – at least it seemed that long to me. We're standing there, he's cuffed up, he's not going anywhere, but it was so much silence. He did not say one word the whole time he stood there with us. Not one word.'

'We were standing around him, like in a semi-circle,' said Chaput. 'His eyes went from person to person . . . from face to face. I was at the end, and when he got to me I was hoping, you know, that he would key in for a while. But he just started going back the other way. It felt like it was intentional. He couldn't have forgotten me because I sat in the courtroom through both his trials, plus there was the initial interview. I was thinking, should I take this as an insult? He knows who I am. But at the same time, I knew he was a very calculating person. I think he was already starting to figure out what his next move would be, how he was going to get through this, alibis, stories, whatever.'

The patrol car arrived. Frediani was pushed in the back. They drove to Burlingame station, led him to an interview room and unlocked his handcuffs. It was an unfamiliar set-up to Laura and Vic: a large reclining armchair on one side of the table, two hard metal chairs on the other, a bottle of mineral water on the table. Frediani sat in the big chair, leaned back; in his suit and tie, legs crossed at the ankle, anyone looking in through the glass square in the door would have seen a confident executive interviewing two hopefuls for a junior position.

He looked bored as Laura read him his rights. To her surprise, when she asked whether he wanted a lawyer, he said no, 'Sure, I'll talk to you.' For the next four hours, Frediani sat back while first Laura, then Vic, then Laura again, asked him question after question. Where had he been the day of the murder? Did he commit the sexual assault? He consistently denied any involvement.

High in one corner, the red light was on above a video camera. The interview was being filmed and relayed live into a side room. Chaput watched for a time. Martin Murray stayed for most of it, joined, straight from the airport, by Valerie Summers. The San Diego deputy district attorney has a vivid memory of that first impression of her new prey. 'He was arrogant, slick. A lot of that is his persona, but it was exaggerated by him being in this big chair, swilling water in his glass as they were talking to him. He didn't admit a thing during the entire interview.'

Laura and Vic were trying every tactic they could: cajoling, riling, persuading, threatening. But Frediani did not break. At one point, Vic jabbed his finger at the man sitting opposite: 'You're nothing but a crook,' he said. 'Granted you wear nice clothes, but you're still a crook, a crook in a nice suit.' Frediani barely raised an eyebrow. They asked about his relationships, his work, the indecent assaults, then returned to the murder.

'I didn't do it,' he insisted.

'Then how come we have your DNA?'

'As far as DNA evidence, oh, I'm sure you've got some DNA evidence that probably points to me.

Where you got it, how you got it, that's a whole different matter. I've been in your custody for a long time.'

'Why would we want to plant evidence?'

'To close the case.'

From time to time, Laura or Vic would leave the interview and pop into the other room where Valerie Summers was talking to Martin Murray, with half an eye on the video relay. 'The officers are conducting the questioning,' Valerie explains. 'They are professionals and you don't tell them what to ask, although you might give them ideas about where they might go to cover all the bases. At that stage, we didn't know whether it was going to be a death penalty case. And if it was, we would need personal information, a complete family history, mother, father, place of birth, where he went to school, friends, all that kind of stuff.'

Murray felt as good about the arrest as if he had personally placed the handcuffs on Frediani's wrists. For him, the saga had been ongoing for nearly fifteen years. 'When Laura first contacted me, to tell me that she was working on the case, I couldn't believe it, that after all those years, someone was still looking at it. I was thrilled. And little by little, as the evidence built up, I became more excited. When she called to say they had the DNA match and she was coming up, I was gratified, very gratified.

'It was strange sitting there, watching him on the close-circuit video. He's put on a little weight, he's a bit puffy around the jowls, where before he was athletic. Once again I was struck by his arrogance and how calm he is able to maintain his exterior. He's very glib, very controlled, but if you watch his chest, though, it moves a bit. I thought, this is going to be an interesting trial.'

After four hours, the detectives realized they weren't going to get any further, and terminated the interview. They reclamped the cuffs and Paul Frediani was led away to a cell. After ten years and five months of freedom, he was back behind bars.

For Laura Heilig, the investigation was just beginning: to have been able to interview her suspect was a bonus, but she had not come away with much, just a few pages of names and phone numbers of his friends and family. She made arrangements for her Sheriff's Department to transport Frediani down to San Diego, then she and Vic started searching for further proof of his guilt. 'I hadn't been actively investigating the case before. It just kind of happened. I turned in one lab request and lo and behold, we had our man. Sure we had the DNA, but we also had a lot of groundwork ahead of us. We needed to know what he had been up to. Had he killed again? Had there been other sexual assaults in the area that could be tied to him?'

Frediani had given them permission to search his apartment without a warrant. The San Diego detectives parked their car in his space and rode the elevator up to his apartment. They walked into a neat studio room; the bed against one wall, carefully made, a sofa facing a large-screen TV, wrapped sweets in a bowl on the coffee table. They opened the wardrobe, a battery of suits hung beside an army of ironed shirts. Many were in strong colours: deep purples and emerald green.

But they found nothing to link him to any kind of criminal activity, just one bag containing a torch, two dildos, and a tiny video camera. And among his video collection, a couple of home-made tapes, clearly filmed more than a decade earlier. In one, he was making love to a young red-headed girl; in another, he was masturbating with a wide grin on his face.

That afternoon, they went to see Kathy Clark, the chiropractor. She told them that she couldn't believe for a second that Paul had been involved in any murder. He was kind, funny and gentle, her best friend. Sure he had told her about his time in prison, but it had been a long time before, and he hadn't done it, right? He had also confided his past to Dave Rangwirtz, his colleague and friend from MSAS Cargo. Rangwirtz described him as 'shy but amiable, with a great head for numbers', a regular guy who played on the local softball team, worked hard, and got along great with children. Rangwirtz's kids referred to Frediani as 'Uncle Paul'.

'If my plumbing broke, he'd be out there under the sink for eight hours fixing it,' he said. 'That's the kind of guy he is.' Rangwirtz's statuesque wife Beverley was also astounded at his arrest: 'There is no way the Paul we know is capable of such a crime,' she told

Laura. Over the rest of the week, and on a subsequent visit a month later, the detectives spoke to his work colleagues, ex-girlfriends, former wives and roommates, and with each interview, they got a different take on Frediani. It was as if they were talking about different people.

Eileen, Paul's great love and 'soul mate', said that she had been terrified of him. She called him 'probably the cruellest person I have ever met'. He had thrown a garbage can over her, dumped her in cold water and told her repeatedly how ugly she was. He had been jealous of her daughter, was 'very insecure, very immature'. But in bed, he was never aggressive, never violent, never angry, the 'stereotypical Italian lover'.

Kit, the student who had shared Paul's bed the summer following the break-up of his marriage to Cris, and less than a year before the assault on Helena Greenwood, recalled how he had told her he couldn't reach orgasm with oral sex: and she had proved he could.

As they were building this strange, often contradictory portrait of their murderer, so they were fleshing out the series of snapshots they had of his victim. Tom Adams, who had tempted Helena to Gen-Probe, described her as 'bright, creative and aggressive, with an infectious personality'. Thomas and Patricia Christopher were still clearly mourning her death, and that of Roger, only months earlier. Helena, once out of her serious shell, they told Laura, was 'fun, very caring, able to understand people'. She liked classical music, to cook, to ski, make jewellery. She and Roger had been very close, a 'tight couple', although the sexual assault had affected them. For instance, their bed had become an issue; it was special to both of them, the first piece of furniture they had bought when they moved to the US, but Helena could no longer look at it. Eventually, Roger concurred and the bed was dismantled. Their long-term plan was to move to San Diego, make some money and then have a family. 'They weren't greedy, but they wanted to live comfortably,' Thomas said. 'When we had our first baby, Helena laid down a case of port for him.' He cannot forget the day Helena testified at the preliminary hearing. She and Roger had come straight from the courtroom to the Christophers' house. Helena was quiet, but seemed calm and strong. Roger was visibly relieved: 'I was so proud of Helena,' he told Thomas and Patricia. 'You should have seen how she handled herself. She was incredible. She got up there and those nasty guys, the lawyers, were trying to make out like she asked . . . trying to undermine her and she just stayed totally calm. She made them look like fools.' Thomas gave Helena a hug then turned to her. 'I said to her, "You know that was the worst thing that could happen to you and now it's over – lightning never strikes twice in the same place." Well, I was so wrong,' he told the detectives fifteen years later.

He still finds her death hard to accept; for a long time, he would look for her around every street corner. Roger had not dealt with it well at all; he could not even bear the idea of a memorial service. The Christophers were in touch with Cathy Franklin, Roger's widow and mother of his daughters, they told Laura Heilig. She was living in the aftershock of her husband's death, and with no one else to blame, lashed out against Frediani. Roger's cancer, she blamed on 'the horrific experience of Helena Greenwood's murder'.

But while the central characters were becoming real people to Laura, she still had not found what she had hoped for and expected: corroborating evidence of Frediani's trip down to San Diego, or anything to link him to other crimes. 'People like that do not just stop offending,' maintains Laura. 'He had to have been up to something – but he was lucky enough to have gotten away with it.'

Paul telephoned his parents from jail. He hadn't seen them for a number of years, but he had called them just the month before. His mother had answered the phone. 'What's wrong?' she had asked at once.

'Nothing. I'm just looking for Donna's number.' He had not been in contact with his sister for some time either.

She had audibly exhaled.

This time, however, her fears were confirmed. Paul called on the evening of 16 December 1999 with news of his arrest for murder. He did not make light of his predicament. He was in jail in Redwood City, but would shortly be moved down to San Diego. He needed to make arrangements to clear out his apartment. Whatever happened, he would not be back for a while.

Paul Frediani's parents believed their son when he said he was innocent. To do otherwise would be to question their role as parents, the values they had instilled in their eldest son, the genes they had passed on to him. And as parents, it was their desire and responsibility to do everything they could to ensure he had the best possible chance of being declared innocent in a court of law. Their first aim was to find him a good lawyer. They knew a decent private attorney would be expensive, but they had some money put away for their retirement and a pension which they could cash in, and they did not hesitate to use it. Donna volunteered to match their donation. Paul's father was more physically and mentally devastated by what had happened; Paul's mother channelled her distress into action. She contacted the County Bar Association in San Diego, who recommended a local lawyer with a good reputation and plenty of courtroom experience, David Bartick.

When Mrs Frediani called, Bartick was at first unsure whether he would have the time and resources to be able to give their son the assistance he would need. He said he would find out a bit more about the case, talk to Valerie Summers and Paul when he arrived at Vista, and then let her know his decision.

The next week, once they had endured the forced conviviality of Christmas, the Fredianis packed up their big jeep and drove for three days across the country. They did not sleep; they couldn't when they tried, so it made better sense just to stick to the freeway and keep going. Quite apart from everything, the end of December was looming and they did not want to have to pay the $1,100 for their son's January rent. When they arrived at the apartment, on the evening of 30 December, they found a terrific mess. The police had turned everything upside down in their search. Paul's clothes had been flung from the closet, each video cassette opened, every computer disk pulled out of its place. Carefully, methodically, they packed it all up; his personal stuff would come back with them to the East Coast, his car was to be returned to the leasing company, his apartment keys to the letting agent. By the evening of the 31st, their job was done and as most of the world was celebrating the new millennium, they drove down to San Diego to see Paul and David Bartick.

They met Bartick in his downtown San Diego office. They liked the energetic lawyer. He was a one-man band, but his polished desk and framed newspaper cuttings of past courtroom successes spoke of quiet confidence. He was polite and reasonable, and did not give them false expectations. He had spoken to Valerie Summers at the DA's Department, he told them. She had a strong case and was determined to press for the death penalty. The crime qualified, unfortunately; not only was Paul accused of first-degree murder, but there was a special circumstance, that of killing a witness to a crime, which made the offence especially heinous in the eyes of the law. 'It will be a high-profile case and they will be very keen to get a guilty verdict,' Bartick told the Fredianis.

He believed, however, that in the event of a guilty verdict, a jury would not pursue the death penalty. In the California courts death penalty cases are treated almost as twin trials; only after a guilty verdict in the central murder case would the jury then consider the death penalty, and this would be almost like a trial in itself. It had been fifteen years since the crime and Paul had not been accused of anything in that time. He had a good job, a supportive family, children, good friends – and all this would count in his favour. Bartick was confident that he had a better than evens chance of persuading the jury of Paul's redeeming characteristics – in the event that he was found guilty of murder.

The Fredianis then visited their son in Vista jail. It was the first time they had seen him in prison scrubs, and it was a shock. They told him they would be there for him every step of the way, and would see him at the trial. Then they got back on the road east, leaving their son to wait, alone, his future blocked by another trial. This time, it had the potential to end in his death.

16

15 March 2000. I am back at the beginning of my story, at a blameless spring day in southern California. I am driving down the coastal highway to San Diego, heading for the preliminary hearing on Paul Frediani's murder charge. I had read an article about Helena Greenwood's murder the day before, and for some reason it had grabbed me and demanded more attention. I don't know what it was specifically. That she had been the same age as me when she died? That she had grown up just sixty miles from where I had? That she had been killed in the very same southern California village where my husband and I had spent the previous two winters? Certainly the scientific aspect of the story had intrigued me: this woman, who had staked her professional future on DNA, was even now, fifteen years after her death, using it to catch her killer. There was a symmetry about it, an irony, that was undeniably alluring. And there was DNA itself, that spinning double helix which was beginning to pirouette into our daily consciousness. The Human Genome Project. Dolly the sheep. Gene therapy. And then the forensic aspect: I had always revelled in the science of crime detection, the procedure, the teasing out of clues from tiny specks of mud or fibre, facial reconstruction from a bleached and weathered skull, or passing fingerprints on human skin. Here, surely, was the future: in DNA. What effect would it have? Was it already having? In Helena Greenwood's murder, perhaps, I would find some answers.

I contacted David Bartick, who told me about the preliminary hearing, set for that very morning. The timing is serendipitous; I am only a hundred miles away. As I make my way south from Los Angeles, the scent of citrus blossom seeps through the windows. It is a familiar drive, and I always look forward to the point, around about half-way, near the swallow's springtime roost in San Juan Capistrano, where the air clears. It is as if an invisible curtain, sky-high, separates the pale ochre smog of the city from the fresh blue sea air of the lower coast.

I am thinking about our first child as I drive, growing invisibly inside me. Inside the nucleus of every cell in his body, he displays a microscopic facsimile of me, and one of his father. Which aspects of either picture will be visible will depend on chemistry, chance, fate, whatever, but everything physical and most of his emotional, spiritual and mental make-up will be derived from a combination of our genes. It is a strange, sobering thought, especially when seen through the prism of this murder trial. The defendant, Paul Frediani, is just a product of his parents' genes and from what I have read, they are normal, law-abiding people. What went wrong?

At this point, Frediani is not a real person to me; just a man accused of murder, approaching his day of judgment. My thoughts and sympathies are with Helena Greenwood, the victim, the person I am already relating to. It would only be later, as I spun backwards through the story, starting near the end and working my way to the beginning, that the other characters would come to life. Each is unique, genetically and emotionally, with their own hopes, fears, ambitions and achievements. Every one is affected by this murder: families, friends, colleagues, detectives and attorneys. Its tentacles have crawled into their lives like a parasitic bacterium: for some, it is a passing stage; for others, a nightmare for life.

By the time I have parked my car in the crowded forecourt of an imposing building – five storeys of brick and glass, stretching horizontally along echoing corridors – and found the courtroom, the players are in place, the morning session has half-passed. I feel as if I have entered the final dress rehearsal of a play without permission. Even the scant handful of spectators – I do not know who they are or what their role is – seem, by virtue of their prior presence, to be a part of what is going on. I am the outsider.

It is a spacious, modern courtroom, echoes of art deco in style: wooden inlays, shallow mottled glass shades softening the overhead lights. At the back, on a raised dais, the judge looks like an efficient private school headmistress. To my left, a woman, long dark hair, a dark jacket, stands at a table, talking and waving a sheaf of papers. On the right, two men. My eyes are drawn to the defendant, clad in a blue cotton prison T-shirt, his head held high. He sits very still, and it is only occasionally that I catch a half-glimpse of his face: a straight nose, slightly hooded eyes, his neck beginning to take a short-cut between his chin and collar bone. I don't know whether it is him, or his role in the proceedings, but he is an imposing physical presence. He says not a word throughout. He sits beside David Bartick, a smaller figure with a thick moustache and polished shoes. Bartick is leaning to whisper to his client, his arm draped around his back.

As I tune in, a slight blonde woman is sitting at the witness stand, answering questions put to her by the dark-haired woman. I later learn they are Laura Heilig and Valerie Summers, key characters in the unravelling of this case.

'Has the use of DNA advanced greatly with regard to law enforcement and forensic applications since the time of the original crime and the time you started reviewing the case?' Summers asks.

'Yes.'

This is the core of this case. In chronological terms, it tracks neatly the history of forensic DNA. Like the two strands of the double helix, the hunt for Helena's killer cannot be separated from the development of the science that has delivered Frediani to the doors of justice.

David Bartick is out of his seat now, questioning Detective Heilig. He is not trying to trip her up, just to elicit as much information as he can, information that might be of use to him when the case comes to trial. I like David Bartick on sight, he reminds me of an inquisitive field mouse near a pile of grain. He seems straightforward, un-showy and, of course, his is the hardest job. Paul Frediani has entrusted his fate to his legal skills; if he fails, his client has no future.

Laura Heilig is now sitting beside Valerie Summers at the prosecution table. A man is on the witness stand, an investigator from the District Attorney's office. He is talking about a conversation he had with a scientist at Cellmark, in which he learned the results of the DNA tests on Paul Frediani's blood sample. Much of what he is saying makes no sense to me, but I write it down, hoping that at a later date it will.

'... DQ Alpha, one point one, one point two. LDLR or LDL receptor, AB ... D3S1358, fourteen, fifteen. VWA, fourteen, seventeen ... D7S820, ten, eleven.'

I know nothing about DNA fingerprint analysis at this time, I have not yet met Alec Jeffreys, or Kary Mullis, or Ed Blake, or Peter Gill. I have never heard of probes or alleles or markers. It is a foreign language. I notice that one of the reporters, sitting across the aisle from me, has dozed off; another is covering his pad in intricate doodles. For them, it is just another case.

During the lunch break, I drive the twenty minutes south along the freeway to Del Mar. I slip down to the beach, my thoughts on Helena Greenwood. How many times had she walked on this same stretch of sand, run into the same ocean? How many of these people surfing in front of me knew her? If she had not been killed fifteen years ago, would I have met her some time over the past two years, when we too lived in Del Mar?

I am back in the courtroom for the afternoon session and this time, I feel more of a part of the proceedings. A reporter says hello, asks me what I am doing here. Another introduces himself. The bailiff returns, a tall man in a Sheriff's Department uniform, and with him, even taller, Paul Frediani. The heavy handcuffs are unlocked and removed from his wrists after he sits down, but the bailiff is never far away.

Valerie Summers has just one more witness, Gary Harmor from Seri in Richmond, California. He talks more DNA, which again I write down. He is going through the procedure for testing samples: the blood presumptive test, methods to extract DNA, how to perform PCR. I grasp some of what he is saying, the rest drifts over my head. His voice is measured, soporific. '. . . PCR is only useful in copying strands that are under a thousand base pairs in size. So the markers that are utilized in PCR are chosen based upon their size and their variability in the population . . . Population studies are done on them to make sure that they do have a widespread discrimination potential . . . Six of the markers that we used rely on a population study collection that was done nationwide from different agencies and produced by Dr Ed Blake.'

He talks about the individual pieces of evidence that he was asked to analyse, each tiny fingernail clipping or scraping taken from Helena Greenwood's lifeless hands the day after her murder. One right-hand clipping, we learn, has no DNA present, another has DNA consistent with the victim's. On the left hand, one sample proved to be a mixture between two different people, Helena Greenwood and a foreign donor. 'And then in sample 4–10, which was a piece of dark material that was loose in the left-hand clippings box which had blood in it, turned out to be a profile completely different from Miss Greenwood.' I notice David Bartick sit a little straighter in his seat. Harmor explains that he tested sample 4–10 then compared his results to the profile of David Paul Frediani that had been faxed to him from Cellmark. 'I determined that they were the same through all fifteen markers, as well as being from a male.' He ran them through the population frequency tables.

'Now, based on that calculation and your testing in this case, are you able to form some conclusions with regard to who left that DNA at the crime scene?' Valerie Summers asks.

'Yes. I determined that David Frediani left that debris from the fingernails at the crime scene.'

'And to what degree of certainty would you have with that?'

'One hundred per cent, to the exclusion of everyone else . . . The statistical analysis that was conducted reproduced a genetic frequency that was extremely rare for this particular profile of fifteen markers. And no one else in the world in my opinion could produce that DNA profile but David Frediani or possibly an identical twin.'

Valerie Summers closes her questioning, leaving Bartick to ask the question that is dangling in front of us all: what exactly was the population frequency he had calculated?

'Estimation', Harmor replied in an even voice, 'is that one person in every 2.3 quadrillion [1:2,300,000,000,000,000] people.' Bartick asks no further questions; there is nowhere else to go.

With those potentially fatal words ringing in his ears, Paul Frediani is handcuffed once more and ushered out of the side door, presumably back to his cell in Vista jail. The judge has ruled that there is sufficient cause to believe that he is guilty of the offence he is charged with, and to proceed to trial. He must now await a decision on whether the District Attorney will try for the death sentence.

The judge leaves the room, the attorneys pack their files and start to walk out. The reporters are hovering around Valerie Summers, pressing her on the likelihood of this being a death penalty case. She says she is hopeful; the special circumstances make it eligible. 'He wanted to stop the victim from testifying against him at trial,' she says. 'She was an essential witness in that case. The trial without her would have been severely hampered.' She will not say more at this stage; she is polite but unapproachable.

David Bartick is more friendly. He says that the defence will dispute vigorously the DNA statistics and the methodology employed. 'There are going to be some surprising developments presented at trial,' he promises. I am hooked. I know I will have to return for the trial.

A week later, I am back in England. I find Sydney Greenwood's number. I arrange to see him, and one spring day, with a makeshift picnic, I drive through the New Forest and along the coast to Lymington. Sydney's house is functional, anonymous, his front garden tidy. My ring is answered after several minutes by a slim man in an old tweed jacket, a silk cravat wrapped around his gaunt neck. 'The nurse has just left,' he explains, after welcoming me into his sitting room. He carries himself straight, but it is clearly not easy to walk. 'They come every morning to help me get up. I have cancer, you know. I'm feeling better at the moment, but I'm in and out of hospital.'

His voice slips from distinct to a mumble and back again. It is possible, beneath the educated cadences, to catch a whiff of a soft northern accent. He had met his wife Marjorie, he tells me, when they were both teaching at Manchester Grammar School – he the boys and she the girls. He had spent time in the army, fought for his country, then devoted himself to his painting and teaching art. Helena was a brilliant girl, their only child. He hadn't been sure whether he had wanted children at first, but Marjorie had persuaded him. 'Most men are different,' he says, with a laugh that expires into a painful wheeze. 'They don't like their noses being put out of joint, but when it first says Dada, they begin to take an interest. That was very naughty of me. But I was always drawing them – that is how I showed my love for them. Pictures of Marjorie and child – mother and child. I've sold a lot of them, I've got none left.' He talks about Helena's love of science and shows me a cutting from a newspaper about Rosalind Franklin that he has kept. At one point, he drifts into sleep mid-sentence, and I leave him for a while, his armchair now moulded to his frail figure, under a portrait of Helena as a young child in a blue dress.

When he wakes, he apologizes. 'I am tired these days. I know I am dying, but I am not ready, just yet, to go.' He talks a little about her death, and tears drip, unbidden, down his cheeks. 'There's enough sadness in the world without people killing each other. It's like throwing stones in a pond, the ripples as they grow outwards bring misery to everyone.'

A few weeks earlier, he was contacted by a woman working for David Bartick, asking whether he thought Frediani should receive the death penalty. He had been taken by surprise; had no time to collect his thoughts. He worried now that he had not expressed himself clearly; he knew he was not well enough to be able to go to San Diego for the trial, and was anxious to tell somebody his views. I suggest we write to Valerie Summers. 'I said on the telephone that I couldn't give a fair statement on the penalty because I don't know all the details on the crime and what followed it. I have always felt that if he was mentally ill, then perhaps the sentence should take this into account. Then I wanted to say that if, as appears probable, the man had been guilty of repeated violent sexual crimes, he therefore deserves the death penalty, but she shook me off. What I really want is for justice to take its proper course and for the courts to decide what is appropriate. I feel it was unfair to try to get my opinion on this most important matter suddenly, and without giving me time for consideration.'

He turned: 'Is that all right?' It is clear that he wants to make his contribution. His daughter's death inevitably, and obviously, affected him profoundly. He suggested, just as Cathy Franklin had of Roger, that his cancer might have been brought on by the anger and anguish. His only consolation was that his wife had been spared the pain of Helena's death. Now, at this late stage, with this unexpected development, he wanted to do right by his daughter. He fully appreciated the irony of the role that DNA had played, both in Helena's life and her death.

'She always told me her work would prove valuable. She firmly believed in the power of DNA. She told me, "This is going to change the world." At the time, I had no idea what she was wittering on about. I was just proud that I had produced such a smart and lovely girl. Well, she was proved right. Nothing can bring Helena back, but I know she is looking down on me now. She was a fighter. Her killer took her life, but he did not silence her. It has taken fifteen years, but I know Helena has spoken from the grave to indict her killer.'

I leave Sydney Greenwood to sleep, and on subsequent visits, we talk more. We eat bread and cheese at the bottom of the garden and discuss art and history as well as death. When I tell him that we are planning to go to San Diego for the trial, he says he wishes he could come too.

'Why can't you? We will look after you.'

'No, my doctor would never let me. But you must promise to call me with the verdict. It has haunted me for too long. I've been told over and over to forget it. It's not been easy, and now I am determined to see it through.'

I stay in contact with Sydney, and correspond regularly with David Bartick. He is helpful, but guarded. Any publicity before the trial could taint the juror pool. Both he and Valerie Summers are engaged in backroom work to predetermine the sentence. There are only two options for first-degree murder in California: death and what is less than affectionately known as L-Wop (life without the possibility of parole). Valerie Summers wants the death penalty.

'I was particularly angry about the facts of this case, that she was a witness,' she tells me later. 'We ask witnesses every day to come forward, to tell police officers what happened to them, and then to repeat it to a judge. It's a very hard thing to testify – that's a true test of courage and character in the first place –

and it shouldn't come with a health risk attached. The sexual assault on Helena Greenwood did not happen here, in San Diego, but she came into our community to start her life over, and he got to her here. The reality is that we can't protect them – there's no 24-hour guard for witnesses. We can't relocate every witness and give them new names, nor would they want that. But when a crime disrupts someone's life horribly like that, then to have the person come and kill them, that's very bad.'

In the weeks following the preliminary hearing, she put together a presentation to take to a case review team comprised of senior prosecutors. Behind closed doors, they discussed the evidence, the strength of the case, the heinousness of the crime, and came up with a recommendation on sentencing to take to the District Attorney. It is an open secret that on the Frediani case they voted unanimously for death.

At the same time, David Bartick was mining his client's past for reasons why, in the event he was found guilty, he should be spared execution. He spoke again to the Frediani family, to Kathy Clark and Dave Rangwirtz, to college friends and fraternity brothers. Their testimonies, collated into a glowing report, would, he hoped, be enough to sway the DA's decision.

It makes emotional reading, not so much for what it says about its subject – for it would have been failing in its purpose if it portrayed him as anything but a much-loved hero – but what one learns about the effect his imprisonment has had on the lives of the people who love him. Mrs Frediani, through tears, says she 'find[s] it hard to believe that the Paul I raised and loved was capable of doing something like this. He was never a fighter and he never presented himself as a severe discipline problem. I love him and I find it difficult to get past this. I just want him to come home . . .

'All that has been important in Paul's life are his twin boys, working hard and trying to get ahead. His kids mean the world to him,' she continues. When they called to say they would not see him any more, 'it broke his heart. My husband and I used to send the twins gifts for their birthdays and Christmas and we never heard from them. We tried calling them on the phone . . . It's been two to three years since we last had any contact with them. We miss them terribly.'

Paul's sister Donna recalled as a child doing everything with Paul. 'We had chicken pox together. We played in the snow and during the summer, when we were out of school and our parents worked, Paul was pretty much in charge of me . . . Over the years, we have been by each other's sides whenever one of us has had to have surgery. I underwent two serious surgeries between my sophomore and senior year and Paul was right there all the way offering me his support.'

Over the last few years, Kathy Clark had begun to regard Paul as 'just like one of the girls. He loved shopping with all of us. We loved having him around . . . When I heard about Paul being arrested and what the charges were, I thought back over the years I have known him to see if perhaps I had been wrong in my judgment of him. My answer to that is *no way*. I never saw him lose his temper, everything just always seemed to roll off his back. This whole incident came as a great shock not only to me, but to everyone who knew him. His friends were in tears when they heard the news and were genuinely saddened by this turn of events. Most everyone I introduced Paul to grew to like him.'

Whether the District Attorney of San Diego, Paul Pfingst, would do the same, on the basis of a written report, was Paul Frediani's current concern. David Bartick turned in his report on 19 April 2000; the review team of deputy district attorneys had already made its recommendation. Pfingst said he would get back to them.

I sat in England waiting to hear his decision, and to pass on the news to Sydney Greenwood. He had spoken once to Laura Heilig and once to Valerie Summers, but he was not in constant contact with the forces of San Diego justice. This case, however, was the focal point of his life.

That summer of 2000 was the season of the gene. It was nearly impossible to open a newspaper or magazine, listen to the radio, or have a conversation without DNA or genes or the genome, somehow entering it.

As Paul Frediani sat in Vista jail, awaiting the decision which could determine whether he lived or died, the race to map the human genome, between the $3 billion publicly funded Human Genome Project and Celera Genomics, the private operation run by bio-entrepreneur Craig Venter, was entering the finishing straight. Both were claiming imminent victory at the same time as shooting aspersions at the rival effort. The multi-national public project was an inefficient dinosaur, according to Venter, spread between sixteen different laboratories primarily in the US and UK. Celera, based in Maryland, was a 'cowboy operation', the opposition countered, not only using the results of the HGP's work, which was posted on the internet for public consumption as it came through, but seeking to make financial gain – by patenting individual genes – out of what were essentially the most universal of entities.

The two teams were employing similar approaches. Both started with blood and sperm samples; the HGP used a combination taken from a dozen anonymous donors, while Celera advertised in the *Washington Post* for volunteers and announced that it had selected six men and women from a variety of ethnic backgrounds.[1] The HGP scientists took a short piece of

1. At the end of 2002, the maverick founder of Celera, Craig Venter, revealed that he had overridden the decision to use a selection of anonymous donors, and instead substituted his own DNA for the most detailed analysis of a single individual's genetic make-up yet performed. Asked why, he said: 'How could one not want to know about one's own genome?' As a result of the work, he discovered that he has inherited a variant gene from one of his parents, associated with an abnormal fat metabolism and an elevated risk of Alzheimer's. He is taking fat-lowering drugs in an attempt to counteract its effects.

a chromosome and, using PCR, made thousands upon thousands of incomplete copies, all starting from one end. To the other end, they attached fluorescent tags, using different colours for each of the four base letters. The fragments were separated according to size – in the same way as RFLP – allowing the sequence of highlighted base letters to be read out, then these short sequences strung together to give the chromosome's code. To do this, latterly, they used giant computers, made by PE Biosystems, working day and night. Even here was a link to the Greenwood–Frediani case – PE Biosystems is the same firm that manufactured the DNA testing kits most widely used by forensic scientists, including those used at Seri and Cellmark to match Paul Frediani's blood to the scraping from under Helena Greenwood's fingernail. The code they arrived at for each chromosome was by no means the complete sequence, but an abridged version.

Celera shortened this process further, using what is known as the 'shotgun' sequencing technique. Instead of sequencing adjacent segments of chromosomes, they chopped the entire genome into pieces and sequenced that. The computers then had the task of reassembling the random bits, by looking for overlapping fragments. It was faster, but gave an even more incomplete picture.

On 27 June 2000, two days before our baby was due, the HGP scientists and Venter apparently put aside their differences – in public at least – to announce that a working draft of the human genome was complete. Bill Clinton and Tony Blair held a joint satellite press conference to praise the latest giant leap for mankind. 'Today we are learning the language in which God created life,' Clinton said. 'We are gaining ever more awe for the complexity, the beauty, the wonder of God's most divine and sacred gift. It is conceivable that our children's children will know "cancer" only as a constellation of stars.'

For his part, Blair acknowledged that many people, himself included, were uneasy about the implications of this knowledge. 'The role of science is to inquire and discover and it is the role of society, and government on behalf of society, to make judgments on what we then do and how we respond. I don't ever want to see science limited in its inquiry.'

Inevitably, there were fears that this Brave New World could start to manipulate the same divine process of creation that Clinton had lauded. Improved pre-natal genetic screening, some claimed, could lead to pressure on parents to abort foetuses that did not pass some arbitrary 'quality test'. Also to genetic discrimination, with the possibility of a 'genetic underclass' being unable to get insurance, private health care or employment.

These fears were mere squeaks from behind the skirting board, however, on 27 June 2000. What James Watson called 'a great moment for our understanding of life', Professor Richard Dawkins described as 'along with Bach's music, Shakespeare's sonnets and the Apollo Space Programme ... one of those achievements of the human spirit that makes me proud to be human'. The focus was on the potential benefits of being able to read what had been dubbed 'the book of life', the promise of cures for previously incurable diseases, infallible organ transplants and life-prolonging elixirs. As Helena Greenwood had predicted it would to her father twenty years earlier, the ability to read and control DNA was indeed changing the world.

Yet most people, if stopped in the street and asked what DNA was, would have said something along the lines of, 'It's that thing they're using to catch criminals.' On the cusp of the new millennium, DNA was also setting them free.

In the United States, Governor George Ryan of Illinois, a pro-death-penalty Republican, imposed a moratorium on capital punishment after the thirteenth wrongly convicted man was released from death row in his state following DNA confirmation of his innocence. Even George W. Bush, then still governor of Texas, by far the most committed employers of the electric chair, pardoned A. B. Butler after he had served seventeen years in prison for a sexual assault he did not commit. In April 2002, a national landmark was reached when the one hundredth person was freed from death row, after DNA had proved him innocent.

In the United Kingdom, a build-up of pressure had finally persuaded the Criminal Cases Review Council, an official, government-backed equivalent of the Innocence Project, to order the exhumation of James Hanratty. The so-called A6 murderer had been hanged at Bedford prison in 1962, after being found guilty of rape and murder. The case for a long time had been considered 'unsafe' – since prosecution witnesses had been discredited, and since the discovery of a significant amount of evidence suggesting that Hanratty was nowhere near the scene of the crime when it occurred. By 1997, investigators for the CCRC had become convinced that a miscarriage of justice had taken place. But to their considerable surprise – and the continued disbelief of many commentators – the results of DNA tests performed on Hanratty's remains matched those done on fragments of clothing worn at the time by the raped woman. DNA, it would appear, had confirmed the court's original decision.

Forensic DNA was once again in the news in early 2001, when a Spanish waiter, Francisco Arco-Montes, was arrested in Florida and charged with the rape and murder of a thirteen-year-old British schoolgirl, Caroline Dickinson, five years previously in France. Montes had been arrested in Miami for burglary and lewd and lascivious behaviour. Those charges turned out to be the least of his worries; DNA tests done while he was in custody and fed into the international databank, tied him to the Dickinson murder. It was a popular triumph of detection – and another boost for the profile of forensic DNA, in the UK, France and America.

On the western side of the Atlantic, the Forensic Science Service was continuing to develop new techniques. Unlike the rest of the world, Britain now uses DNA as a method to solve even petty crime, like burglary or car theft. 'These days, we can get a DNA profile from a couple of cells,' Peter Gill explains. 'If someone has stolen a car, for example, you know they must have touched the steering wheel, so we target the steering wheel. If they've broken into a house, they may have touched a door handle. Whenever you walk through a room, down a passage, across a field, you leave behind a trail of cells. They are like invisible calling cards, they lie scattered across the floors and walls and furniture, just waiting to be picked up and read. Where burglars have learned to wear gloves, they rarely bother with masks, and we can catch them from particles of saliva on their breath.'

Gill believes that it is only a matter of time before it will be possible to get a DNA profile from a single cell. With PCR, the potential is there; the present difficulty lies in the interpretation of such microscopic tests. But they're working on it, developing methods to improve accuracy, reduce the risks of contamination. They are also looking at single nucleotide polymorphisms – or 'snips'. These are a single-base pair change – each therefore only having a 50 per cent variability. But with 9,000 Snips on one microscope slide, each describing a different piece of genetic information, their power increases dramatically. They are cheap and fast and may one day replace STRs, Gill believes. 'What they give you, in principle, is a way to discover anything that is genetically encoded.'

Some progress has already been made in the quest to identify a person physically from their DNA profile – to shade in between the dots. Race has been there for some time, but now they can determine hair colour too – if it is red. Gill has tracked down a red hair marker. On a gene romantically known as MC1R, it has been shown that there are two metabolic pathways: the first produces U-melanin, which is brown, black or blond hair, the other Pheomelanin, which, with two mutations, tends to produce red hair. This is already being used in casework – putting red-headed criminals at a distinct disadvantage.

'The research that is already being done into building an identikit based on a DNA profile does seem to suggest that, say, facial characteristics are genetically encoded. In principle, therefore, you could find the genes that suggest a high forehead, or eye colour, for example. It's my guess that we may be looking at this in the next twenty years or so.'

Paul Frediani spent the weeks following his preliminary hearing waiting anxiously for news from the District Attorney's office. As a remand prisoner in a county jail, he had privileges denied to the convicted criminal. He had daily newspapers and no work duties, and was allowed into the yard twice a week. For the rest of the time, however, he was inside, denied even a breath of fresh air. Still, his lot was better than that of more than 3,700 prisoners across the United States – 607 of them in California – locked up in high-security cells twenty-four hours a day, under sentence of death.

In June 2000, he had been attacked by a fellow prisoner, who scratched his face and inside his lower lip, and as a consequence, Frediani had been assigned to a wing for detainees with 'sensitive needs', away from the main body of prisoners. There, he spent his waking hours in a recreation room, watching television, playing Scrabble with whoever would take him on – and inevitably winning – and talking on the telephone. At least once a week, he would reverse the charges to Kathy Clark, the Rangwirtzes, Diane Christiansen – an old friend in San Francisco – and his family. These were the people he could trust; his comfort at a time of extreme anguish.

In May 2000, Paul Pfingst made his decision. He had read the representations from his own attorneys and from David Bartick, spoken to both sides and, after reflection, he had decided not to pursue the death penalty. The Frediani camp was relieved. Valerie Summers and Laura Heilig were disappointed. 'I thought he deserved it,' Heilig said. 'What he did was terrible. It was cold-blooded and calculated. He destroyed the life of a brilliant young woman purely to protect his reputation.' Valerie Summers was more guarded in her reaction: 'Look, our county is very conservative in that way. When it is a death penalty case, the whole process is different – it becomes bigger and more complicated. But here, the fact that she was a witness in a pending trial . . . When someone kills someone because they're going to testify against them, if the criminal justice system does not respond to that with the full force of vengeance that we have, then what do you reserve it for?'

Pfingst had made his ruling, however, based on more practical grounds: he did not think a jury would have been able to sentence Frediani to death. 'Every case is unique,' he said later. 'What a district attorney has to consider is that a decision to seek the death penalty is a decision to ask a group of jurors to recommend the execution of another human being. I know how difficult this is for jurors. A guilty verdict ultimately requiring a substantial period of imprisonment – perhaps as long as the remainder of a person's life – is very difficult. Asking the jurors to kill someone raises that difficulty by a factor of many, many times.

'I try to look at the decision from the perspective of the jurors, and they're confronted with perhaps the most difficult choice any of them will make in their life and one that will stay with them for ever, in one way or another. In this case, the defendant brought to the courtroom a history of personable relationships and friendships among people who were highly regarded in his community. He brought children into the world during this period, and if those children, who had not been born when the crime was committed, asked the jury not to kill their father, that would be very compelling testimony.

'What we would have had to prove, for a jury to vote for execution, was that this person had no potential for redemption. I don't think that would have been possible in this case.'

The trial date was set for the autumn. My first child had been born and we were all ready to go, when it was delayed. New evidence had come to light, and required additional testing. The date was moved to November. We bought our tickets to San Diego – our small family was set to move for the winter. The date was once again moved back. Our tickets were unchangeable, we had rented a cottage in Del Mar from mid-November. We decided to go anyway, and hope there were no further delays. On 22 November 2000, the day before Thanksgiving, we arrived in San Diego.

17

In *The Sign of Four* Sherlock Holmes said that '... when you have eliminated the impossible whatever remains, *however improbable*, must be the truth'. Finding these explanations for his client's innocence was David Bartick's challenge in the run-up to the trial. However, as the start date loomed, the impossible – Frediani's guilt – kept rearing up in entirely plausible guises. In the early autumn, the prosecution had sent additional blood samples from Helena Greenwood's clothing up to Seri, and the remaining fingernails to Ed Blake's lab for DNA testing. The results were looking ominous for the defence. Bartick argued successfully for yet another postponement. The trial was rescheduled to begin in early January 2001.

The Frediani case was David Bartick's fourth murder, but the first that looked set to go the distance. In one, he had been able to prove that his client was nowhere near the scene of the crime, and the state had dropped charges a week before it got to court; both of the others had been settled out of court in mutually satisfactory plea bargains. For the rest of the time, Bartick's one-man practice represented people accused of a wide range of crimes: corporations and drug dealers, bankers charged with money laundering, judges with domestic violence and domestic cleaners accused of murder. Unusually for a defence attorney, he commands respect across the board: from his peers, DAs, policemen, journalists. He is always busy, but makes it a point of pride to devote as much energy to each of his clients, whatever their crime and whatever their circumstances. He is known as a professional – who fights hard, without ever crossing the line, or compromising his ethics.

His first loyalty, however, is always to his client. He had never asked Frediani whether he murdered Helena Greenwood. 'Nor would I ask any client whether they did the crime. That's my own practice. If I think there's a possibility they might take the witness stand and testify they did not do the offence, I do not want to put myself in some sort of ethical predicament, because I can't. I put myself in a state of mind that I need to, to believe in my client. Perhaps I wish I were stronger mentally so that I could argue something different to the jury, but I can't expect the jury to believe something if I don't believe it myself.' Nevertheless, in the year-long run-up to the trial, he had spent many, many hours with Paul Frediani, learning about his life from childhood to arrest, his jobs and relationships. 'I don't know if I have to like all my clients, but I generally have some kind of rapport with them, and as heinous as their crimes might be, they are still people. You learn to attach yourself to that part of them you're able to identify with. With Mr Frediani, that was not a problem. He was always a pleasant individual, and he treated me with the utmost respect and I found him to be very personable in many different ways. That was not difficult.'

He takes his responsibilities seriously; he knows that not only is Frediani's future in his hands, but the hopes and expectations of his friends and family rest on his actions. A private defence, inevitably, does not come cheap, especially where DNA and the death penalty are involved. On top of Bartick's basic rate, there are the laboratories to pay, the expert witnesses, who charge anything up to $5,000 for a court appearance as well as an hourly rate for their pre-trial time. In Frediani's case, a special firm had been retained to draw up the lengthy document sent to the DA arguing against the death penalty, there was a jury consultant, private investigators in San Diego and San Francisco. And then Bartick himself had to be educated in the minutiae of forensic DNA. There was no shying the issue: with no eye-witnesses to the murder, and no fingerprints, DNA would be at the heart of the trial, and Bartick had no option but to confront it head on.

He knew the worst from the preliminary hearing, and it was a figure: 2.3 quadrillion. There was no chance of arguing a one-in 2.3 quadrillion coincidence that the DNA matched his client's, especially when Frediani had a known link to the victim, and a motive, whether plausible or not. *Eliminate the impossible: search for an explanation.* If Frediani did not commit the murder – and Bartick could not let himself believe otherwise – then how could the presence of his DNA under Helena Greenwood's fingernails be explained? Was it planted, or was it the technology itself that was at fault?

Soon after accepting the case, after Paul Frediani's parents had driven down to San Diego to meet him, Bartick started looking into the history of forensic DNA. He read about Alec Jeffreys and the invention of DNA fingerprinting and profiling, about Kary Mullis and PCR, about alleles and multi-locus probes, about O. J. and Castro and the Innocence Project. He learned both the strengths and the potential pitfalls of using cutting-edge science in a courtroom in front of a jury of twelve normal people.

'From the first, I was hampered by the fact that I never had any raw material to work with. I retained the services of different experts to retest the work that the prosecution had done. But with regard to the fingernail scrapings, they had consumed all of that for their testing. All I had to work with, basically, was their extracted DNA. I would have preferred to have started with the sample, untested. Of course, while that was going on, I was also pursuing other angles – looking for an alibi to place Mr Frediani up in the Bay area on the day, trying to locate the young girls who had seen the black Porsche park in Ms Greenwood's driveway on the morning of the murder.'

The Alton girls, Kati and Kyri, had been six and seven years old at the time of the crime. Fifteen years later, they had moved away from Del Mar, their memories of a morning more than two-thirds of their life ago probably scorched. Bartick's investigator managed to track them down: Kyri to Los Angeles, Kati to Las Vegas, where she was working as a performer at Cheetah's Gentleman's Club. He spoke to both of them. 'It is very difficult to get reliable alibi witnesses in a case this old. And those girls were so young at the time. It was inevitable that their recollection would not be too clear.'

Paul Frediani had always maintained that he had seen Barbara Powell – Barbara Kenney as she is now – at the apartment complex up in the San Francisco area on the day in question. 'Obviously, it was of paramount importance that I contacted her. But she refused to speak to me, and I can't force her to speak to me before the trial. There is no question that she was interviewed at the time of the murder. But it is interesting that all I have in regard to her statements is one very brief page of notes, which are not specific. I wonder whether there was someone else she spoke to, in the manner of providing some sort of alibi? It says in her statement that she had seen his vehicle – that's not an alibi but it helps.' As to whether she remembered talking to Paul Frediani, Bartick would have to wait for the trial to find out.

With question marks over the witnesses, Bartick turned back to the science. A planted evidence defence is always tricky to sell to a jury, especially in a predominantly middle-class, law-respecting area like north San Diego, and there seemed to be no written evidence to substantiate it. His alternative would be to attack the technology, to make it seem fallible to a panel of people who probably had little in-depth knowledge of DNA. For this, he would need his own expert to explain the procedure. He had met Marc Taylor at a death penalty seminar a few years earlier. Taylor, who owned an independent DNA lab, had given a presentation on DNA evidence, pointing out the potential problems of the technology. Bartick asked around, spoke to various colleagues who had retained Taylor in the past, and then made an appointment to see him.

It was sitting with Taylor, in his lab south of Los Angeles, that David Bartick felt the defence's luck beginning to turn. Taylor told him how, in the preceding months, courts in three states had refused to admit evidence produced by DNA testing that used automated equipment to analyse STRs. The Profiler Plus system, employed in tandem with a 310 Genetic Analyzer, was the new generation in DNA analysis. But it had been rushed on to the market by its manufacturers, PE Biosystems (known at various times as Perkin Elmer Corporation and Applied Biosystems), in a bid to beat its rival system to be the FBI's supplier. Any lab that works with the FBI – has any need to produce DNA profiles to be stored on CODIS – would necessarily have to invest in the new and expensive machinery, as well as the mass-produced testing systems, and would probably start using it exclusively. In the hurry, the new system,

Taylor maintained, had not received adequate validation. And more than that, PE was continuing to refuse to disclose both the results of the validation studies it performed and the chemical formulae for the primers and probes the kits employ. Only a handful of PE scientists, sworn to secrecy, knew exactly what went into them. The customers were supplied with prepackaged kits, and asked to follow the instructions booklet – to mix phials of chemicals with test tubes of extracted DNA – and to trust them that the results displayed on the 310 Genetic Analyzer would be correct. A trained monkey could have followed the procedure and come up with the same results.

Taylor's laboratory had spent the last year running all sorts of tests on the Profiler Plus system and the 310 Genetic Analyzer, he told Bartick. On numerous occasions, the results had been, at best, ambiguous. Amplifying and testing multiple loci is problematic using the new automated technology, Taylor claimed; the multiple systems create multiple reactions and to some extent the additional primers compete with each other, which may ultimately result in mistyping. Typing samples containing more than one person's DNA – mixed samples – increased the potential for errors still further.

It was on these grounds that courts in Colorado and Vermont, and San Francisco and Fresno in California, had rejected the technology during admissibility hearings, and refused to admit the DNA analysis produced by it in court. Taylor had been involved as an expert witness in these cases, as well as a similar one in Australia.

Bartick checked his files: both Seri and Cellmark had used the Profiler Plus kit and the 310 Genetic Analyzer. This, he realized, would be his defence: he would show the science to be untested, persuade the jury it was voodoo. It was the strongest argument he had. If a court in San Francisco could reject it, then there was a chance that the traditionally more conservative San Diego circuit might do the same. And without the DNA evidence, there was no way his client was going to prison.

Bartick hired Marc Taylor as his expert witness, and started preparing his defence. The first step was the Frye hearing, in late summer. Bartick knew it was not going to be an easy ride. Valerie Summers was not only an exceedingly able prosecutor, but she had the best possible help at hand. Among her colleagues at the DA's office was George 'Woody' Clark, who had been one of the two specialist DNA lawyers brought in by the O. J. prosecutors to tackle the scientific evidence, and attempt to counter the Scheck and Neufeld effect. Whenever DNA came into a trial, Clark was on hand for advice, tutoring and even courtroom assistance. Bartick had no doubt that Valerie Summers would be taking every advantage of this resource.

It was a blow for him when, after two days of intense technical argument, the trial judge denied his attempt to have the DNA evidence excluded, but he knew he would have another chance to argue his case to the people who really mattered: the jury.

In northern California, Ed Blake's lab had been chosen to look at the additional evidence. He had been sent the fingernails to see whether he could find any DNA present that did not belong to Helena Greenwood. It was the sort of challenge he relished. The work itself was not particularly taxing, but here was a case with a good story behind it, that promised to have a high media profile, which always added a touch of spice to the proceedings.

Blake enjoys testifying at trial, and he has gained a reputation as the best and the worst of witnesses. As the first forensic scientist to use PCR, he knows the technology better than anyone else. He has worked on over a thousand cases – both for the prosecution and for the defence. His evidence has sent men and women to prison and condemned them to death, but he has also given back life, to the more than fifty wrongfully convicted people whose innocence he has proved through DNA. He is the Innocence Project's favourite uncle, but he could never be accused of bias. And that comes across on the stand; if an attorney from either side hasn't done his homework, asks an inappropriate or meaningless question, Blake does not hesitate to pull them up on it. He is outspoken and, by his own admission, impatient. 'There's hardly ever a case that I'm involved in where anyone in the courtroom has been involved in more litigation than I have – usually by a factor of ten. It's a constant battle dealing with lawyers. I like it, though. Both sides are always making what I consider to be incredible errors in judgment about how they approach their presentation of information to juries. And if they ask me some stupid question, then I say to them, "That's not what you want to ask. What you want to ask is . . ."'

'The Frediani case shows some of the flaws in our system,' Blake continues. 'Wouldn't it have been nice at trial to have had a DNA analysis of the semen from the original sexual assault? Modern science is never going to cure idiocy, unfortunately. What would possess somebody to throw away evidence in a case like that? That kind of attitude, to me, is unacceptable. I've seen it happen for so many years, and damage so many cases, on both sides. There are numerous defendants out there who are claiming their innocence, and if society decides they have the right to investigate that innocence, then to destroy evidence that would make that investigation impossible, is an outrage.'

Even judges do not escape his opprobrium. After the court ruling in San Francisco which excluded DNA evidence on the basis of Marc Taylor's assertions that the Profiler Plus technology was inadequately validated, Blake vented his spleen to the *San Francisco Examiner*. 'What you have here is an arrogant, ignorant, stupid judge who is unable to get through the smoke thrown at him by a very skilled lawyer,' he said.

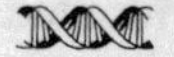

I wait for the delayed trial start in Del Mar, enjoying the typical San Diego winter – sunny days perfect for long beach walks, crisp nights. I walk often to 23rd Street. The cottage at the end on the left has not changed at all. It is a simple structure, with the same tall reed wall around the inner compound, the same gates behind which Roger found his wife sprawled with her legs apart, fifteen and a half years ago. I walk across a single sleeper bridge, over the small channel to the railway tracks. It is scrubland, with trees and long grass: it would not be hard to hide here, to see into the garden of 260, waiting for the road to clear, for someone to come out. I find the jog in the fence, with the tubular terracotta tiles. An easy entry point. Few people pass by. In the daytime, most houses appear to be empty. I walk into the drive and up to the gate without challenge.

I drive past the old Gen-Probe building on Chesapeake Drive, but the company has long gone, to a shiny glass building on Genetic Center Drive, in San Diego's own mini Biotech-Valley. I had heard that there was a plaque commemorating Helena there, but I decide against going in to ask: it looks too big, too professional. Gen-Probe is now one of the most successful biotechnology companies in the city. From a tiny start-up, great things have come. The original triumvirate have moved on to new ventures of their own. Helena Greenwood set the ball rolling on Gen-Probe's first products; she would have been gratified, I am sure, at their success.

I meet David Bartick, who gives me fat files of transcripts from Frediani's sexual assault trials. I call Valerie Summers, but she says she cannot talk to me until after the verdict, and warns me from contacting any of her witnesses. Most of the key characters in the case are testifying for one side or the other, and are thus barred from comment.

At one point, Bartick had considered hiring Kary Mullis, but his budget would not stretch to a Nobel laureate. Since the PCR revolution, Mullis has become a sought-after speaker on the international lecture circuit. No one falls asleep in a Mullis talk. He is entertaining in presentation, eclectic in choice of subject matter, and has a reputation for slipping in slides of naked women between diagrams of molecules and chemical reactions. Three years ago, he moved from his beachside apartment in La Jolla – just a few miles from Del Mar – north to Newport Beach, to work as a consultant for a biotech company. He is an infrequent visitor to the office these days, and rarely spends more than a few days at a time at home, between speaking engagements around the world.

I am lucky to find a window in his schedule. In person, he is every bit as charming and roguish as his reputation has promised. Over midday bottles of wine, he talks about astrology, AIDS and PCR. He has just returned from Australia, where he had been hired as an expert witness for the defence in a murder case. He was sure his man hadn't done it: the only evidence linking him to the crime was his DNA on the victim's towel. 'But there wasn't much left, and my contention was that the towel, after fifteen years in an unconditioned warehouse in the tropics, in fact didn't have any DNA on it. But the prosecution had this forensic pathologist who had become some sort of hero in Australia by solving all these old cases. He was an authority figure and the jury believed him. But I thought it was suspicious that he had found this DNA. I thought I had figured out an experiment which would prove that the lab work had been concocted – but unfortunately, it didn't work.

'The independent labs have an economic motivation to come up with a result,' Mullis warms to his theme, 'and most of the time, they're being paid by the prosecution. They can fake results easily enough. What I think should happen – and I've just written a paper about it – is that when blood samples are taken in the first place, they must be somehow tagged. You could drop in a plasmid that has a synthetic sequence in it that tells you that it was taken from this guy – and the defendant's lawyer should be there to witness it. It's the only reasonable and economic thing to do. That's the only way I would give blood in a case like that. Otherwise, I would say, forget it.

'Look, PCR has had a massive impact on the criminal justice system. Now, police all over the world know the power of DNA. The trouble is that in the courtroom, there's always going to be some people saying one thing, and some people saying another. The jury's job is to look at the people and figure out who is lying. Now, these molecules have made their job a whole lot easier, because they don't have the capability to lie. However, you have to trust the people who collect the samples, do the analysis, and come into the courtroom; you have to assume that all those people have no good reason to tell you a lie. The trouble is that in a courtroom you know that half the people have to be lying.

'I don't enjoy testifying in criminal cases,' he said. 'I like my science to be airy and inconsequential and fun. I don't want someone to hang as a result of it.'

Yet, that is what forensic DNA, using his fun and airy invention, is doing. The consequences of Mullis' science have sent countless people to the execution chamber or into a long-stay prison cell. They have also freed many from unjust punishment. In giving apparent certainty, it is creating a whole new kind of justice, in which we can turn back the clocks, rewrite history. Without this new science, Paul Frediani would still be driving his Lexus to work in San Francisco every day, wearing black tie to the ballet, diving into love and crawling painfully out. Instead he is facing the possibility of a lifetime in prison. Is this what Mendel and Mullis, Watson and Jeffreys foresaw?

On the eve of the trial, I telephone Sydney Greenwood. My call is answered by a neighbour: he passes the phone across, and between shallow breaths, the old man asks me to let him know as soon as there is any news.

On Thursday 11 January 2001, I am waiting outside court 18, kingdom of Judge John Einhorn, before the bailiff has unlocked the doors. In the corridor, milling around with polystyrene cups of coffee, are close to a hundred people. The jury pool. They have been given numbers and are called to preassigned seats. I follow them in. Standing, like a wedding receiving line, are Valerie Summers, David Bartick and Paul Frediani. Their faces look as if they have been composed into practised expressions, serious but winsome. Over the following weeks, as I am allowed into the court before the jury, I watch them prepare this face. Valerie's is the most obvious. As soon as the bailiff goes to open the doors, whatever expression has been there before is immediately replaced with a look of concerned empathy.

The judge enters at the back and climbs up to his boxed-in throne on a raised dais. He is a small, beady man, balding, with a little fluff of hair on top of his head: he looks like a baby eagle. When he welcomes the jury, his voice is courteous, precise and even. He introduces the attorneys and then David Bartick introduces his client, Paul Frediani, to the potential jurors. Frediani is wearing a suit and a tie. He looks less bulky and broad than he did in his prison pyjamas, but his head is still inclined ten degrees too high. It gives that impression of arrogance that so many people have noted.

The judge explains what is going to happen. '. . . Parties have the right to select a jury of their own choosing . . . series of peremptory challenges . . . Both attorneys, without disclosing their reasons, can ask for jurors to be excused.' Each potential juror has filled in a questionnaire, devised by the defence and prosecution, asking about everything from their education to their opinions on the O. J. Simpson trial. Now, the judge, prosecution and defence have an opportunity to ask further questions. 'We do not attempt to overly pry into private lives,' Judge Einhorn says, 'but there might be some things in your feelings, opinions, life experiences, employments . . . which may make it impossible for you to serve on a jury in a case of this kind . . . to be fair and impartial . . . The test I like to use is: "If I were in the unfortunate position of Mr Frediani, would I be willing to have twelve people of my state of mind stand judgment on me?"'

He starts with a general question: is there anyone who feels they might not be able to look at graphic pictures of death and violence? Three raise their hands, and are excused. He moves on to individual questions: one juror, a black woman, says that she distrusts all police officers; another, a distinguished-looking older white man, thinks the criminal justice system is too lenient. Juror 31's neighbour was murdered recently, but believes that wouldn't affect her judgment.

David Bartick is next. He asks several potential jurors if they can 'promise to be fair and not let other experiences cloud your judgment?' Does juror 3 accept that police have the same frailties as normal beings? Yes. What does juror 14 think about defence attorneys?

'They don't have the best reputation in town.'

'But you won't hold that against me?'

A laugh. 'No.'

Some, it is clear, want to avoid jury duty; others are doing their best to appear reasonable and responsible. I have heard it said that juries are composed mainly of people who don't have the wit to get out of it.

It is Valerie Summers' turn. She smiles, and comes across to the jury as warm and easy-going. Her hair is blow-dried, her suit smart. She is every inch the professional. Her questions focus on each person's education. I cannot work out whether she sees some scientific knowledge as a bonus or a hindrance. Slowly, I am getting to know several salient facts about each juror, which I come to think of as their defining characteristics. Juror 10, a handsome man in his forties, tall and outdoorsy, majored in biology at college, and now works as a fire-fighter captain. Juror 29 is blonde and well-dressed, a ringer for Jessica Fletcher in *Murder She Wrote*. Her former husband was a police officer, but she also had a friend charged with issuing a terrorist threat – which made her see the law from the other side. Juror 47 spent a single term at college, 'majoring in pub and cafeteria', before realizing he had better get on in life. He now works in hazardous waste disposal.

Once the questions are over, it is time to pick the jury. Each attorney has a number of peremptory challenges – opportunities to expel potential jurors without having to explain their reasons. It is reminiscent of picking teams at school. Valerie Summers and David Bartick take it in turns to stand up and say, 'I would like to thank and excuse juror . . .' In short sequence, they get rid of sour number 2, economist number 7, the black lady with the grievances against the police, the man who thought that only guilty men would opt for a jury trial and the redneck whose nephew set fire to a portaloo. Out go the man who thought the criminal justice system stank, the innumerate golfer, and the desperate-looking forty-something with the tight black clothes and dyed vermilion hair.

And then there were twelve. The jury chosen by default, almost, to stand judgment on Paul Frediani's future; numbers 3, 5, 10, 14, 23, 29, 31, 32, 42, 47, 61 and 64. Eight women, four men. All but one white, mostly middle-aged, predominantly overweight. They look particularly unexceptional. Judge Einhorn asks them to stand, to raise their right hand and to solemnly swear to see justice done. He warns them against discussing the case with anyone, and asks them to avoid all media coverage of the case. All nod solemnly. They are perceptibly cloaked in pride; the disciples of Judge Einhorn.

I bump into David Bartick in the car park and ask how it went. He shrugs, 'Not bad. They already hate my client. That's a fact. They come in, the judge reads out the charges and they know he is up for murder.' So much for innocent until proven guilty. 'There's not much I can do about that. The best I can aim for is for them to like me a bit. Look, I have an uphill struggle, I know that. The O. J. trial was the worst thing that could possibly have happened to us, to defence lawyers and the legal system as a whole. Most of these jurors are white, pretty conservative, and to them, O. J. showed the system up as a farce. In the face of that, the best we can hope for is to get a jury of unopinionated people.'

With the trial slated to begin the following week, Bartick is busy with pre-trial motions. Both he and Valerie Summers are attempting to lay the ground rules in their favour before the trial starts. Each is trying to deny the other opportunities to raise certain aspects of their cases. Both have pretty good ideas of the opposing cases – from the preliminary and Frye hearings, the witness lists that by law they have to supply before the start of trial, from the files and files of police reports and interviews – 'discovery' – that both sides have the opportunity to work from. They know what the flash points are going to be.

Bartick is keen to avoid a replay of the sexual assault trials. Summers argues that the assault is key to the defendant's motive for murder. The judge treads the narrow beam between them: he does not want a full-blown rehash of the old case, but agrees that the prosecution can present an outline of the events, in order to establish the connection between the defendant and victim. He passes the defence's motion, however, to exclude as prejudicial two of the more lurid details of the assault: that Helena Greenwood had been forced to strip and walk naked around the house prior to the attack, and that her assailant had ejaculated on to her face.

For her part, Valerie Summers argues energetically for the exclusion of two of the central tenets of the defence case: the strange, threatening phone call made to Helena Greenwood's successor the year after her death, when Frediani was safely incarcerated, out of reach of a telephone; and the timing of his plea of no contest to the sexual assault. Bartick had wanted to use the first as evidence of third-party culpability; if Frediani could not have made the call, then the person who had must have knowledge of the case, and a motive to make the call. The judge, however, rules that the call was unspecified and untraceable and as such, blatant hearsay. He also bars Bartick's plans to draw attention to the timing of his client's no contest plea – to emphasize it was done after two sets of trials, two appeals, and offered Frediani an opportunity for almost instant freedom. By doing so, Bartick would raise the whole spectre of the sexual case, the judge pronounces.

With the jury chosen, the battle lines drawn, we are left with a long weekend to await the start of the trial. David Bartick has his opening statements to prepare, and his clients to brief. The Frediani family are flying in from the East Coast. He has given them regular progress reports over the preceding year – the successful avoidance of the death penalty, the search for witnesses, the Frye hearing, technology defence – but it is now time for an honest appraisal of their son's chances at trial. He is not sure that they are prepared for even the possibility of defeat.

18

16 January 2001. At the jury selection, I was the only spectator, but an article in the *San Diego Union Tribune*, heralding the start of the trial, indicates that Frediani's fate will not pass unnoticed. When I arrive at the courtroom on the first morning, the jury are waiting around outside. They appear to have spruced up for the occasion – juror 42, the nursing teacher, has had a haircut. I immediately recognize the Frediani family: it is not just that their son's features shout out from their faces, but everything about them signals that they want to be left alone. It is as if they are surrounded by an invisible high voltage fence, labelled Keep Out. Even in the corridor, they sit as far away from everyone else as they can, and make sure their lines of sight cannot be intercepted. They are well turned out: Mr Frediani's shoes are polished to a high gloss; his wife wears a large turquoise and silver ring on her middle left finger. Their clothes are tidy, respectable, though not cut from the same cloth as their son's. Paul's sister, who shepherds them around, is elegant yet wan, her make-up a shade obvious, perhaps to compensate for a lack of sleep. They walk into the courtroom as soon as the doors are open and sit a few rows back, on the defence side. No one sits near them.

When Paul Frediani is led in, he gives them a faint nod of acknowledgement, then takes his place, facing forwards. David Bartick asks the bailiff for permission for his client to greet his family. When it is granted, Frediani turns stiffly around, and smiles. His face is blotchy. He does not look well rested. Of the four chairs lined up behind the prosecution and defence tables, his is the only one that does not swivel.

A television camera is being set up, a press photographer leans against the barrier between the court and the spectators. Four reporters take their seats across the aisle from the family, behind the prosecution table and near the jury box, and chat like old friends. As the judge calls for the jury, the room subsides into silence. Solemn-faced, the twelve file into their seats on the first morning of their duties and listen as the judge instructs them of their powers, that they must apply the law without being influenced by pity or passion, and based on the facts and the evidence presented to them.

In the quiet that follows, Valerie Summers walks to the back of the room, brings out an easel and sets it up before the jury. On it, she places a blown-up colour picture of Helena Greenwood, lying in the dirt of her front yard, her face bloody and bruised, surrounded by the scattered contents of her handbag. She walks over to a portable hi-fi, and pushes the play button. The trial opens with Roger Franklin's voice: 'This is an emergency. My wife has been attacked. She's lying in the garden. I think she's been killed . . .' I am struck by how controlled, how rational he sounds.

Valerie Summers clicks off the recording, walks up to the jury. 'So many times in a murder case, you're left asking a lot of questions: what exactly happened right before the person died? Why? Why did that person have to die? Well, in this case, I can tell you why she died. She died because she was going to testify against this man here, David Paul Frediani.' The jury turn, as though drawn by a magnet, to where Frediani is sitting, staring straight ahead.

They hear, for the first time, the victim's name, Helena Greenwood. They learn that she was a DNA scientist, and that a year before her death, she was sexually assaulted. Valerie Summers deftly outlines the story of the assault – the teapot, Thomas Christopher, her trip up to San Mateo to testify in the preliminary hearing. 'Everyone is getting ready for trial, tensions are rising, and he starts getting desperate. He approaches his friends to lie for him in that trial, and they refuse. He's getting desperate. And so what happens?'

She describes the murder, Roger's hasty return from work to find Helena, the police arriving while he is sitting beside her in the dirt, holding her hand and stroking her hair. The police investigation, collection of evidence and the reopening of the case, fourteen years later, in the era of DNA. The scrapings are sent off to Seri, Frediani's known blood sample to Cellmark, 'And lo and behold, they match. On every marker . . .

'We'll show you the DNA evidence from the experts and they will tell you the numbers of what this means. But what you need to know is that he left behind in the sexual assault case in 1984 a little piece of himself. He left behind his fingerprint. He didn't make the same mistake twice; he didn't leave any fingerprints at the murder scene. But the desperate David Paul Frediani, who didn't want to get convicted of forcing her to orally copulate him, didn't want his family and friends to know the monstrous thing he did, who was desperate to make this trial go away, left a little bit of himself behind at the murder too. He left his blood. Thank you.'

Her opening statement had taken less than half an hour. She had spoken fluently and without notes and the power of what she said was not lost on the jury, nor on any of the spectators. I could not bring myself to look across at the Frediani family during that opening salvo: Paul Frediani had not flinched, had shown absolutely no emotion. But I cannot believe they could have been that strong. How would David Bartick match that?

His style is immediately different to Valerie's; he is more theatrical, he walks up and down, uses his hands vigorously, and varies his delivery far more. It is as if she had only to let the story come through her narration, whereas he needs to make more of an effort to capture the jury's attention.

'Ever since the popularity of various television shows and movies that have had a way of dramatizing or sensationalizing court proceedings, I have always been a bit hesitant about beginning a jury trial such as this. And the reason why is that I cannot promise you the excitement or the drama that you might see in one of those shows. But I can assure you that your role, as a juror in this case, is much more important than any role of any actor or any cast member of any of those shows. At this time, I would like to truly thank you for accepting this solemn responsibility.

'This case, as far as the homicide, occurred a long, long time ago, in 1985, more than fifteen years ago. It will be important for each and every one of you to realize that things are much different from how they were, back in 1985 . . .'

He starts to outline the case that he will present to the jury. Unlike the prosecution, he cannot tackle it chronologically, and he does not want to dwell on the sexual assault: for a start it provides his client with a motive, and one that he can no longer deny in court as a result of the no contest plea. So, he focuses instead on specific instances and people, highlighting their importance.

'You will hear from three young girls . . . who lived in the neighbourhood. And these girls observed something very unusual that morning. These girls had chicken pox . . . and they happened to observe a vehicle drive up Miss Greenwood's street. This vehicle was a Porsche, black in colour.' David Bartick holds up to the jury a poster advertisement of a red Porsche. 'These girls observed this vehicle drive into Ms

Greenwood's residence, and park. Then it left. Mysteriously, a couple of minutes later, this Porsche drove back into Ms Greenwood's driveway. A person got out – and this person was described as having long white hair, pulled back in a bung. This person was observed leaving the vehicle and approaching Ms Greenwood's home. It was after this person with the white hair left that Ms Greenwood was found murdered in her front yard.'

He moves on to the crime scene. 'You will hear that there were fingerprints found at the crime scene. Ms Summers said that there were no fingerprints belonging to Mr Frediani – and she is absolutely correct. You will hear testimony that there were fingerprints taken off items that were spewed across the front yard . . . Specifically, fingerprints on a belt that was found not on Ms Greenwood, but beside her, and very possibly was used to strangle her. There was a thumbprint on that belt, a thumbprint that does not belong to Mr Frediani.'

He launches into DNA, the hub of the prosecution case. 'It is very important that you listen to the experts in regard to the DNA testimony,' he tells the jury. He walks across to his desk and picks up a large white board, which he holds up to them. 'DNA stands for deoxyribonucleic acid, but in this case, what the DNA is going to stand for is, DOES NOT APPLY.' These words are printed in coloured ink across his board. As a visual aid, it does not have the shocking power of the photograph of Helena. He goes on to talk about the procedures used in STR testing; the 'cocktail' kits containing primers, supplied blind by PE Biosystems to the laboratories, their contents a secret, and the 310 Genetic Analyzers which are used to analyse the results. He calls them 'black boxes', two unknowns, rushed on to the market without being subjected to rigorous scientific scrutiny. 'Why? The company that disseminated [the technology] was concerned that another manufacturer was going to come out with a typing procedure that would be in competition. You will hear an expert testify that what PE did was distribute their solution to different labs across the country before they had done scientific validation on it.'

He walks back across the room to stand behind Paul Frediani, a hand on his shoulder. It looks like a calculated gesture, a 'would I be touching him if he was a murderer?'.

'Mr Frediani is forty-six years old, and was raised in the same home that is still occupied by his family. He had a normal upbringing, and despite the fact that he had a club foot, a disability . . .'

Valerie Summers is on her feet: 'Objection, Your Honour.'

'Overruled.'

'Ladies and gentlemen, you will hear testimony that on the morning of this murder, August 22nd 1985, Mr Frediani's BMW was located in the carport of his residence in Belmont, California, 500 miles away from Del Mar. You will also hear testimony that Mr Frediani himself was at his residence in his Belmont condominium. Ladies and gentlemen, I am confident that, after hearing all the evidence . . . you will realize that Mr Frediani is not guilty of any of these charges, and that he will be acquitted, and you will find that not only have the People not met their burden but that Mr Frediani is not guilty on each and every count. Thank you.'

It was an intriguing conclusion. I had certainly never heard of this witness to Frediani's presence in San Francisco. It appeared that there were two horses in this race.

The first prosecution witness is Martin Murray. On the stand, he looks distinguished, confident and calm. He answers the questions put to him in a precise manner, his voice rarely rising. Similarly, Valerie Summers sounds more matter-of-fact than she had in her opening, less emotional. As first one speaks, then the other, the jury turn their heads from side to side, like spectators at a tennis match. At the defence table, Frediani makes notes on a yellow legal pad. But Murray has nothing dramatic to contribute: he identifies Helena from a photograph – the carefree one that had been pinned to Laura Heilig's office wall. He points out Atherton on a map, explains that he had been the prosecutor in the sexual assault case.

'Was she a special witness to the prosecution in this case?'

'Yes.'

'Why?'

'There are two issues that occur in a sex assault case; one is, did a crime actually happen? And two, the identity of the perpetrator. In my experience of sex assault cases, the identification by the victim is the critical factor in gaining a conviction.'

'So she would be a special witness in this case?'

'Yes.'

'At some time after the litigation, did the defendant enter a plea in this case?'

'Yes, after protracted litigation, he eventually entered a plea of no contest.'

'And did that plea include prison time?'

'Yes. Six years . . . and lifetime registration as a sex offender.'

Valerie walks over to the easel and replaces the photograph of the healthy, smiling Helena, with the one of her dead body.

'Do you recognize this person?'

'Yes, that's Dr Greenwood.'

'Thank you.'

David Bartick has only a few questions. 'Mr Murray,' he begins. 'Would it be fair to say that you are a lifetime prosecutor?'

'Well, I've still got some years . . . I don't know how I'll spend the rest of them, but, so far, yes.'

He asks whether, as prosecutor in the case, he would have been present at all of Frediani's court appearances.

'At all of the more important court appearances, yes.'

'And Mr Frediani also would be required to appear personally at these court procedures, correct?'

'I think he was present, yes.'

He agrees that they had both been at the pre-trial conference on 4 September, less than two weeks after Helena Greenwood's death.

'And you had an opportunity to observe Mr Frediani to see if he had any facial markings or scratches, is that correct?'

'Yes.'

'You do not have any independent recollection of whether Mr Frediani appeared to have been in any type of violent event?'

'I didn't see any scratches.'

The next witness is the ghost of Helena Greenwood. For the third time in open court, her preliminary hearing testimony is reread, this time by a young, dark-haired woman from the DA's office. She is well prepared and fluent. Hearing it spoken for the first time, I am filled with admiration at how composed Helena must have appeared, in a courtroom much like this, sixteen years ago.

'And what happened?'

'He quickly undid his trousers and pulled out his penis and asked me to suck his penis.'

'What did you do?'

'I put his penis in my mouth.'

'How long did that activity continue?'

'It was very short.'

'And what happened?'

'He pushed my head back on to the pillow and he ejaculated on to the pillow.'

There follows a series of prosecution witnesses. Their testimonies are straightforward, and they are disposed of promptly: policemen from Atherton, Thomas Christopher – a gentle, serious-looking man – Steve Chaput and a triumvirate of fingerprint examiners and analysts. At one point, David Bartick asks for the photograph of Helena, still haunting the easel at the end of the jury box, to be removed.

Then in walks Arthur Settlemeyer. Like his friend Jim Thoren, Art Settlemeyer has not weathered as well as Paul Frediani. Decades of drinking and partying have left their legacy in the pouches under his eyes and over his belt. With his grey beard, and shiny leather jacket, he looks like the sort of person who would be left in the bar at closing time.

'Are you familiar with a man called David Paul Frediani?'

'Yes,' Settlemeyer replies. He points towards the defence table.

'At some point in 1985, did you become aware that the defendant had been charged with a crime?'

'I was aware that they had been investigating him.'

'Did you find that out from the defendant?'

Settlemeyer's eyes slide across to Frediani, then back to Valerie Summers.

'Yes. I was outside one day and he approached me and asked me to do something for him. He said he was being investigated by the San Mateo Sheriff, for a breaking and entering at a house, and they had found his fingerprints outside the house. He asked me to go to the Sheriff's station, and tell them that he and I had been over to look at the house – it was supposedly for sale. And that he was looking at the house, he was considering buying it.'

'What was your job at the time?'

'I was a general contractor.'

'Did you ever go with the defendant to do a home inspection?'

'No.'

'So you knew he was asking you to lie for him?'

'Yes.'

'Tell me about his demeanour when he was asking this.'

'He seemed a little frantic, maybe. Something expedient about his nature. Maybe I was caught a little off guard. It was kind of a strange approach. I told him I would think about it.'

'Did he approach you a second time?'

'A day or two later, he approached me and asked me if I had thought about it. I told him I had, but I wouldn't.'

'What was his demeanour like at that time?'

'A little more frantic, or desperate. He tried to convince me to do it for him.'

It is the first major blow to the defence. Throughout, Frediani had sat at his table, occasionally shaking his head, whether in response to what his erstwhile friend had to say, or to his own plight in being caught out trying to fabricate an alibi, it was hard to say. But it was a rare movement.

Bartick has little to work with. Still, he peppers Art Settlemeyer with questions. About his friendship with Frediani, about Paul's car crash – while he had been on a trip, supposedly to Tahoe, a week before Helena's murder – about the alibi request.

'You must have been rather surprised and shocked that Mr Frediani might be asking you to do this? You're telling the jury at this point that Mr Frediani was asking you to commit perjury. Is that true?'

'He didn't walk up to me and ask me if I would commit perjury for him. He asked if I could help him out . . .'

'Were you ever interviewed by detectives back in '84 or '85?'

'I have some recollection. I recall being interviewed but not any specifics.'

'When you were interviewed, you certainly did not tell investigators that Mr Frediani asked you to provide him with an alibi. Is that correct?'

'I don't recall.'

'You were interviewed by San Diego Sheriff's detectives in December of 1999. Would it be fair to say that that was the first time that you told anybody that Mr Frediani attempted for you to create an alibi for him?'

'Probably yes. I don't recall having said that to anyone.'

'It is now fifteen years later, in 1999, that you had this recollection of this conversation?'

'Yes.'

Bartick looks doubtful as he sits down.

Valerie Summers bustles back to the witness box. She shows Settlemeyer a photograph.

'Do you recognize that person?'

'That is Paul Frediani.'

'Does this picture accurately reflect how he looked back then?'

'Yes.'

'A little younger?'

'Yes.'

'A little slimmer?'

'Yes.'

'A little tanner?'

'Yes.'

I look across to the defence table again. For the first time, Paul Frediani's mask has cracked. But is he smiling, or biting back the tears?

As Settlemeyer leaves the stand, the judge calls the proceedings to a close. It has been the prosecution's day. Frediani's attempts to fabricate an alibi for the sexual assault have been exposed, his reliability tarnished. But a liar is not always a murderer. We leave the courtroom – the jury to their homes, me to our cottage in Del Mar, the Frediani family to their hotel, the defendant to his jail cell.

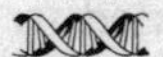

If the prosecution's opening salvo had been targeted at the sexual assault, the second wave focused on the murder. One by one, Valerie Summers called witnesses to piece together the events of 22 August 1985. Sam Morishima, earnest, still youthful, described seeing Helena the night before, at a barbeque at her house. 'She was excited, celebrating, toasting, comfortable,' he recalled. The next morning, she didn't turn up at work.

Her former boss at Syva, Richard Leute, confirmed that he had spoken to her by telephone on the morning of her death, around 8.30 a.m. Douglas Perkins, a neighbour on 23rd Street, remembers hearing an extraordinary cry that morning, some time soon afterwards.

'I heard a sound I will never forget . . . a muted scream. It caused me to look out of the windows. The sound didn't go away. I dressed, took the dog out, walked to the end of the cul-de-sac, but saw nothing unusual.'

'What did it sound like?'

'Something that shook me up, concerned me. I couldn't figure out what it was because I hadn't heard anything like it before . . . It was a muffled, guttural kind of yell.'

Roberta Loiterton, Helena's old secretary at Gen-Probe, flown over business class from Australia by the DA's office, described how, as the morning had passed, and Helena failed to arrive at work, she had become increasingly worried. At first, she had thought her car might have broken down, but when she hadn't heard anything by lunchtime, she called Roger at his office. Some time later, he had phoned her, frantic and hysterical.

'He said to me, "Robbi, I think she's dead." '

On the witness stand, unwillingly, Robbi Loiterton started to cry.

'I don't know why I cried,' she tells me later that week, when we meet to talk about Helena. 'It wasn't as if I was particularly close to her or anything. To be honest, I think she was irritated by me. She worked late and expected me to hang around, but I would sneak off to my gym class when she wasn't looking. I wasn't one of her favourite people. But when I walked up to sit in the chair, they'd left a photo of . . . of Helena there. A before photo. A really nice photo of her. And I sort of saw it and did a double take. And then I sat down and I could feel myself getting all emotional. I mean, I was fine when I was answering the questions . . . until I actually had to say those words that . . . thinking back . . . I could remember how Roger had said it. "Robbi, I think Helena's dead." I was a mess.

'I was nervous before, but Valerie had told me it would be kind of cosy in there. But when I went in my stomach was churning, my hands were shaking and my throat was dry. I sat down and poured myself a glass of water, and smiled at the jury and smiled at Valerie, and smiled at Sam Morishima, who was sitting at the back. And then I looked at the . . . David

Frediani. And he just stared at me. It was just horrible. I thought that I could outstare him, that he'd look away, but he just wouldn't stop staring at me.'

Detective Dave Decker followed Robbi Loiterton's emotion on the stand with professional calm. He described being called out to the crime scene, his initial investigations. A paramedic told how he had been the first to arrive, and had pushed down the fence to get to Helena's body. It gave Valerie an opportunity to put the photograph of Helena, crumpled behind the gate, back on to the easel. For the rest of day two, the jury was confronted with this constant reminder of the pathos of violent death. Various police officers and emergency staff painted a verbal picture to accompany the photograph.

'The only thing missing in the picture is the husband,' one officer commented.

'What was he doing?'

'He was crying. He was visibly upset. He had a hold of her hand and he was sobbing. As I watched, his hand periodically reached up to her face and pushed away the ants that were in her partially open mouth.'

On the third day, Valerie Summers held her breath and dived into her scientific evidence. However much she had managed to blacken Frediani's name – however horrendous the crime – it was still only science that linked him to Helena Greenwood's death, and she needed to ensure that the link was unbreakable. The rest was window dressing. She was visibly more uptight when she called Dr Robin Cotton to the stand.

Cotton, of Cellmark Diagnostics, was immediately recognizable to anyone who had followed the O. J. case on television: a neat-looking, schoolmarm type. As a prosecution witness then, she had spent more than a week in the witness box, being grilled by Scheck and Neufeld about every minute detail of the tests that her lab had carried out. Since that time, she had testified about DNA in hundreds of cases, in every state in America. This, however, was Valerie Summers' first big DNA trial.

She needn't have worried. All Cotton needed was the merest prompt and she took over, listening attentively to the questions as if they were the most intelligent she had ever been asked, then turning to the jury to give her answers. Concisely, clearly, like the best kind of teacher, she gave us a primer in DNA; its history, uses and the current forensic techniques. In the Frediani case, Cellmark had performed two sets of tests on the sample sent to them at the end of 1999; the DQα and polymarker, and the STR 'Profiler Plus', utilizing thirteen loci. From the combination, they built up a genetic profile of the suspect. When, on 28 January 2000, they were sent a fresh sample of Frediani's blood, and performed the same tests, the results were 'completely consistent'.

Bartick handed Robin Cotton a fat marker pen and asked her to write down the chronology of DNA on a large display board – from the discovery of its structure in 1953, to the appearance on the market of Profiler Plus less than a year earlier, in 1999. He did his best to sound sceptical, tried to needle her on the lack of published scientific validation of the technology, but Robin Cotton remained resolutely unpricked.

'How much has your laboratory paid to PE Biosystems?' he asked.

Certainly an amount in the range of hundreds of thousands of dollars, she replied.

Detective Decker was back on the stand. He described what he had found at the crime scene: the broken fingernails, the blood spatters, an overturned flowerpot, the gold wedding ring on Helena's left ring finger, a fine necklace around her neck, a pearl stud found under the wooden decking. How he had gone back the next day to check that the shape of the gate latch matched the wound on Helena's head. (The judge admonished him for calling her Helena, as if he knew her – asked him to be more formal.)

They had begun by looking at Roger Franklin, he admitted. Statistically, spouses are the most likely murderers. But this husband had been eliminated from their inquiries when his account of his departure for work was verified, and checked against Helena's phone records: he had arrived in San Clemente while she was still talking to Richard Leute. Decker had looked carefully at her business associates at Syva and Gen-Probe, but found no one with a strong enough motive. Then he turned to Frediani.

David Bartick waved some pages at Decker. They contained his crime report, dated 11 February 1986.

Where had he written about the collection of the hairs? And the hairs were booked into evidence in a Carlton cigarette packet. Where had that come from?

Decker said he didn't know. Maybe from the back of his car.

Was this procedure, Bartick asked?

Not exactly, but it seemed practical at the time.

Did Decker smoke?

Only a pipe.

The defendant didn't smoke, the victim didn't smoke, nor, as a rule, did her husband. David Bartick paced around the courtroom, spitting questions about the cigarette packet at David Decker, stressing its potential importance, building up to a crescendo, then nodding, as if he had made a point.

If the packet had been unimportant, picked out of Decker's car, then why had it been powdered for prints?

Who was this Donald Van Ness, to whose fingerprint card the prints on the Carlton cigarette packet had been compared?

Who had left the 6½ inch footprints in the recently raked sand around the side of the house?

Decker's replies were innocuous. But it sounded as if Bartick was heading towards some white rabbit that he would produce with a flourish at a later stage.

The prosecution's next key witness was Barbara Kenney (née Powell), Frediani's roommate at the time of the murder. He had moved into her second bedroom, she explained, on 1 July 1985. In August, she became aware that he had been in a car accident. 'He was very upset about it,' she testified. 'He was upset that a report had been filed. He said it had destroyed his plans.'

What had those plans been?

'I don't know exactly. I remember he said he went to LA "to take care of some business". '

Did she see Paul Frediani in the apartment on Thursday 22 August?

Not as far as she could remember.

Bartick referred her to a statement she had given Detective Joe Farmer on 26 August 1985, four days after the murder, in which she said she had seen the car in the garage on the 22nd.

'I have no independent recollection of that,' Kenney said. She remembered going to her apartment twice that day, however, to collect clothes. She remembered it was in the afternoon. But did she see the white BMW?

'I have no independent recollection.'

Did she not, in fact, see the defendant standing by his car that same afternoon?

'I have no independent recollection.'

'Have you tried to remember?'

'I was interviewed by Detective Heilig on February 7th, last year. I found it overwhelming. I have done nothing, unfortunately, other than think about what happened in August '85, since February until now. I do have an independent recollection of a conversation with Mr Frediani about his car, but I can't remember whether I spoke to Mr Frediani at 4 p.m. on August 22nd.'

Bartick continued to hammer away. Barbara Kenney appeared more and more flustered, but did not falter in her testimony.

Valerie Summers stood up: 'Are you able to provide an alibi for Mr Frediani for August 22nd, 1985?'

'No.'

In the car park that evening, David Bartick looked shattered. 'Was that as bad as it looked?' I asked.

'You don't know the half of it.'

The court reconvened after the weekend. The Frediani family had spent Saturday with their son in Vista jail. Bartick was with him for most of Sunday. Valerie Summers appeared confident on Monday morning. Her skirt was shorter, less flattering, but she seemed relaxed, her smile less forced. Before the jury was called in, she disappeared through a back door and emerged carrying a mannequin, dressed in a bright blue cotton suit, the skirt below knee-length, gathered with half pleats, the jacket short with padded shoulders and a frilly lapel, a black and white pin-striped shirt: the clothes Helena was wearing when she was killed. Bartick objected on the grounds that it felt like a presence in the courtroom, and as such was unduly prejudicial. The mannequin Helena was returned to its place behind a closed door.

When Frediani was led into the courtroom, he smiled at his sister, sitting in the front row. She smiled back, continuing to look at him with warmth as he sat down, stretched his legs in front of him and began flipping pages in the files. It was as though they had come to some sort of closeness over the weekend; the bond between them was perceptible for the first time.

The prosecution's first witness that day did not have far to come. Detective Laura Heilig stepped from her seat beside Valerie Summers and into the witness box. As the investigating officer, she had the right to be present throughout the trial. She smiled at the jury.

'By whom are you employed?'

'I am a deputy sheriff at the San Diego County Sheriff's Department.'

She had been, she explained, a homicide detective for the past nine years. 'During that time, I received training in blood spatter analysis, interview and interrogation, evidence collection, shooting courses, things of that nature.'

'Approximately how many homicides have you participated in the investigation of?'

'Well over a hundred.'

She explained she was now on the archive team. She had first read the Greenwood case in 1992, and reopened it in 1998. First, she had sent items from Helena's bag off for fingerprint analysis, then entered them into the central computer system. There were no matches. She had next turned to the biological evidence.

Valerie Summers brought over two plastic hinged boxes, one box labelled as 'RH Fingernail Cls' and the other as 'LH Fingernail Cls'. 'When I first reviewed the evidence in the case, these two plastic boxes were in evidence. I viewed the contents and placed the boxes into this envelope and identified them as Item 8 and sealed the envelope.' Over the next few questions, she stated that there was documentation to show that the boxes had been stored in the evidence warehouse since the time of the crime, until she had withdrawn them and sent them to Seri. When she had heard that an unknown suspect's DNA had been found on the scrapings, she had contacted the DOJ DNA lab to ask if they had a reference sample from Paul Frediani on file.

'Did you request that that reference sample be sent to Cellmark in Maryland?'

'Yes.'

'Did you receive the defendant's reference sample before it went to Cellmark?'

'No.'

'It went directly from the Department of Justice in Berkeley to Cellmark in Maryland?'

'Yes.'

'Was there any sample of the defendant's blood in your case file, or in your evidence?'

'No.'

Laura Heilig testified about the results coming through as a match, and her subsequent trip up to Burlingame to arrest and interview Frediani. On

22 September 2000, she had met crime scene reconstruction expert Rod Englert to go through the physical evidence in the case, to see whether there was additional material to send out for DNA analysis. The mannequin was brought back into the courtroom. As Valerie Summers pointed to holes in the jacket and sheer grey tights, the detective explained that there had been splats of blood which Englert suggested might contain the murderer's blood, as well as the victim's. She had cut around the stains, and sent them off to Seri for analysis.

Under cross-examination, she reiterated that the evidence from the Greenwood case had been stored in a warehouse attached to the Sheriff's building. The fingernail scrapings and clippings had been kept in a freezer. Bartick asked question after question about the chain of evidence, about the cigarette packet, the mysterious Donald Van Ness, whose fingerprint card was included in the case file. On none of them had Frediani's fingerprints been found. Prints had been found, he was able to elicit, which did not match either Helena Greenwood's or Paul Frediani's. In total, eighteen different prints had been entered into the automated system – but none had found a match. Bartick had the jury's attention, and when Laura Heilig returned to her seat, they looked almost disappointed.

She was replaced at the stand by Mary Pierson, who had been the crime scene investigator called out to 260 23rd Street on the afternoon of 22 August

1985. Pointing to the Spectre of Dead Helena, as I had begun to think of the photograph, Pierson pointed out the pieces of evidence that she had collected, from the fingernails to the plastic yoghurt spoon. The following day, she had collected all the 'loose trace evidence' from Helena's clothes and body, from under her fingernails, prior to the autopsy. One by one, while Mary Pierson described them, Valerie Summers displayed blown-up photographs of Helena Greenwood's hands, her head and neck, the cuts and bruises on her legs and feet, a close-up of the laceration to her scalp, and two haunting pictures of her haemorrhaged eyes – pools of black where there should have been white.

Bartick bounded up to Mary Pierson like a greyhound released from a trap. He waved his evidence sheet at her and asked repeated questions about the Carlton cigarette packet. Why, he demanded, was there no item number attached to it? The witness looked a little taken aback. It was labelled 7 on her sheet, she said. He directed her to her testimony at the preliminary hearing. She had described then how she had collected the fingernail cuttings and scrapings and put them in paper bindles. Now they were in clear boxes. When had they been transferred? Mary Pierson said she had no independent recollection. It was a phrase that was becoming familiar in the trial. Again and again, Bartick hammered home his point: no one could explain how the fingernails had come to be in plastic boxes when they had been stored originally, according to Mary Pierson's initial testimony, in brown paper bindles.

When she got up for her redirect examination, Valerie Summers could not elicit an explanation for that, though she did manage to clear up the missing number 7 on the evidence sheet. It had been removed by a hole puncher. She showed an embarrassed David Bartick her copy.

Next on the stand was the Chief Medical Examiner of San Diego County, Dr Brian Blackbourne. He first detailed the autopsy findings – the haemorrhaging in the whites of her eyes, abrasions on her lips, marks under her eyes, chin, jaw. Internal injuries to her neck, petechial haemorrhaging, bite marks on tongue and inside mouth; more haemorrhaging within the neck muscles, in the oesophagus and larynx. He had no hesitation, he said, in backing up the original autopsy conclusions: cause of death was asphyxiation by manual strangulation.

'How long does it take to strangle someone to death?'

'Between three and five minutes.'

Valerie Summers let his answer hang in the air for what seemed like a long time.

In the changeover between witnesses, a well-dressed blonde girl walked into the courtroom, sat down beside Paul's sister and handed her business card to the Frediani parents. There was immediate speculation across the aisle as to who she might be. A defence investigator, was one reporter's suggestion.

I thought she might be a family counsellor. No one dared ask.

She sat through the testimony of Mary Buglio from the Sheriff's Department crime lab, and was there the next morning when Gary Harmor, from Serological Research Institute, came to the stand. Frediani smiled at her when he was led in, dressed in a new charcoal double-breasted suit and an expensive-looking tie, dark with a golden geometrical pattern. He appeared pleased with his outfit; David Bartick complimented him on it.

Harmor's recitation was less than exciting. He covered much of the same ground as Robin Cotton, describing methods of DNA extraction and analysis, but if she was the inspirational teacher, he was the one whose lectures were sparsely attended. At one point, when I looked around, three people were dozing, including the blonde. But the jury appeared attentive; many took notes.

Harmor described how, in October 2000, he was sent the additional material for testing: the bits of blue jacket, skirt, slip and pantyhose. Most of the bloodstains were consistent with the victim's DNA profile; on one, however, the left back pantyhose, he had detected a mix of two profiles: Greenwood's and Frediani's. Analysis of the tiny sections of stuttered DNA found beneath Helena Greenwood's left fingernails, at the thirteen different loci targeted by the Profiler Plus kit, Harmor explained, produced a DNA profile that, after calculation of the population frequency using standard methods, could have come from only one in every two comma three quadrillion people. Again the magic figure was brought out and this time dangled in front of the jury who would decide Frediani's fate.

David Bartick appeared eager to take on Gary Harmor in a way he had clearly not thought worth his while with Robin Cotton. After asking for his qualifications, and finding – as he clearly knew – that they did not include postgraduate degrees, he said, 'So you are a lab *technician*, then?'

When Harmor said he had attended a course at UC Berkeley, Bartick responded, 'This wasn't a degree course, was it? You do not have a degree from UC Berkeley like I have a degree from Berkeley?' Harmor admitted that he did not.

'You are not an expert in . . . molecular biology . . . biochemistry . . . population studies . . . demography?'

'No.'

Over the next half an hour, Bartick managed to jab away at Profiler Plus – which he referred to as 'the cocktail kit' – how it had not been scientifically validated, that Harmor and his fellow 'technicians' had to rely on the maker's instructions to work it, that Seri had not been an accredited lab until after it performed the tests. But he could not dismiss that figure: one in 2.3 quadrillion.

If Harmor was a sedative, Ed Blake, who was the next in the witness box, was a box full of fire crackers. Unlike Harmor, Bartick could not attack his credentials; Blake had a Ph.D. from Berkeley in criminology, where he had studied under the father of modern American forensic science, Paul Kirk. He had started his own firm, Forensic Science Associates, in the 1980s, 'And the rest, as they say, is history,' he told the jury. He had been instrumental in the development of PCR as a forensic tool, worked with the Innocence Project on many cases . . .

'Does your company . . .' Valerie started to ask.

'My *firm*,' Blake cut in. 'A *company* makes widgets.' It was clear that he wasn't going to be as generous as Cotton had been in making the attorneys look good.

He had come into the Frediani case at a relatively late stage. At the end of October 2000, he had been sent four of Helena Greenwood's fingernails, with the brief to attempt to recover microscopic particles of DNA from them – particularly any biological material that may originate from anyone other than the victim – and to design a mechanism whereby that DNA could be analysed. He was initially hired as a mutually agreed independent lab, he said, and only later, when the results came through, retained by the prosecution.

Blake was an entertaining witness; sharp and illuminating, and obviously experienced. Valerie Summers had to do little more than pull out the string behind his back and then sit down as he filled the jury in on his work in this case, the history of DNA, Mendelian genetics. It was an education.

He had taken the extracted DNA from the

fingernails and divided it in half, then analysed it using half-volumes of the primer kits. On one of the right-hand fingernails, he had found DNA that appeared to emanate from three sources – two female and one male. STR analysis had come up with a DNA profile that did not exclude Paul Frediani, with the random probability of it being someone else around one in 780 million. He explained that analysis of mixed samples – and the resulting population frequencies obtained – was generally less sensitive than those of single donor samples, leading to lower probabilities. Helena Greenwood was not excluded as one of the female donors, while the third profile was unknown. Tests had excluded everyone who had had access to the evidence – Laura Heilig, Mary Pierson, Mary Buglio. The third profile remained a mystery.

Might Helena Greenwood have scratched a third person, a woman, the same person who had left the small footprints in the sand at the side of the house?

There was little to do about Blake on cross-examination, and Bartick's attempts occasionally ended up backfiring. At one point, when he was trying to pour scorn on PE Biosystems (a *company*, as Blake agreed), he slipped up, and the witness cut in: 'There is some confusion on your behalf that I can help you with . . .'

'No,' Bartick replied, before moving swiftly on.

Blake also managed to add a little mystery into his testimony: the other half of the samples, he said, had been delivered to Lisa Calandro's lab at the request of the defence.

During the lunch interval, the blonde said goodbye to the Frediani clan and left. If she had any emotional investment in an innocent verdict, she would have been relieved to miss the next witness, the prosecution's last. Rod Englert was described as a 'crime reconstruction expert'. Before he climbed into the witness box, he set up a mini-theatre in front of the jury, draping cream canvas over tables and chairs.

He had worked in law enforcement for thirty-eight years, he said. His speciality was bloodstain interpretation, which he had taught around the world, from Scotland Yard to Moscow. Drops and splatters of blood were for him like a Fodor's city guide: by examining them, he could discover the significance of what did and did not happen during a crime. Different types of drops, made in different ways, form different shapes. Low-velocity blood loss – drops, transfers, swipes – show directionality. Vertical drops make round marks; angled drops make tear-shaped stains. Medium-velocity spatter – when an instrument hits a blood source – always occurs away from the attacker.

Englert then pulled on white latex gloves and stood in front of his stage. Bartick and Frediani walked over to the jury box, where Frediani leaned against the back wall, apparently nonchalant, like a playwright standing at the back of the stalls during a performance of his own work. Englert filled pipettes with stage blood, then spattered it on the canvas with different swipes of his hand to demonstrate the origins of the different types of bloodstain.

'Blood dries in three to six minutes,' he said, splashing more red liquid. It is another well-rehearsed act. (That night, when we turn on the television, to one of the innumerable true crime shows, there is Englert giving the same performance, almost word for word.)

For the Frediani case, Englert had first studied 203 photographs, from the crime scene and autopsy. He had come down to San Diego from Oregon to meet Laura Heilig, Valerie Summers, David Decker and Mary Buglio on 22 September 2000. Together, they had gone to 260 23rd Street, and with Laura standing in for Helena Greenwood, and Decker for Frediani, acted out the assault, as Englert read it from the blood spatters. For Helena's head to have been bashed against the latch – and that, Englert agreed, was the most likely weapon – she would have had to have been on her knees. The blow to the head – the only source of blood – would have been violent to have caused the blood pattern that was found. She was attacked while standing and kneeling. There was a pool of blood at the base of the gate, satellite spatters radiating out to the side, and on the front of her skirt. 'The contusions were consistent with a struggle in a combatant scenario, where there is intimacy between the attacker and the victim, meaning that they were close, that there was a transfer of evidence – could be blood, hairs, saliva.'

The hand transfers of blood around her neck were consistent with strangulation, the chipped red toenail polish and injuries to her hands indicated defensive wounds, where the victim put up her hands and legs to guard against a weapon. 'With fighting in a mutually combative situation, the attacker can also receive defence wounds,' Englert continued, 'mostly on the appendages: hands and arms.'

'Based on all of your examinations of the crime scene, have you formed opinions with regard to this crime scene?'

'Yes.'

'And what are they?'

'That Helena Greenwood was attacked by the gate . . . and that she fought very, very hard, went down on her knees, abraded her knees, used her legs to support her to fight. She received the bruises to her hands, the cuts on her hands, also the bruises on her face, at which time she was also being strangled. The evidence here indicates that she resisted very, very violently.' I looked across to Frediani. He was leaning against the wall, scratching his cheek. If he was shaken by Englert's very vivid description of Helena Greenwood's last minutes, he did not show it; if he wasn't, he would have been alone in the courtroom. And it was not over.

'When she finally went down, she was lying on top of all those papers, the contents of her purse. But the position she was found in was not consistent with the position of a strangled person . . . That is an awkward position. That's not the position someone lands in. That's a posed position.'

'Did you observe any particular blood pattern on the pantyhose?'

'Yes, Ma'am . . . there were two hand transfer patterns around both ankles. And they were just around the ankle bones on each side, as though someone with bloody hands grabbed the ankles and just pushed the knees up and left her in that position, with her legs spread apart . . . That is a posed position.

'. . . Due to the violence of this and the nature of it – there was a lot of interaction between the attacker and the victim, especially to Helena Greenwood's hands, to which she received cuts – one can also know that that same propensity is possible with the attacker, that he or she in a case like this would get cuts to their hands. And in looking at something like that, and knowing that there is a possibility that the attacker may have been bleeding, you look at certain areas where, if a person was bleeding, and had his own blood on his hand, where would he transfer that blood on her clothes? The last area that was touched – according to the crime scene reconstruction – was her ankles. So it was requested that her hosiery go to a DNA lab to do a search and see whether there was any other donor of blood on her ankles . . . As well as under her fingernails.'

19

24 January 2001. On the sixth day of his murder trial, David Paul Frediani gets up from his seat, pulls down his suit jacket and walks across the courtroom to the witness stand. He is followed by a guard, bald-headed and black, who sits unobtrusively between him and the back door. He raises his hand and swears to tell the truth, the whole truth and nothing but the truth. His voice is deep and smooth, like espresso coffee; it matches his clothes rather better than his current situation. He speaks quickly and fluently, turning to address the jury with his answers, but his face gives nothing away.

'Mr Frediani, how old are you?' his attorney asks.

'Forty-six.'

'Where were you born?'

'Denver, Colorado.'

'Do you have any siblings?'

And so we ease into the defendant's testimony. That he would take the stand had never been sure. From the beginning, David Bartick had said that he would decide as the case went along, depending on how things were going.

Rod Englert's performance with the stage blood the previous evening had had a powerful effect. As he talked through the crime reconstruction, the violent struggle between Helena Greenwood and her attacker swam before the court like a strip of cine film. 'She fought for her life. And she lost.' Those haunting words. But it was the posing of her legs, propped up and spread apart, that was the most chilling aspect. For someone to do that was beyond understanding.

That evening, I went to the library to try to find out whether there was any accepted psychological explanation for what the action meant. The only mention I could find of the posing of a murder victim was in a book written by John Douglas, the FBI's former profiler-in-chief, inspiration for Special Agent Jack Crawford in *The Silence of the Lambs*. It was, he wrote, like a killer's signature. 'We don't get that many cases of posing, treating the victim like a prop to leave a specific message . . . These are crimes of anger, crimes of power. It's the thrill of the hunt, it is the thrill of the kill, and it is the thrill afterwards of how the subject leaves the victim and how he's basically beating the system.' But had Frediani killed Helena for a thrill, or out of desperation? And if the latter, was that any mitigation?

Valerie Summers knew how to quit when she was winning. Englert was her last witness, her final flourish. The drama of his performance had appeared to add substantially to the body of the prosecution case. It was slick and shocking; Helena Greenwood had been brutally murdered. But it hadn't actually linked Paul Frediani to the crime. Only invisible molecules of deoxyribonucleic acid had done that. As with the single fingerprint in the sexual assault case, it was science that pointed the accusing finger.

David Bartick was not just facing an uphill struggle, it was the north-west face of a dozen Eigers – without crampons. To make matters worse, he was having problems with his witnesses. He had decided against calling the younger Alton girl, Kati – six at the time of the murder and now working in a strip club in Las Vegas – but now the older sister, Kyri, had apparently taken off to Europe and left no contact address. The third young witness, Rian Alworth, was still living in Del Mar, but was showing reluctance to obey the subpoena summoning her to court. The previous night, her father, the former San Diego Chargers footballing star, had called to say that she would not be coming. Bartick now had no alternative, he told the judge, but to ask for a bench warrant to be issued, much as it had been to the strange eye surgeon in Frediani's second sexual assault trial. Judge Einhorn concurred: a deputy was dispatched to the Alworth house, with a warrant to compel Rian Alworth to attend court. If she continued to refuse, she would be arrested on a $50,000 bail.

With that business out of the way, Bartick's first witness was an investigator he had hired to determine whether Helena – or Hel-ay-na, as he always called her – Greenwood's address was listed in the 1985 telephone directories. It was not: she had only lived there for a month prior to the murder.

Now Frediani is on the stand. There are no television

cameras, no photographers, just the usual stalwart reporters. If Bartick's aim was to escape the pressure of publicity, he is certainly succeeding.

'I have one sister and a younger brother.'

'Where did you attend school?'

More questions about Frediani's background; more innocuous answers. Valerie Summers jumps up and down from her seat with repeated objections, like an overexcited child in a game of musical bumps. Most are overruled.

Frediani is not distracted. He sits quietly, slowly swivelling on his chair a few degrees from side to side, waiting patiently for the judge to rule each time before answering the questions Bartick puts to him. They cover college, his work history, his move to San Francisco.

'Now, Mr Frediani, in 1985, were you arrested for the sexual assault of Helena Greenwood?'

'Yes I was.'

'And did you, in fact, enter a plea of no contest to that assault in 1989?'

'Yes I did.'

In August 1985, he explains, he was sharing an apartment with Barbara Powell-Kenney, as she now is. He was on paid leave from Lincoln Properties. On 15 August, at the suggestion of his girlfriend, Andrea Goodhart, he had decided to take the weekend off and go on a trip in his white BMW 320is. But just north of Los Angeles, a driver had crashed into him, leaving his car a virtual wreck.

'After this accident, was this car ever again capable to driving long distances?'

'No. I could drive it around town, but not much further.'

'From 15 August, for the next few weeks, did you have a vehicle available to you?'

'No.'

'Mr Frediani, I want you to focus at this time on 22 August 1985. Specifically, where were you on that date?'

'I was home at the complex, in and about, playing tennis, lying out at the pool.'

'And your white BMW, where was this on that date?'

'It was in my assigned parking place in the carport, right below my apartment, next to Barbara's car.'

'On this date, August 22, did you have the occasion to speak to Ms Kenney?'

'Yes I did. Around 4, 4.30 in the afternoon, I pulled into the carport on my bicycle. It was the first time we had actually spoken since my accident, and she said, "What happened to your car?" I told her the situation about the car. She expressed her condolences for it. I asked her where she was going – she was all dressed up. She said she was on her way to meet friends for happy hour. About a three-minute conversation, that was it.'

Was this the alibi that Bartick had promised in his opening statement? If so, his mountain was growing ever taller. And steeper.

'Mr Frediani, in August of 1985, did you know where Ms Greenwood lived?'

'No, absolutely not.'

'In August of 1985, did you have any opportunity to drive to the city of Del Mar?'

'No, I did not.'

'Mr Frediani, specifically, have you ever in your life been to Del Mar, California?'

'No I never have.'

'In August of 1985, did you have the occasion to rent an automobile?'

'No I never did.'

'In August of 1985 did you ever board an airplane destined for San Diego?'

'No I didn't.'

'In August of 1985, did you ever go to any type of public transportation, such as a bus system, to come to southern California?'

'No absolutely not.'

'Specifically, on the morning of August 22 1985, were you in the presence of Ms Greenwood?'

'No I was not. I had no idea where she lived.'

'Mr Frediani. Did you assault Ms Greenwood?'

'Absolutely not.'

'Did you murder Ms Greenwood?'

'Absolutely not.'

I could not keep my eyes off Frediani. His answers were firm, and so was his gaze. He did not scratch his cheek, or pull his ear or rub his nose. He did not seem in any way agitated; this was his very last chance to save himself from a lifetime of incarceration. He knew that. And he just sat there, answering the questions, briefly and clearly and without visible emotion.

Bartick pulls back, asks where Frediani has been living since 1989, whether he has ever tried to relocate abroad, about his master's degree in Business Administration. Then it is back to the front line.

'Let me direct your attention to the day of your arrest, December 15 1999. Where were you the night prior to your arrest?'

'We had attended a black-tie affair at the San Francisco Ballet, the opening night of *The Nutcracker*.'

'And you were confronted as you were approaching your car the morning of 15 December?'

'I was walking out to my car around 8 o'clock. They were parked right beside my Lexus. All of a sudden I saw two guys get out of the car.'

'Were you shocked and surprised?'

'Very.'

'Did you deny any involvement in Ms Greenwood's death at that time?'

'Yes, I did. Later, when I was questioned, but at the time, they just took me down to the police station.'

'Thank you. No further questions.'

Behind the defence table, both of his parents are crying, holding on to each other. Mr Frediani, with his face buried in a handkerchief, is shaking. His wife strokes his arm. Donna sits behind them, her hands clasped together, knuckles white. Valerie Summers, arms crossed, all business and barely stifled aggression, walks towards the witness box.

'I would like to start with the sexual assault of Dr Greenwood, which occurred in 1984.'

Bartick is on his feet. 'Objection. Beyond scope.'

'Overruled.'

'Do you remember that?'

'Yes I do.'

'And you were arrested for that?'

'Yes I was.'

'And you are aware that your fingerprint was found at the point of entry on a teapot?'

'Objection. Beyond scope.'

'Overruled.'

'It wasn't at the point of entry,' Frediani counters.

'Where was the teapot?'

'On the deck.'

'Is that where you touched it?'

'Yes.'

'And you were at the preliminary hearing in 1985, where Dr Greenwood testified that the teapot was inside the window sill before the sexual assault?'

'Yes. I was.'

'And you are aware that your fingerprint was found the next day on the teapot on the deck?'

'Yes.'

'You are aware that the screen was in place when she went to bed that night?'

'Yes.'

'And when she was attacked in her bedroom, it was no longer there?'

'That is what I understand.'

'You are also familiar with the fact that you are blood type O?'

'Yes.'

'And that blood was taken from you?'

'Yes.'

'And the donor of the semen on the pillow was blood type O?'

'Right.'

'And that you are a secretor?'

'That is what I understand.'

'And it was a secretor who left the semen stain on the pillow at the point where she was forcibly orally copulated?'

'Yes.'

'And that your PGM type is a 1 + and that is the same as the evidence that was left behind in that case?'

'Yes.'

'Do you remember when you were arrested for that case?'

'Yes I do.'

'Tell me, when you were arrested, were you asked whether you were familiar with Atherton?'

'Objection.'

'Sustained.'

Both attorneys are getting agitated. They appeal to the judge for a conference. He dismisses the jury. Prior to the start of the trial, Judge Einhorn had told both sides that he didn't want to retry the sexual assault case in his courtroom. Bartick is complaining that this is exactly what it appears the prosecution is trying to do.

'I was very cautious, Your Honour,' he says. 'I believe I asked two questions with regard to the sexual assault. From there, my questions went straight to 1985 . . . I followed it up with the question, did you murder Ms Greenwood? . . . I don't believe I ever asked a question about whether he assaulted her, in reference to the 1984 case. There were only two questions in regard to that and everything else was directed towards August 22 1985, and I believe I made that very clear to the jury.'

But Valerie Summers thought not. The sexual assault case, she maintains, was his motive for murder, and as such, central to the People's case; the reason for the special circumstance in the charge. Furthermore, Bartick's question "Did you assault Ms Greenwood?" opened the door to cross-examination about the early case. 'I take issue with counsel's suggestion to this court that that question was in reference to the 1985 killing, because if it was, it is duplicative of his following question: "Did you murder Ms Greenwood?" Assaulting Ms Greenwood is a separate thing from murdering Ms Greenwood. A separate and distinct incident.' It is a semantic point. Bartick was referring to the day of the murder, but he had indeed omitted to preface that one small question with, 'On August 22nd 1985 . . .'

The judge has to decide which corner justice should take: 'The concern this court has is whether the answer to the question about whether Mr Frediani assaulted Ms Greenwood is referable to the homicide, or referable to the sexual assault, or to both? Were you to ask him on cross-examination whether he committed the sexual assault and burglary, and he were to deny that, then I agree that it would be appropriate cross-examination to question him about the statements he made after his arrest for the sexual assault.' He seems to be championing the prosecution's cause.

'Based upon Mr Bartick's statements to this court, there is a concern as to whether he has denied the homicide and admitted the sexual assault – and accordingly, unless or until there is a denial of the sex crime commission, you are precluded from cross-examining Mr Frediani about post-arrest statements he made to law enforcement concerning the sexual assault.'

Valerie Summers thanks the judge. She will get her opportunity. Bartick looks shaken. He has fallen into a trap. He tries once more to extricate himself: 'For clarification, I believe that Mr Frediani admitting that he entered a plea of no contest is an admission of the offence and I don't believe that Ms Summers should be able to go into more specifics about his culpability – whether he feels bad about it. I think he has admitted that. I think that in response to any question about whether he assaulted Ms Greenwood in 1984, he could answer – and properly so – "I entered a plea of no contest."'

'Your Honour, however, the plea of no contest is a plea of not contesting the charge,' Valerie insists. 'It is not an admission of the underlying facts.' Despite David Bartick's continued protestations, the judge sticks to his decision and rules it goes towards motive, allowing the prosecution some latitude. Bartick asks for a recess, to allow him to look over the morning's transcripts. As the judge leaves the room, I see Bartick and his client talking intensely together, shaking their heads.

Word of the dramas in Court 18 has spread. By the time we reassemble after lunch, a handful of television cameras are vying for the right to film the proceedings, and for the first time, almost every seat in the gallery is filled. Frediani, trailed by his guard, walks back to the witness box.

'On April 7th 1984, did you break into Dr Helena Greenwood's house and force her to orally copulate you?'

Frediani replies, as planned: 'I pled no contest to that charge.' Valerie Summers was never going to let him off that easy.

'Did you force Dr Helena Greenwood to orally copulate you?'

'Isn't saying no contest an admission of guilt?' He is starting to get riled, but she is straight back in his face.

'No. I am asking you directly; did you force Helena Greenwood to orally copulate you in 1984?'

Frediani turns in his seat to address the jury. 'For

the purposes of these proceedings I will admit guilt so we can get past this because it has nothing to do with the murder.'

The judge intercedes: 'Mr Frediani, is your answer yes or no?'

There is a pause.

'It is yes.'

'Did you also break into her house and commit the burglary?'

'Objection.'

'Overruled.'

'Yes.'

'You had seen her testify at your preliminary hearing, did you not?'

'Yes I did.'

'Face to face?'

'Yes.'

'Heard her testify in front of a court as to what you had done to her?'

'Yes I did.'

'Were you worried about the coming trial?'

'Of course it was a concern.'

'Did you feel any remorse over what you had done to her?'

'Objection.'

'Overruled.'

There is another long pause. It is as if everyone in the room is holding their breath. Contrary to what David Bartick had warned in his opening statement, this is a dramatic moment to rival any film or television show. Frediani seems to come to some conclusion. He turns to the jury, his jaw set. 'Yes.'

'Yet you asked Arthur Settlemeyer to concoct a story to say you had been there, looking over the house. Why would you do that if you had actually done this?'

'I believe Arthur was mistaken. When I mentioned to Arthur: we need to come up with my alibi for a year ago – because I was arrested a year later – at the time I had thought I was with him, because it was Saturday night, and Arthur and Jim and I used to go out on Saturday night a lot.' Frediani is back in his well-worn groove.

'So you admit, you asked him to concoct an alibi for you?'

'I wouldn't say concoct.'

'You told him you needed to come up with where you were a year ago, but you didn't ask him that. You asked him to say he had inspected a house for you.'

'As I said before, later on, he knew what my alibi had become and somehow he got confused with one thing and another. I did not tell him that we went to a house together. We never did.'

Valerie jumps on the discrepancy. She is flying by now, shooting out her next question before Frediani has an opportunity to think. 'Are you telling me you had a different alibi for this? Did you have another story that you gave out with respect to this forced oral cop?'

'Well, I've admitted guilt and therefore, I guess my alibi is no longer current.'

'What was your alibi?'

'That I was there.'

'And now your story is that you did it?'

'Objection – argumentative.'

'Sustained.'

'Why would you ask Arthur Settlemeyer to lie?'

'I already stated that I didn't ask him to lie. I wholeheartedly believed that a year prior to my arrest that Arthur, Jim and I were going out on a Saturday night like we always did. It was a month later that I told him about the fingerprint, about going to an open house.'

'You didn't go to an open house at that location, did you?'

'It wasn't exactly an open house. The house was for sale – there was a "For Sale" sign in the front yard. That was my understanding that I must have been there.'

'That has been your story all along, hasn't it, that you were there for an open house? Up until December 15th, when you were interviewed by Laura Heilig. You in fact told her, "Hey I was there at an open house. I had nothing to do with that oral cop." Right?'

'That is what I said. And that is what I said fifteen years ago, when I took the no contest plea and I was allowed to take that plea because I wanted to get past that.'

'But that wasn't true. Was it?'

'For the purposes of these proceedings, I am accepting responsibility. What do you want from me?'

'I want the truth.'

At this moment, Valerie Summers is magnificent. Until now – except when she was playing to the jury – she has come across as rather cold, unemotional, professional yet somehow uninspirational. But in this cross-examination she has proved herself a queen among lawyers. She strides around the courtroom, firing questions at a man she has broken. If Frediani has been anything throughout the proceedings, he has been proud. Now she has ripped that pride into tiny little pieces.

'I have already answered the question.'

'That wasn't the truth, that you had been there at an open house. The truth is that you went in and forced Dr Helena Greenwood to orally copulate you. Isn't that true?'

'Yes, that is true.'

'Then why for all these years have you continued to stick by a lie?'

'Objection. Argumentative.'

'Sustained.'

'You would like this jury to believe that you didn't commit this murder. Is that correct?'

'Yes.'

'And you are a convicted felon?'

'That is correct.'

'You have been convicted of burglary?'

'That is correct.'

'You have been convicted of forced oral copulation, have you not?'

'Yes.'

She asks about the preliminary hearing, about the terms of his bail, about his job. It seems innocuous enough, as if she is taking a breather, but Val the impaler does not need to breathe, and Frediani gets sucked right in.

'Was it a good job?'

'A very good job.'

'Did they know you had been arrested?'

'No they did not.'

'How did you get a leave of absence?'

'Well, I was working there for a few months, and I believe something came out in the paper. Since I had such a good rapport with my boss, he wanted me to still get paid, but he thought it would be best if I took a leave of absence.'

'And in that paid leave of absence, wasn't the arrangement that if you were convicted of these crimes, of course your job would not be waiting for you, but if you were acquitted of these crimes, of course you could have back your job?'

'Well yes. I mean I couldn't do my job from the jail.'

'And during this time, you found out that your girlfriend was pregnant, did you not?'

'Yes.'

'You don't see those kids any more . . .'

'Objection.'

'Sustained.' But the point was made.

'So you were waiting for trial, you've been to the preliminary hearing, your job was waiting for you if you don't get convicted, and your girlfriend is pregnant. I can imagine that was a tremendous amount of stress?'

'Yes.'

'Your next court appearance was scheduled for September 4th, was it not?'

'If you say so.'

'During that time, you were out on bail?'

'Yes.'

'And did you have any conditions to your bail?'

'No.'

'You knew Dr Greenwood was living in southern California, didn't you?'

'Yes, it came out in the pre-trial hearing.'

'And you took a decision on August 15th that you were going to take a drive, did you not?'

'That is correct.'

She goes to a map of California, points out San Mateo, and Valencia, scene of the accident.

'You told your friends you were going to Tahoe, is that correct?'

'Yes.'

'So why change your plan?'

'I just didn't feel like going there any more.'

'So what was your plan?'

'By that time, I didn't have job responsibilities, I knew the trial was coming up, I was going on vacation.

I suddenly realized there was nothing in Tahoe for me to go for. I decided it would be more fun to go to southern California instead.'

'To do what?'

'Basically be a tourist.'

'Where were you going to go in southern California?'

'I had no specific plans, but if I was going to southern California on vacation as any tourist might do, I could go to Disneyland, I could go to Magic Mountain, I could go to the beach. I have never really spent much time in Los Angeles and I wanted to do that.'

'You knew Dr Greenwood was living in southern California and you were out on bail for forcibly orally copulating her, and you decided you were going to drive more than 300 miles to be a tourist?' Her question is straining with incredulity, her voice almost breaking from emotion. Either she cares deeply about this case, or she is an incredibly skilled actor. At this time, I am sure it is the former.

'Were you afraid of being convicted of that offence?'

'Of course it was a concern.'

'You were so afraid that you asked Arthur Settlemeyer to lie for you?'

'I think we already covered that.'

Quietly, scornfully: 'I am asking you a question.' She continued: 'Did you ask anyone else to participate in this lie?'

'No.'

'Did Andrea Goodhart testify that she went with you to this open house?'

'Yes.'

'I want to talk to you about Dr Greenwood's murder. You have heard testimony that your DNA, to the exclusion of everyone else, is under her fingernails, is on her pantyhose, and is on her shoulder. How can you explain that?'

'Well, if you believe the tests . . . which are highly debatable. I have my own theories as to where the DNA may have come from, but I am not so sure they would agree with your theory.'

'Mr Frediani, you would have been humiliated in your community if everybody had known that you had broken into Dr Greenwood's house and forced her to orally copulate you, wouldn't you?'

'Yes, that would be very humiliating.'

'You would have been humiliated in front of your common-law wife, your girlfriend, wouldn't you?'

'It would have been very humiliating, yes.'

'And you would have been embarrassed in front of your family and friends, is that right?'

'Yes, it is very humiliating in front of everybody.'

'Nothing further, Your Honour.'

It has been twenty-four and a half minutes of riveting theatre. I almost feel sorry for Frediani at the end. His defeat is absolute. If it is science that has tapped on his shoulder, it is an attractive dark-haired woman in her late thirties who finishes him off. It is some kind of poetic justice, I suppose.

At his table, David Bartick looks resigned. His chin is in his hands and he is fiddling with his wedding ring, as if for solace, to remind himself that when this is over, he has a wife, two children, a lovely house. He made a tiny slip in his direct examination – more of an ambiguity than a slip – and as a result of one short question, a trial that he might have escaped from with dignity has turned into a debacle. And it is not over yet. He gets up for his redirect examination. It is now a matter of trying to stick small fingers into gaping dykes.

'Mr Frediani, during this time, specifically the week of 22 August 1985, did you ever leave the Bay area?'

'No.'

'Did you ever drive south on I5 on August 20th or 21st?'

'No. Besides, I didn't have a car anyway.'

'Back in 1985, did you know where Del Mar was located?'

'I had heard of the racetrack, and I knew it was in the San Diego area, but not specifically.'

'You worked at Lincoln Properties . . . Was there any information available to you at that time that would allow you to discern addresses of private residences?'

'No, we had nothing of that kind.'

'Did you even attempt to discover the address of Ms Greenwood?'

'No, I had no need to.'

'And the first time that you became aware of her death was in court, is that correct?'

'It came from my attorney – I can't remember whether it was in the courthouse or in his office, but it was definitely from my attorney.'

'It was approximately a week later that you appeared in court in the Bay area?'

'Yes.'

'No further questions.'

Predictably, the prosecution had some.

'You talked about the automobile accident report. Did you have any alibi for the day of the murder?'

'I do.'

'And what is that?'

'OK, when I found out about the murder, my attorney called me and said I had better mark down where I was that day. I had better think real quick, because they might arrest me. If I could not come up with a decent alibi, I could expect them. I remember my car was at the body shop all week. I remember I picked up the car Wednesday night. I remember specifically that Barbara talked to me the very next day after I got the car home – that was how I remembered it was Thursday. I backtracked from that day. I was doing the very same thing I did every other day. I knew she was home that day. I heard her that morning and I assumed she heard me; taking showers, et cetera, et cetera.'

'Now, of course, since you knew this was of dire importance to your future, you had her sign some sort of declaration?'

'Actually, I mentioned this to my attorney, how

unfortunate I didn't do that, because never in my wildest imagination did I think that I would need it. I don't think a common citizen would think that fifteen years later, I would need documentation to say where I was. I knew. I told my attorney. My attorney was in contact with the District Attorney's office. I assumed that, when they didn't come and question me until many years later, that Barbara had verified my story. Because I knew that if she hadn't, I would be arrested.'

'You told the court that you weren't down in Del Mar on August 22 1985, is that right?'

'Yes.'

'But on August 22 1985, you were in fact at the house of Helena Greenwood, is that correct?'

'It is not.'

Valerie walks to the back of the courtroom, picks out the photograph of Helena, resting in the sun in a pair of running shorts.

'Do you recognize this woman?'

'I wouldn't recognize her except for the fact that I know it is Helena Greenwood from this trial.'

'You have no independent recollection of her face?'

'No.'

'You don't remember the face of the woman who you forced to . . .'

'Objection.'

'Sustained.'

'Mr Frediani, on August 22 1985, you in fact drove to San Diego, did you not?'

'No.'

'You in fact waited inside the enclosed patio of 260 23rd Street and waited for her husband to leave, did you not?'

'No.'

'And in fact, when she came out, carrying her papers in her purse, and her yoghurt, and her spoon, you attacked her, didn't you?'

'That is absolutely not true.'

'She fought for her life, didn't she?'

'I wouldn't know. I wasn't there.'

'She scratched you, trying to keep you from killing her, didn't she?'

'If she had scratched me, people would have noticed the scratches, believe me.'

'Nothing further.'

'Mr Frediani, you are excused.'

What can Bartick do from here? Frediani has admitted the sexual assault, for the first time, in court, at his murder trial. With that motive and the DNA evidence, the case is over. I cannot help but think of Mr and Mrs Frediani, sitting here, having to witness this. From what David Bartick has intimated, they have made considerable sacrifices to come up with his fee, cashed in their retirement plans, blown their savings. They have flown across the country, even hired a brand new white Lincoln Continental, for the privilege of watching this. What can they be thinking? As parents, they must not believe it. Yet, in this courtroom, for the past week and a half, they have been force-fed clear evidence that their son is a murderer. How could there be any alternative explanation? Bartick's feelings are written in his drooped shoulders. He is an honourable man; he has done what he could. But it appears that he has run head-first into the immovable barrier of truth. The impossible appears to be the likely explanation after all.

Rian Alworth is on the stand. The ten-year-old of 1985 is now twenty-five, a mother. But she clearly has no sympathy for the Frediani plight. She is annoyed at having been dragged into court against her wishes, and it is obvious that here is a woman-child who is used to getting her wishes. Yes, she admits, she remembers the day of 22 August 1985. She remembers talking to the police officers afterwards. She saw a car in the drive of 260 23rd Street. She thinks it was a black sports car. A Porsche? She is not sure. Bartick asks whether she would like to refresh her memory by reading her original statement. 'No,' she replies.

'Do you remember seeing a person with white hair getting out of that car?'

'I think the person had dark hair,' she replies, glaring at the defence table.

Donna Frediani is crying now, clutching tissues.

Bartick has one more witness – his defence will have taken a single day. Marc Taylor walks to the stand. Bearded, confident, he explains that he is a forensic scientist with his own DNA laboratory. Recently, he has been involved in researching the Profiler Plus system. He talks on and on about inadequate validation studies, the rush to the market, lack of publication in peer-review journals, but it comes across as irrelevant now, hollow in the shadow of Frediani's witness-stand admission. Even Taylor argues with less conviction than he had shown to David Bartick in his laboratory months earlier. What he cannot get away from is that, even if the tests are unreliable, the chance of them producing a false positive to match the profile of the one person now proven to have a motive to murder Helena Greenwood is zero.

'DNA is a miraculous technology in the field of forensic analysis,' he admits, but when the Profiler Plus system is used on mixed samples, particularly, it can cause confused results and errors.

In her cross-examination, Summers cuts straight to the point.

'Is Profiler Plus reliable when used on single-donor samples?'

'Yes.'

The defence rests.

Closing statements are scheduled for the following afternoon. Valerie Summers is in the courtroom early. She appears rested. Her hair is freshly blow-dried. She is wearing a navy suit with a hot pink satin camisole – a hint of triumphalism? She arranges her props: the Spectre of Dead Helena on an easel at one end of the jury box, the mannequin dressed in her torn and bloodstained clothes at the other. As soon as the jury take their seats, she starts, very quietly. We have to strain to hear her: she has our attention. For the next forty minutes, as her voice rises and falls, we do not dare to move: 'What happened to Dr Helena Greenwood is every woman's nightmare . . .'

She leads the jury through the sexual assault. 'She had to tell the police what this man did to her. A trying experience. You think that you can go to the police, that everything will be all right . . . the person will be caught and you will be safe. That is how our system is supposed to work . . . But he wasn't caught for a year, and in that year she moved to the safety of our community, to Del Mar, a place where things like this [she points at the photograph of dead Helena] should never happen. This is our community. Witnesses don't get killed here. But she did. Then on August 22nd, her husband says goodbye to her for the last time. He leaves for work, never to see her alive again. You can imagine the defendant standing there, waiting and watching while her husband leaves, waiting and watching for the opportune time to take care of this witness. We heard him say it: he was going to be humiliated. Can you imagine if his work, his family, his friends, his pregnant girlfriend were to know the monstrous deeds that he had done back there? His life was going to be over. He would have been shamed in front of his family and friends.

'Imagine what he thought for the 500 miles that it took to come down here and commit this crime: the fear, the fear that he was going to be convicted in that courtroom. The trial was a short time away. It had to be done. He had to take care of it. So he waits . . . Imagine Dr Greenwood coming out of her house, with her papers for her meetings, and her lunch, her yoghurt in a baggie, and her spoon to eat her yoghurt, her keys in her hand. And she almost gets to the gate, when she is ambushed by this defendant . . . Imagine the fear in her heart when she saw the man she had testified against only a few months earlier. Imagine in that closed patio what she must have been thinking. She almost made it out. She was right at the gate. She must have known that she had to fight for her life. And she did. She fought so hard for her life that his blood, his body is embedded in her fingernails . . . Imagine her fear as he is taking her head and slamming it, not once but twice, on that latch. Imagine how she must have felt with his hands around her neck. And you heard the doctor say that it would have taken three to five minutes of continuous pressure. She is struggling. Imagine those three to five minutes as her life, slowly, is taken from her. He took her dignity and then he took her life. And we know he did it because he left a little bit of himself behind.'

She is fluent, confident, talks without notes. She stands between the picture and the mannequin like the dominant figure in an avenging triptych. 'The crux of this case is an identity case. The defence is going to get up here and say, "It's not him." But how do we know it's him? That this monster, this sexual predator also is a killer? Well, one, he had a motive.

He told you, begrudgingly, that he committed that offence . . . he finally admitted after fifteen years that he's the one who forced her to orally copulate him. That he's the one who broke into her house in April of 1984 . . . What else did we know? We know, from his mouth, that he knew she lived in San Diego. And we know he was in an accident a week before the murder. He knows at that point that she's down here in southern California. He knows that he is out on bail. He knows that his trial is coming up in a couple of weeks . . .

'How did he track her down? I can't tell you how he found her; whether it was his contacts from the field of being in real estate. I can't tell you whether he followed her home from the prelim. I can't tell you whether or not, knowing that she worked in the field of genetics, he worked it out, called the company where she worked. But we know he found her. And then, August 22nd, he travelled 500 miles down to San Diego . . . And years later, after Helena Greenwood is long gone, and her family has mourned her death, and the defendant is walking around among our community, the archive unit at the Sheriff's Department picks up the case. As their expert, Marc Taylor, said: DNA is the most powerful tool in criminal evidence. DNA has the power to exonerate someone, the power to exclude someone as the perpetrator of an offence. But it also has the tremendous power of pointing the damning finger and saying, no one else, no one else but you.

'And that is what it did in this case. You can see it in fingernail 4–10. You can't recognize it as the defendant, but truth and science recognizes it. And that is subjected to DNA analysis. The newest and most powerful DNA analysis known to forensic science. Science that is used by everyone around the world; science that is used to make life-and-death decisions in the medical field every single day. Science that could either have exonerated this defendant or found him to be the one.

'It found him to be the one . . . not the one in a thousand, million, billion, trillion, but 2.3 quadrillion. And there's six billion people on earth. And his genetic profile is so unique that it's one in 2.3 quadrillion. That is to the exclusion of everyone else walking this earth. Now and ever.

'But killing her wasn't enough. After breaking into her home a year earlier and taking her dignity by forcing her to orally copulate him, that man', she jabs a finger at Frediani, 'came down and killed her. And with her lying there dead, what did he do to her? You know what he did. He took his bloody hands, the hands which had her last life blood mixed with his, his guilty vile blood, and he grabbed her around the ankles – because he left his blood mixed with hers on her ankles – and spread her legs as the final insult. This is every woman's worst nightmare. We should respond with all the force that our justice can muster.'

With one last hate-filled stare at Frediani, Valerie

Summers goes back to her table. The judge calls a brief recess. It is a moment of relief. Then it is the defence's turn. Bartick looks alone suddenly, small in a room full of people who have surely already committed themselves to disbelieve him. Still, he has a job to fulfil.

'The one thing we all agree on is that this is a case regarding circumstantial evidence,' he begins. This time, he cannot start with any statement about how the real-life courtroom can never match up to the fictional one. 'In this case, there is no direct evidence. It is completely based upon circumstances. A circumstantial evidence case is based on the evidence, and what they attempt to do is to stack it together like a house of cards. But the difficulty is, that if one of the cards does not fit properly, or is not wedged properly, the whole stack of cards falls to the ground. Ladies and gentlemen, the prosecution asked you to throw out certain evidence . . . I am requesting the very opposite . . . that you take the time to look at each and every piece of evidence that has been submitted . . . and the reason why, is that I am confident that once you have looked at each piece of evidence, and had the opportunity to analyse it, you will clearly see that Mr Frediani is not guilty of these charges.

'This is like a jigsaw puzzle, and what the prosecution has tried to do is fit all the pieces together.' Bartick had clearly decided that one metaphor was too few. 'In this case, we not only have pieces that simply do not match, which I contend to you is the reason why this case took fifteen years without even the issue of an arrest warrant . . . [but] if you look at each and every piece of evidence, you will also see that this case is missing evidence that would point to Mr Frediani. For that reason, ladies and gentlemen, he is simply not guilty of this offence.'

Bartick has a display board, which he props on to the easel until recently used to hold Helena's picture. 'The prosecution has the burden of proving this case beyond reasonable doubt. It accepted that responsibility and it is your obligation to hold them to it. But this case is full of reasonable doubt. I have outlined here nine different areas of doubt,' he points at his board. 'Each one of these is enough to acquit Mr Frediani.'

By the number one, he has written: 'No scratch marks on Mr Frediani.' At the time the murder was committed, he contends, there was no question that his client was the prime suspect. 'How come there were no witnesses who had the opportunity to observe any kind of scratches, any abrasions on Mr Frediani? We know for a fact that the authorities interviewed many people straight after this incident, people very close to Mr Frediani and I assure you that Mr Frediani himself was under very close surveillance.' But no one had mentioned scratches – at least in court.

Point two: 'Footprint found, 6½ inches.' Clearly not Frediani's, and not the victim's either. 'Does it make sense that this footprint, this very important piece of evidence does not match Mr Frediani?' Bartick asks.

Three: 'Carlton cigarette packet.' Bartick calls it 'a mysterious item that does not fit'. Why was it there? Why was it fingerprinted if it wasn't part of the crime scene, as Decker had suggested. Why were the fingerprints entered into the computer? Why was it preserved for so many years?

Four: 'Print card of Donald Van Ness.' Who? Why had his print card been kept as evidence for fifteen years?

Five: 'Fingernail clippings.' Mary Pierson originally testified that she had put them in a coin envelope or paper bindle at the time of the autopsy, but when Laura Heilig had opened the evidence bag more than a decade later, she found them in plastic containers, and dated the day of the homicide, and not the day they were collected. 'This is very suspicious. Something is not right with this,' Bartick said, in a perhaps conscious echo of criminalist Henry Lee's words at the O. J. Simpson trial.

Six: 'There is also reasonable doubt that Mr Frediani knew where Ms Greenwood lived. This is a very important fact because they are unable to place Mr Frediani in southern California. The People have produced no evidence at all that Mr Frediani was in the area that week.'

Seven: Bartick pointed at his board. 'How would he have got to the Del Mar area? His vehicle was disabled and the People were unable to demonstrate how he could have come down to San Diego, and the reason they could not do that was because he was not here.'

His eighth 'missing piece' related to the absence of Frediani's fingerprints at the crime scene. Many prints had been found there, but none matched the defendant's. 'The prosecution say it was because he must have worn gloves. But there was also testimony about his blood being on the clothing. If he had worn gloves, then how could his blood have got on the clothing? It doesn't make sense. It simply doesn't make sense.'

Bartick had purposely missed his ninth – and penultimate – point off his list. He had done so, he explains, because it shouldn't be there. 'The DNA evidence should not even be considered by you. As my expert testified, I am not trying to demonstrate that DNA is not a good science. My contention to you – supported by many different individuals – is that DNA does not apply to *this* case. This Profiler Plus test kit is what was on trial here. The People asked you to rely on this test kit, which scientists themselves fail to agree is scientifically valid.' The kit, he reiterates, pronouncing the word from the edge of his front teeth, as if too frivolous for his mouth, was only disseminated to the community in 1999. It consisted of three test kits, combined into a 'cocktail'. Bartick takes a jug of water and pours first one glass, which turns yellow to represent the original yellow kit, then another which turns green, and a third, blue. Then he pours each glass back into the jug, which turns an indefinable green colour. 'No one knows what is in them – but the corporation asks us to trust them. And what they are using to prove that it works is that one lab using this test kit will get the same results as another lab. But because the results are consistent does not mean that it is accurate typing. The prosecution is asking you to accept in this case scientific evidence, but what I am asking you to consider is whether it is appropriate for you to accept its reliability before scientists themselves do. Their case relies on this "cocktail" and yet they will not tell you what is in this "cocktail" or how it does its work. They ask you to trust this machine called the 310 Genetic Analyzer and we don't even know the software. Ladies and gentlemen, that is not science. Are we going to take this science that has not even been validated and use it to convict Mr Frediani? Because that is all the People have.'

He turns back to the board for his tenth point: the mysterious third person's DNA which was found by Ed Blake under one of the fingernails. To whom did it belong? The owner of the footprints? Was she the murderer?

'Ladies and gentlemen, you heard from Mr Frediani himself. He did not have to testify, but he wanted to face each and every one of you, to tell each and every one of you that in fact he did not commit this horrendous offence. That he was at home – and apparently there's no indication that he wasn't. He sat on the stand and was forthright and honest with you. He admitted some things that are difficult and also things that he admitted years ago. I want you to use your common sense. The People tell you the reason why Ms Greenwood was killed was because Mr Frediani did not want to embarrass his friends or family, and Mr Frediani was concerned about losing his job. Now, does that make sense to you? Is that a motive for murder?

'You heard that at the preliminary hearing, she indicated that she really couldn't identify him. Ladies and gentlemen, her testimony was really not that damaging. Does it make sense that an individual of Mr Frediani's stature, his intelligence, to avoid the shame, to avoid losing his job, would have murdered this woman? It simply does not make sense.

'I am asking you to look at this case with common sense, to look at every piece of evidence, look to see which pieces fit – and which do not. I am confident at the conclusion of that evidence, you will realize that Mr Frediani did not commit this horrendous offence. The People have not proven their case and he should be found not guilty of each and every charge, and each and every allegation.'

His voice rises at the end. Sitting behind the defence table, Mr Frediani senior grabs his wife's arms, and she turns to kiss his shoulder. They could not be holding out much hope, but at least Bartick has given them a crack of possibility on which to focus. He has done a solid job, mustered the fragments at his disposal and presented his collage clearly and fluently. He must have known there was not much he could have done; known from the start. But he has done what he could, and that was all he could do. There was only Valerie Summers' final reply to get through and then it would be over, but for the verdict.

She is predictably efficient and professional. One by one, she picks up Bartick's points, then neutralizes them, as if killing mosquitoes with a giant can of Doom. 'Counsel says we are unable to place him in southern California. Well, yes we are. I am able to place him in southern California from August 22 1985 until today. Because he is still here. His blood, his cells, his body, his unique mix of his mother and his father is still here, and it's been here ever since he squeezed the life out of Helena Greenwood . . .

'The fact that there are no prints left . . . is inculpatory to this defendant. Because he was not going to let himself get caught for the same thing again . . . He didn't know that science was going to catch up with him. There was no way for him to know that in 2000 the human genome would be completely mapped. There was no way to know we could exclude someone to the exclusion of everyone else . . .

'Lastly he attacked the science . . . What's the mystery about this? Again I would ask you, how many of us use a camera? How many of you know the emulsion for a film? Of course not. Can you still use a camera? Same thing . . . Let's say you have a doubt about that; you say maybe the science isn't quite ready. So was it done right in this case? Well, it didn't pick any of us out. The defendant's genetic profile was done by Cellmark on the other side of the country, and done from a sample from the Department of Justice lab that was got from the defendant years and years ago. And then later, when Cellmark does another test with a current sample, it doesn't come up with a different result . . . it comes up with a match on each and every marker. And we know that the unique array of the defendant's markers leads to the exclusion of everybody else . . . Well, that's validating. And then on the other side of the country, the original sample, the small fingernail scraping, is analysed. It doesn't come up with your DNA . . . it comes up with one person's: that man's,' she points the accusing finger at Frediani again, 'the man who has the motive to kill her . . . And for defence counsel to say he admitted it a long time ago is simply not true: that's the first time he has ever said he broke in her house. That's the first time he's ever said, "Yes, I made her orally copulate me."

'There is no doubt in this case . . . He travelled 500 miles to wait in her patio. Then he came up, then he grabbed her, then he beat her, he got her down on the ground, he banged her head twice on that gate. Then she got up – because there was blood on the bottom of her shoes – and she fought for her life. And then he put his hands around her throat and squeezed every last breath out of her. And he got away with it; got away with it until now. Thank you.'

20

The jury was given the weekend off before being sent into a windowless room to decide Paul Frediani's future. It must have been a strange couple of days for them: they were still forbidden from discussing the case with each other or their families. Yet every day for the past two weeks, they had lived with it, hour after hour, testimony after testimony. For most, it was the first time they had been forced to consider such gruesome reality, the closest they had come to violent death. For the Frediani family, it must have been hell.

With Sydney Greenwood back in England, Roger dead, it was like the bride's side of the church was empty, while across the aisle, the Fredianis loomed live and anguished in our daily presence. It was impossible to escape the pathos of their situation. The last weekend, at least, gave them time to spend with their son in Vista jail. They did not know when they would be able to see him again.

We are all there early on Monday morning. The jury listens to the judge instruct them of their duties, before sending them off to deliberate. There is nothing for us to do, but wait for their verdict. The Frediani parents sit in the corridor, clutching their privacy to them. Donna is not with them. The handful of regular reporters hang around the coffee machine, exchanging case gossip. Alex Roth, the journalist who wrote the original story in the *San Diego Union Tribune*, received a threatening letter two weeks after his article appeared. He called in the FBI, who fingerprinted the letter, but found no matches. Then, this morning, Kelly Niknijad from the local wire service received a pager message. It was just three figures: 187, the police code for homicide. There was no phone number attached. She is feeling a little shaken. Onell Soto, who took over Roth's beat of the north county courthouse, is in regular contact with the *Southampton Echo*, Sydney Greenwood's local paper; a journalist there has promised Soto he will drive straight over to the old man's house to get his reaction upon hearing the verdict. Fred Dickey, whose piece in the *Los Angeles Times Magazine* set me off on this ride, confides that he is talking to a Hollywood agent about writing a screenplay based on the Helena Greenwood story. As soon as this is over he is going to approach Laura Heilig and ask for the exclusive rights to her life story.

Around mid-morning, a note is sent out from the jury room asking for Marc Taylor's testimony to be read back to them. What could that mean? Had the jury been convinced by the defence theories?

By lunch, still no verdict. We walk across the road to a hamburger restaurant. The jury are sitting around a big table in the corner. I stop to say hello as I pass, but I get no clue from their expressions, and they do not seem to have lost their appetites.

At 3.30 in the afternoon, they announce they have reached their decision. I am waiting as they file from their deliberation room into the glass-walled corridor in front of Courtroom 18. As they walk past the tidily dressed couple in their early seventies – waiting for what is probably the most momentous event in their lives – they seem relaxed. They are chatting amongst themselves, a couple are laughing. Only one, a middle-aged blonde woman, juror 7, the former nursing teacher, looks as if she has been crying.

We are called into court. The Frediani parents are first through the door, Mrs Frediani leaning heavily on a metal cane. They take their usual places behind the defence table, and sit silently, holding hands and staring straight ahead. A host of reporters from every local paper and TV station, a phalanx of deputy DAs from their fifth-floor offices and various onlookers file in. The gallery is full. Paul Frediani enters, blowing out his cheeks. He nods at his parents, sits down in his chair for the last time.

The jurors come in through the back door. None look at the defendant as he stands facing them. The judge asks if they have elected a foreman. Juror 10 puts up his hand. The jury have put their faith in a fire-fighter, a man of action. 'Has the jury reached a verdict?'

'We have, Your Honour.'

The bailiff walks across the courtroom, takes a

piece of paper from the foreman and hands it to the judge's clerk. She reads out the verdict.

'We find Mr Frediani guilty of murder in the first degree. We find the special circumstance of killing a witness to a crime to be true.'

Bartick is asked if he would like the jury polled. He says yes. One after the other, they repeat the damning word: guilty, guilty, guilty, guilty, guilty, guilty, guilty, guilty, guilty, guilty, guilty, guilty – like a volley of shots from a disciplined firing squad. Paul Frediani sits back in his chair, his right leg hooked over his left knee, his hands apparently relaxed. Behind him, his father is crying openly. The verdict is recorded, stamped, the sentencing date set. Frediani is led away. As his parents, still weeping, leave the courtroom, the predatory video cameras fall on them, despite David Bartick's best attempts to prevent them.

In the car park, I run into Laura Heilig. She seems relieved more than anything. 'I was so happy to hear him admit to the sexual assault,' she says. 'To hear him say that brought tears to my eyes.' We make a plan to talk the next morning. 'I want to telephone Mr Greenwood first thing. I want to tell him that his daughter's killer will never get out of jail.'

Later that evening, my phone rings. It is Sydney Greenwood's neighbour. 'I just wanted to find out what happened,' he says. 'We're here with Sydney and I can't sleep.' I tell him the verdict. 'Thank you. I will pass on the news to Sydney, although I don't know if he will be able to take it in. He is very weak.' As I put down the phone, I realize that it is 3 o'clock in the morning in England.

The next day, I find out that Sydney Greenwood died – sixteen hours after he heard the verdict. The neighbour told him, and the old man nodded. He gave no comment. That evening he passed away in his sleep. I cannot believe it. I knew he was ill, I knew he wanted to hang on to see the resolution of the case, but I did not realize just how much effort that was. I wish I could have seen him once more; talked him through the case; explained how Helena's science had reached out and touched her killer. I hope that learning the verdict will let him rest in some measure of peace. I cannot help but remember his words the last time we met: 'It has haunted me for too long. I've been told over and over to forget it. It's not been easy, and now I am determined to see it through . . .'

That should have been it. It would have been in crime fiction. Case closed. Neat ending – an old man receives his dying wish. Triumph of the forces of good over evil. I could go home to England, write up the story, move on to the next thing. But I realize I can't. It isn't the end for me: I have become so involved that I cannot now leave it behind; the verdict provides no resolution. Sydney Greenwood died with his neighbour at his bedside. It should have been his daughter, his family; it should not have been a murder trial that kept him going through the last decade and a half of his life. The Fredianis gave their son everything they could; they should not have to live in this shame and sorrow for the rest of their lives. It has become clear that this story is about more than forensic science and the final slamming of a judge's gavel – it is about human make-up and the effects of one person's actions on a host of others. I am one of those others, and now I need to find out more, to talk about it with the people who have shared the journey.

At her desk on the second floor of the Sheriff's Department Laura Heilig has heard about Sydney's death and is most upset. 'I knew Mr Greenwood was ill, but I sure feel bad that he died,' she says. 'It's sad everything had to end like this. I just pray he found some comfort in knowing that the case was done before he died. It would have been terrible if he had died before the verdict had come in – oh, that would have been worse.

'We might have caught the killer, but that will never bring his daughter back. Look at what he has lost: sixteen years with his only child, the possibility of grandchildren. Nothing can make up for that. I called Valerie as soon as I heard and she was in tears. She is real upset about it too.'

We talk about the trial, about her investigation, how she got involved in police work in the first place. Occasionally, she checks something in one of the oversize white ring binders filled with case notes and clearly labelled Greenwood I, II, III and IV. This is the 'murder book'. It contains every police report and interview in the Frediani sexual assault and murder cases. After sentencing, she says I can come and look through it.

From their desks, Vic and Curt occasionally interrupt, tease her. It is clear that she is a much-loved member of the team. 'She's already had some phone calls from Hollywood,' Vic says. 'Go on, Laura, tell her who you want to play you in a movie.'

'Pamela Lee Anderson.' We all laugh. Laura Heilig may be blonde, but her chest measurements are not quite up to it. And she is not prepared to sell her life story. She is quietly proud of the job she has done, but does not think she should benefit financially from it – beyond what she earns. It is plain to see that here is a woman who really believes in her work; that there is a line between good and evil, and that those who do foul deeds should be punished for them. She clearly feels that Frediani has earned every day of his punishment.

'When I was testifying on the stand, I looked over at him, and he was just glaring at me with that cold stare. I remember feeling really uncomfortable. This guy looks like a killer. I mean you look at him and his eyes, and his whole manner is just killer.'

The jury foreman, juror 10, agrees with her assessment when we meet for breakfast the following morning. He has just finished the night shift at his fire station, but is pleased to be back in his familiar world. 'I think it was a worthwhile experience, though. All twelve jurors agreed that it had been good for us to learn about what's going on, especially in DNA. We all followed the DNA evidence, no problem.'

'Why did you ask for Marc Taylor's testimony to be reread?'

'Well, we immediately discounted Paul Frediani's testimony – he had been proved to be a liar. So it was really all about the DNA. Marc Taylor was the only other bit of the defence case. I was pretty sure that somewhere he had said that for single donor samples, the Profiler Plus kit was accurate, but I wanted to hear it again to be certain. And sure enough, there was the question from Valerie Summers: "Do you have a problem with a single source sample?" and Taylor's answer: "No." After we heard that, I turned to the rest of the jurors and said, "I think I heard him give up all hope that David Bartick was trying to plant." I was 99 per cent sure of his guilt before then, and after the rereading, 100 per cent.

'I think we all knew. I had a feeling right off that if I had polled the jury at 9.15–9.30, we would have had a unanimous guilty vote. But we wanted to make absolutely sure that we weren't giving them any basis for mistrial. We didn't know whether it was a death penalty case. And we had a lively and intelligent discussion. We all contributed – everyone had something to say, and at the end of the deliberations, juror 8 turned around all of the evidence pictures except the one of Helena Greenwood looking alive and happy. We propped it up at the end of the table, like a thirteenth juror, and contemplated it. That was how we thought she should be remembered.'

Almost a year earlier, I had written to David Bartick, asking whether – and if so, how – I might contact his client. He had replied that it was impossible until after trial, but that he would let Frediani know what I was up to. The day after the verdict, I ask again. Now, more than ever, I want to meet the man who has caused this maelstrom. Science may have fingered him as Helena Greenwood's killer, but it gives no clue as to motive. Despite watching him every day for three weeks, hearing his own testimony seal his guilt, I still find Paul Frediani an enigma. Why did a man who apparently had so much, feel the need to creep around in the middle of the night seeking illicit sexual thrills? Why had an intelligent person risked throwing his life away to avoid serving his due time in prison? The forensic use of DNA could not begin to answer these questions, but DNA goes way beyond its forensic use.

Bartick says that he would not advise Frediani to talk to me, but that he is in Vista jail, and there is nothing to stop me turning up under my own steam. I take it as an invitation.

Visiting hours are Monday, Wednesday and Friday afternoons. I quickly learn the drill. You turn up at the courthouse an hour early, fill in a form stating your name and relationship to the prisoner (I put 'acquaintance' – I was worried that if I put 'none', they wouldn't let me in), then you sit on a plastic chair anchored to the floor and wait until it is time. There are ten people waiting with me, two women with a tiny baby, an aged biker, a wizened couple talking quietly in Spanish; mothers, fathers, wives, girlfriends, children. They have all been here before. As the time approaches, they form into a queue, there is a clunking sound, and we are let through. 'Follow the blue line,' the woman at reception says. 'Have a nice visit.'

I am nervous. People I have spoken to think I am odd, or just plain crazy to want to meet a convicted murderer. They do not understand why I feel the need to sit down with him, to try to get to know him. I am not entirely sure myself. At this moment, despite the thick walls and guards, I am scared. I have no idea what to expect, how he will react to me. I follow the other relatives and friends along lino corridors, up a staircase and into a crescent-shaped room. The inside curve is lined with thick plexi-glass; beyond, a glass-walled room: twelve plastic seats facing a matching set on the other side. The prisoners file in, dressed in identical navy cotton pyjamas.

Frediani is the first, and the tallest. He sees me, gives a curt nod and sits down. We both pick up our telephone receivers. I introduce myself, ask if he knows what I am doing. He shrugs. 'A book?'

'Do you want to ask me any questions first?'

'Have you talked to my witnesses, the girls?'

'No, not yet,' I reply.

'Then I have nothing to ask, but fire away if you want.'

He starts out antagonistic, belligerent even. He is making me work to gain his confidence, but once I pass some unspoken test, he warms to his theme: it's a frame-up. Look at the witnesses, he says, everyone changed their story: Barbara Kenney knew he was at home that day; Art Settlemeyer had got it all wrong; Rian Alworth had said at the time she had seen a white-haired person getting out of the Porsche; the Alton girls had mysteriously left town. That phrase they all kept repeating like DA-trained parrots: 'I have no independent recollection.' And Marc Taylor; he had muted his trumpet once he got on the stand.

Then we speak of other things – of his travels to England, his children, how awful he feels for his parents and what they have had to go through. He smiles, starts joking, and it is as if we are sitting across a table in an empty café, with less than an hour to talk about a lifetime. It is probably the most intense conversation I have ever had: I cannot take notes and have to concentrate on every word he says, every nuance and expression. I do not know whether he will talk to me again. But I sense a slight shift in the balance of the conversation: he is trying to win me over.

'I expected a hung jury, at the worst. After David Bartick's closing arguments, I thought I would be acquitted. I was very surprised.' I do not believe him. He feels sorry for Bartick; he worked hard on the case, but nothing went right for him. He played straight all the way, always took the high road.

The siren sounds. There is another deep, mechanical clank, the sign for the prisoners to leave. As I get up, he says, casually, 'You can come by again, if you want to.' It is as if he is asking me to drop round to his house for a drink. And then he files out with the other prisoners. As we leave the room, the navy pyjama-ed men stand to attention, facing us from the other side of a glass wall, a wall separating freedom from imprisonment, their hands jammed into their trousers, in place of pockets. Frediani is looking at me, and as I turn to leave, he gives a slight grin.

I want to talk to him more. I do not feel as if any of my questions have been answered. I find him intriguing, compelling even, but how much of that is due to our strange situation, I cannot tell. In another universe, I can imagine meeting this man, this murderer, around a dinner table. He is smart, funny, tells a good story. Yet, I can also imagine the terror of his rage: up close, his bulk is almost stifling and there is an undeniable strength in his hands. From time to time, a cold shroud flits across his eyes.

The next day, I have lunch with David Bartick. He is still shocked at the way the trial had unfolded, at how his case had crumbled at every turn. Everything that could possibly have gone wrong went wrong: witnesses did not say what he thought they would, he had been prevented from mentioning the phone call, the no contest plea. Then Valerie Summers had wrong-footed Frediani on the stand. And that had shattered his prepared defence.

'I always felt that attacking the technology was the strongest argument we had. The only other way I could see to overcome this type of evidence would have been to say it was planted. But that's a very difficult argument to make to a jury unless you have some kind of suspicious chain of custody, or something else you can document to show it is a possibility.' I tell him that is what Paul Frediani is claiming. 'I would imagine he is second guessing, thinking that at this point we should have gone with the planting. He is probably right: the DOJ has had his DNA since 1989. But that's just something I am going to have to live with; whether I made the right tactical decision regarding the defence. I will never know whether it might have made a difference to the outcome.'

My second visit to Vista jail is less tense. Frediani is warmer, apologizes for being rude when we first met; he was feeling a bit raw about the way his parents had been treated by the media at the trial, and didn't know whether I was one of the pack. He would like to write a book, a thriller loosely based on his experiences, but with a twist at the end. 'A happy ending?' I ask. He laughs. 'You had better believe it!'

'I could write a hundred pages just about my relationship with Andrea.' He explains how she had pursued him until he eventually asked her out, her habitual lying, how the relationship was faltering when she announced she was pregnant. 'And then of course, I wanted to do the right thing.' He has painted a picture of events far removed from what was related in three trials. It is as if it is most important for him to try to charm me on to his side, impress me with his powers of attraction. He has as much as admitted again that the alibi for the sexual assault was contrived.

When he first arrived at Vista jail, he was treated as a normal prisoner, he tells me, and housed with the main body of inmates. 'But then I got into a minor fight in June. This guy threw a kung fu kick and missed. I put him in a bear hug, but he got a hand free and was trying to claw at my face. I shook him off, but not before he caught part of my upper lip and put four deep, long gorges inside my lower lip. It didn't dawn on me then, but at the time, we had been fighting with the DA to turn over the DNA evidence. This guy was a renowned jailhouse snitch and after he scratched me, he immediately went to the cops saying he fell and hurt his shoulder and needed to go to the medical clinic. Now, he was facing fifteen years and was actively looking for his pot of gold. He knew more about my case than I did. It was well known from the investigation papers that the DNA evidence was questionable as to amounts remaining. And then suddenly, they find my DNA on the pantyhose and on the dress, and there's plenty to go around. If that guy wasn't put up to it, he planned it on his own. He was not trying to scratch me for nothing.'

Over the next month, I see Frediani twice-weekly. I am his only visitor. Each time it becomes easier, less nerve-racking. I begin to recognize some of the other regulars, and feel almost like an old hand at visiting time; once I explain to another lady how the system works. When I was signing in, beside the box which asked for 'relationship with prisoner' I still wrote 'acquaintance', but while I was talking to him, I rarely thought of the reason he was there, and after the first couple of visits, we didn't talk about the assault or murder.

Instead, he told me about his friends, his relationships, his family and childhood; what music he likes, his favourite films, restaurants, countries. One time, I asked why, if he hadn't done it, did he think this was happening to him. 'It is the curse of Cris's mother,' he replied, partly seriously. 'She said she would destroy my life, and she has.' He told me stories of his time in prison after the sexual assault, what it was like to get out and think you have a second chance and how he faces the future. I asked what he misses most: and he said hanging out with Kathy Clark, his closest friend, the mystery blonde who had turned up in court and fallen asleep during Gary Harmor's testimony. 'We would go out for cocktails, go shopping together, and when she'd had a row with her old boyfriend, she would come round late at night in her pyjamas and we would watch videos.'

Frediani would talk, I would listen, and then I would go back to our pretty seaside cottage in

Del Mar, to my husband and son, and the piles of trial transcripts and incriminating evidence that I had amassed, and I would be reminded once more what a ghastly thing he had done. It was too easy, seeing him the whole time, thinking about the reality of life in prison without the possibility of parole – a sentence without hope, an existence I could not imagine – to forget about Helena Greenwood, his victim.

On 19 March 2001, Frediani was back in Judge Einhorn's court for sentencing. This time, there was no element of suspense, only verbal humiliation to endure. The judge called Helena Greenwood 'perhaps the most blameless victim' he had ever known. 'The cold, vicious and senseless attack on her . . . is a shock to this community,' he said. 'As Mr Frediani has shown no mercy on Ms Greenwood, this community and this court will show no mercy on you.' He pronounced the predetermined sentence: life without the possibility of parole. Frediani was led from the courtroom without having uttered a word.

On one wall of Valerie Summers' corner office, beside a photograph of her son, hangs a certificate from the County of San Diego, in recognition of her work. She was voted Outstanding Prosecutor of the Year by the local DA's Association, for her performance in the Frediani case. But now it's on to new pastures; she is preparing for a double child murder trial, in which the killer was caught by a random hit on the DNA database.

Frediani had been a big case for her, and an education. It was the first she had prosecuted which relied, almost exclusively, on DNA. 'It's one thing to say to a jury, "And on top of all those eye-witnesses, I've got DNA," and quite another to say, "We only know he did it because of DNA." This case would never have been prosecuted if the DNA had not been found.

'One of the most extraordinary aspects of this case was the timing; it happened too late for Sydney Greenwood to come out and witness the trial, too late for Roger Franklin to know. But if it had been any earlier, we would not have had the DNA . . . DNA has been an exciting forensic application for some time, and it would have been very easy for a police officer to have looked at the file and got excited about it a year too early, before STRs were available. Then they might have sent it off for testing and it would have all been consumed in the process without giving us the figures we needed. He would never have been caught. That's just good luck.'

Frediani's witness-stand confession to the sexual assault was more than she had hoped for. 'Why would you expect an admission from a man who has denied it for so long? Yes, it felt good. But I still walked out of that courtroom kicking myself, because the one question I wished I had asked was "Why? Why did you sexually assault her?" I don't think I would have got a good answer to that, but it eats at me that I didn't ask.'

I go back to see Laura Heilig at her office, to look through her files. Since the Frediani trial, the archive unit's place in the homicide department has been assured, with Laura Heilig as its pin-up girl. I congratulate her on a TV appearance.

'You know, a strange thing happened just after that programme,' Laura tells me. 'A woman rings up. Her name is . . . hang on, I have the report in my files.' She gets out Greenwood IV, turns to the back of the ring binder. 'Oh yes, her name is Kathleen Fischer. She is a vice-president of the trust department of a big bank down here, she's been there for fourteen years. She says she had seen the programme the night before, and recognized Mr Frediani. She used to have a condo at the same George Street complex where he lived at the time of the assault. He wasn't a real close friend of hers, but she knew him as one of the group who hung out by the pool. In November 1984, she moved down to San Diego. She didn't leave her new address with anyone at George Street . . . Then in August 1985, on a weekday morning – she doesn't know the exact date – the phone rang. It was Paul Frediani. She was surprised. "How did you get my number?" she asked him. He said through directory assistance. You're lucky, she said, because I should have been at work, but stayed at home as I wasn't feeling too good. Apparently he wasn't sounding great either. He told her he had planned to come to San

Diego for a vacation, but had got in a traffic accident. He had been up all night working on his car and wanted to come by for a shower and clean-up. She thought it was odd, but said, "Sure."

'When he showed up, he was very agitated and upset. He was perspiring profusely and wearing a white muscle shirt – like a singlet – covered in dirt and grass. They talked for a few minutes, then he had a shower and changed into clean clothes he brought in from his car. He was driving his white BMW, which she recognized. There was damage on one of the quarter panels, which was bent under. He told her that he had been trying to pry it up so as to drive it, and hadn't slept all night. She offered him something to eat, but he refused, saying he just wanted to get home.'

If Fischer's story is true, this is the first time anyone has placed Frediani in San Diego around the time of the murder. It shows him to have lied again in court, to have lied to me.

I spend the rest of the day reading the murder book. In the midst of the catalogue of evidence, I scan what looks like a routine letter from the Department of Justice to Laura Heilig. I am about to turn the page, when something odd catches my attention. I reread the letter more carefully.

'This is in response to your request to provide information relating to the collection, control and disposition of any sample that this laboratory received from David Paul Frediani . . . The Genetic Marker

Card received with this sample indicated that this blood had been drawn from the subject . . . on July 12, 1989 . . . Examination of this sample on January 11, 2000, found it to consist of a single discrete stain deposited on a piece of cloth with 19 other similar stains. This represents the normal manner in which blood samples were processed and stored (frozen) at the time this sample was received. Visual examination of a photograph taken on or about September 5, 1997, of the stain . . . revealed that approximately 25 per cent of the stain had been removed. No records were located detailing the circumstances associated with this removal . . .'

I read to the end, a list of people who had had access to the sample, but nowhere did it mention the missing 25 per cent. I read it again. I copy it down. It seems odd, but the possible implications do not dawn on me immediately. I was just keen to get through the entire murder book before Laura had to leave the office. On the drive back to my hotel, I ask her about it. 'Yes, it was a little strange,' she says. 'I tried to find out what had happened, but they had no paperwork. They said it was probably used in routine staff training.'

That night, I think about the letter. For a committed conspiracy theorist, it provided a theory by which Frediani's DNA could have been found among Helena Greenwood's fingernails. Placed on one side of a scale, with the evidence against Frediani on the other, it would be flung high into the air. But still, it fits the story he gave during his interrogation and has always repeated:

'As far as DNA evidence, oh, I'm sure you've got some DNA evidence that probably points to me. Where you got it, how you got it, that's a whole different matter. I've been in your custody for a long time.'

'Why would we want to plant evidence?'

'To close the case.'

The conspiracy theorist could then explain the presence of Frediani's DNA found on the pantyhose and blue jacket, and the mixed samples found by Blake on the fingernails: the jailhouse attack by the suspicious snitch-type character. It had taken place in June 2000; Englert had come down to San Diego at the end of September, and the further samples only sent to Blake and Seri following that. These, too, could have been Frediani's all along, from the cuts inside his mouth inflicted on purpose during a jailhouse brawl? It is obviously fantastical. Yet, 'when you have eliminated the impossible whatever remains, *however improbable*, must be the truth.' It is the only conceivable explanation for Frediani's innocence. What would Barry Scheck have done with a letter like that at the O. J. trial?

For Professor Bill Thompson, it has wider implications. 'If nothing else, the "missing" portion of the database sample will be of interest to civil libertarians,' he says. 'The government has repeatedly assured the civil rights community that database samples will be held in a secure manner and used only for criminal identification purposes. There is great concern, as you know, about database samples being used for other forms of genetic research . . . It is disturbing that portions of genetic samples in a government database can go missing with no record of their whereabouts.'

It wouldn't have changed the outcome of this trial: Paul Frediani had been proven guilty beyond reasonable doubt, and this was not, by most standards, reasonable. I could not believe that Laura was in any way complicit and I'm sure the jury would not have either. But still . . . it was a loose link in the chain of events that led to Frediani's conviction. The jury should, I believe, have had the opportunity to consider its implications, as it should have been told about the still mysterious and threatening phone call to Helena Greenwood's successor at Gen-Probe. Equally, they should have had the chance to hear Kathleen Fischer's testimony about Frediani's presence in San Diego in August 1985. In an ideal world, there would be no imponderables in the judicial arena: the facts, the witnesses, the evidence would be laid out before the deciding panel. And money would play no part – in the choice of the lawyers the defendant could afford, or in the number and ability of expert witnesses the defence could hire. Justice would be perfect, transparent.

I do not know what to do about this letter from the DOJ. I am surprised that it wasn't used by the defence in court. I am excited to have found this potentially key piece of evidence, but unsure as to how to proceed. My involvement in the story thus far is incidental, not material. If this is thrown into the judicial arena, what effect will it have? Might it improve Frediani's chances of a successful appeal – it is the kind of technicality that I have seen upend the scales on numerous television courtroom dramas? I ask David Bartick about the DOJ's letter. He says he does not recall it, but will check through his files to see if it is there. Either way, he agrees it could have an impact on Frediani's appeal. 'If I missed it, then it could count towards a reversal on grounds of incompetent representation,' he says. 'If I find it, I will have no hesitation in sending it off to the appellate attorney.' We do not even voice the implications of the letter not being in his files.

Some weeks later, he calls. 'I have the letter,' he says. 'It is in my files, with some notations I made at the time on it . . . In retrospect, I certainly could not have done any worse had I elected to utilize this "conspiracy" theory. However, I was worried that to argue that the DOJ, or other governmental agents, would have clandestinely contaminated the fingernails (yet written about the missing stain in the letter) was beyond reasonable comprehension. Therefore, I felt that the better strategy was to attack the science, and ask the jury to use a common-sense approach that there were no eye-witnesses or other "real" evidence to substantiate the People's case.

'. . . Needless to say, I now have sleepless nights as

I ponder what the outcome may have been if I would have taken a different approach. In an effort to fully preserve and protect Frediani's appellate rights, I have discussed this matter with appellate counsel. Therefore, she will have an opportunity to address this matter by means of a writ, if she so believes that it is worthy of an ineffective counsel claim.'

Valerie Summers was ready for a conspiracy theory defence. She had designated several witnesses from the DOJ. 'Training purposes', they would have said.

I had written to Paul Frediani about the DOJ letter. 'Seems to me that it is and should be considered significant. Funny how it wasn't caught before . . .' That was all he had to say. He seemed more interested in my question about when he had last seen Kathleen Fischer. 'The name doesn't really ring a bell. I might recall it if you provide more info. Was she in the pile of police interviews?' he asked. 'I'm eager to hear back, as obviously this person gives you unanswered questions . . . She might be this girl who was friends of a flight attendant I slept with a couple of times. If so, then I don't remember the last time I saw her . . . How is she important?'

His letter turns to news of Corcoran, the Iraq situation, US defence policy: 'I feel a great sense of frustration rotting away in prison. I'd rather be sitting on a mountain in Afghanistan, freezing my butt off looking for Osama than be here doing nothing. Sort of like the Dirty Dozen.'

Later, he returns to Kathleen Fischer. 'The more I

think of it, the more the name brings back my memory of her . . . She was real nice and quiet and professional. We became friends . . . I was sad to see her leave. But then again, I could be talking about the wrong person. Funny how your memories could be swayed . . . Maybe I just choose to forget 1985, one headache after another. I certainly was astounded so many other people had such vivid memories of simple conversations we may have had. They'd say they didn't know things that really they should have known, but get to something that paints me in a bad light, then they have total recall . . . I can't even begin to tell you how frustrating that is. Well, I guess I won't have to deal with it again, and I can just forget them.'

21

As I spent time with Frediani, I realized the truth of David Bartick's words: you do build up a rapport with someone, and attach yourself to that part of them you can identify with. Despite the letter from the DOJ, his guilt was hardly questionable – it was written in the DNA – but I realized that I wished it wasn't him who had killed Helena Greenwood. I could not grasp hold of the idea that someone I knew could have to suffer the rest of their life behind bars. It was a step too close to a reality that I could not conceive. How on earth could anyone face that?

A friend asked me: how would you feel if he had killed your son? Would you want him getting out then? It was a sobering thought. I was afraid I knew the answer. I spoke to someone who had been involved in the case on the defence side, a psychologist. She said that, in her view, Frediani has the personality of a sociopath: charismatic, impulsive, hedonistic, smart, manipulative, faithless in sexual relationships and ultimately remorseless. If he is indeed guilty, he will have convinced himself that it was a righteous slaying. According to studies, around 3–4 per cent of the American male population (and 1 per cent of females) can be characterized as sociopathic; in prisons, this percentage rises to 20 per cent.

Does Frediani fit the definition? Was I being manipulated into feeling empathy for him – an emotion that, as a sociopath, he would not be able to return?

In the spring following the trial, I hire a car and, with my husband and son, drive up the coast to San Francisco. We stay in a B&B in San Mateo – half-way between Atherton, where Helena and Roger had lived, and Paul's last apartment in Burlingame. The area is pleasantly suburban – mainly residential with concentrations of shops. It is not as charming as Del Mar, nor does it have the character and scenic drama of Berkeley, or the overwhelming beauty of San Francisco itself. But it is nice. The main street in Burlingame, especially: crammed with good cafés and delis, and upmarket chain stores. When we had last met, Paul had given me the phone numbers of some of his friends, and a list of his favourite restaurants and shops. We walk by the restaurants – classy but not flashy. We look around the Lauriedale apartments, where he lived first with Jim Thoren and later with Barbara Kenney. As he described, there are sprawling buildings set in a park-like complex, with pools and tennis courts. It is not Holidayville, but I could see that it would have been a fun place for a single person to live. He had told me that after the murder, the police would drive by late at night and shine spotlights through his bedroom window.

He hadn't known Kathy Clark then. They only met five years after he got out of prison, after he had split up with Eileen, when he was picking up the pieces of his life once more. 'He came into my office as a patient,' she explains. We are meeting at her fiancé's house, which is huge and grand, in the hills above Saratoga. There are photographs taken of ski holidays, and private planes. She is immediately friendly, and eager to tell me about Paul. 'We started talking and we clicked right away. He's so funny. I was asking him questions like, "What kind of pain do you have?" And he was replying, "Do you have a boyfriend?" I said, "Yeah," and we were like instant friends. One day, after his appointment, we went out for a cocktail. We had been laughing and joking, but as soon as he gets into the bar, he gets stiff, and looks kind of proud. He sticks his nose up in the air a bit. And this happened whenever we entered a public place; he turned into a different person.

'I think he's really very shy, at least when you first meet him, and he puts up this big defensive front. But I can tell you that when you get to know him, he's just adorable. He makes me laugh like no one else. He's so easy-going, and easy and fun to be with. He is one of the only men I know that truly loves female companionship. He really loves to hang out with the ladies. My boyfriends were never jealous of him, and they liked having him around.'

It was with Kathy and some friends of hers that Paul had gone to the ballet the night before his arrest. They had eaten afterwards, hit a few nightclubs, then driven in convoy back down the freeway to Burlingame. The next morning, she had received a phone call from his work colleagues, worried that he hadn't turned up at the office. 'I was a little disturbed too. He's so responsible and his cell phone is always on. But he wasn't answering it. I drove by his place and his car was there, and I thought, Oh my God, I had better start calling police departments. And then the Burlingame police said, "Yeah, we've got him." I said I was his sister and asked what he was in for. They said, murder of a female doctor or something, but they wouldn't give me any details. I was just blown away. I couldn't believe it.'

Over a year later, she is still struggling to work out what is true and what is not. Even coming down to the trial in San Diego did not bring home the reality of her friend's futureless existence. Most of the time, she argues that he cannot have done it; that the DNA was lying, that it was a frame-up. But every now and then, a little doubt oozes into her mind, and it is almost possible to see her mentally brushing it out. 'I went to the jail later that day and he was in this orange jump suit. I saw him through the glass and he looked very distraught, very suicidal. He looked horrible. I couldn't believe this was happening to him: Paul is the kind of guy who sends Christmas cards and thank you cards on time. I keep thinking, did I miss something? Did I see any anger brewing up to a point where it might have become uncontrollable? And the answer is no.

'I don't know how he's really coping right now, but I can tell you that I really, really miss our friendship. I think back and there were times when I just took our relationship for granted and I feel so bad. It's like I can never get back that time when I'd go for a month without seeing him. It's really weird when you don't have that person around. I can't just pick up the phone and call him, I can't just go and watch a movie or have a slumber party.' As we are talking, she starts to cry.

Diane Christiansen was one of the only friends of Frediani's from pre-prison times whom he had let back into his life after his release. A strikingly good-looking and intelligent woman, she had a brief relationship with him in the mid-1980s. 'We met when I was nineteen; he was older. I thought, "Oh God, he's so sophisticated, very striking." We went out for a short while, a few dates. He was my first real boyfriend and he was a complete gentleman. He was always attentive, and so attractive – so many women liked him. After we stopped seeing each other, we stayed friends.'

Diane married, moved to Canada, came back to San Francisco, and for a while lost touch with Paul. 'Then, one day in 1990, the phone rings. I am sitting on the bed with my three-month-old daughter. And he says, "Diane, you're not going to believe who this is." I was so pleased to hear from him. Later, I took my daughter to meet him, and he held Dominique, and told me what had happened. I was so impressed at how he had pulled himself together after getting out of prison. He had a job, his own place. He told me that he was angry in prison, and all he wanted was to be normal again. Our friendship soon resumed and he would talk to me about everything. He would call up and cry on the phone about Eileen. And later, when that broke up, he came to parties at my place.' She gets a photograph out of her bag to show me. It is Paul, in a dark suit and polo shirt, at a party with Diane on his lap, laughing. 'He was shy. At parties he would sort of keep to himself. My friends would ask about him, say he looked stiff, but when they got to know him, they loved him. I never saw him lose his cool – he was always laughing. Maybe he repressed things, but he never really lost it with me.'

At one stage, Paul offered to be an anonymous case study for a paper she was writing on authoritarian parenting, for her master's degree in psychology. When I ask to see it, we go back to her apartment in a kooky part of San Francisco, and she finds it in a filing cabinet. She hasn't read it, she tells me, for years. When she was interviewing him, Paul had described his parents' style of parenting as 'strict' and 'one way only'. His father was 'a proud Italian' with a 'macho attitude', and his mother rarely stood up to him. He talked about the 'humiliating ultra-short haircuts and conservative clothes his parents forced him to wear throughout his adolescence. He said he would cry every time he went to have a haircut for years, yet this failed to faze his parents.'

'Throughout adolescence he built up enormous resentment towards his parents and developed a rebellious and stubborn attitude,' Diane had written about the character at the centre of her case study. 'All through childhood, he resisted being told what to do, so by adolescence he addressed his parents' endless demands with resistance or aloofness as a way to give the impression he was in control . . . His parents refused to let him date until the senior prom . . . he said when he finally moved away to New Mexico, he felt such an incredible sense of freedom, especially since he could explore his sexuality . . . He continued to be permissive throughout college and well after and added that he has long hair as well to erase further memories of control.'

The description matched much of what I knew about Frediani's past, although to me – and in the long account he wrote of his life prior to the death penalty decision – he had never criticized his parents. It wouldn't be surprising if he had spiced up his childhood for the benefit of a student psychology paper, or exaggerated his woes for Diane's sympathetic ear. It was hard, now, to know which shade of the chameleon family relationship is closest to the truth – perhaps Paul himself does not know.

'One observation made about his current behaviour which reflects his upbringing is that today he is a huge risk-taker . . .' Diane had written in her paper. Was he referring there to his sexual adventures, I wondered? Did the clues to his behaviour lie in his childhood?

Paul calls Diane weekly from jail, insisting upon his innocence. She wants to believe in him, searches for alternative explanations, but I sense that even if she found out that he had done it, she would not give up on him. 'I light candles for Paul every week,' she tells me. 'I cannot bear the thought of him in there.'

That summer, I wrote to Paul Frediani's parents from England. I was worried that their experiences at the trial would make them wary of talking to me, but the response from Mrs Frediani was warm. Paul had told them about me, had sent them a copy of my last book. They would be delighted if I came to see them – and I must stay with them. Since the children left, they have two spare rooms. I booked a flight for the East Coast at the end of August.

I knew that Paul Frediani had been moved from Vista detention centre down to Richard J. Donovan prison, on the Mexican border. There, he was undergoing evaluation to determine which prison he would be sent to. As a lifer with a history of sexual offences, he would not be in for an easy ride at the best of places.

Just before I flew to America, Mrs Frediani wrote to say that he had been transferred to Corcoran, a high-security prison in the desert, about a five-hour drive east from San Francisco. On the internet I found a report entitled 'Corcoran: Hellhole of California', which detailed the conditions faced by high-security prisoners: 22½ hours a day in their cells, no hobbies, few books, and TV and radio only if they can afford to buy their own. Another, 'Corcoran State Prison: 10 Years of Shootings and Torture!!', told of 'gladiator fights' that turned the prison yard into a shooting gallery. Over the last decade, guards had shot and killed seven inmates, the article claimed. Eight officers had been indicted for arranging prison fights for recreation; others, wearing black masks, allegedly abused inmates during cell searches; one officer was convicted of assaulting an inmate by zapping his genitals with a Taser gun. Paul Frediani had been assigned to mainline, and was terrified for his life.

At the end of August I fly to the upstate city where he was born and grew up – not without trepidation. I feel strangely guilty: I am trying not to think about whether their son is guilty of murder at the same time as taking hospitality from the Fredianis. They have not asked for my views, and I have not offered them. I cannot help but feel that they would like me to join their mini-crusade, to feed their hope. Still, I want to see his home, to see where he rode his bike, played basketball, jumped off the roof into the swimming pool he had helped his father to build. To see if there are any clues here as to what happened decades later on the other side of the country.

They are waiting outside the airport in a big Chevy Tahoe, an outdoorsman's vehicle. Mr Frediani limps round to open the door for me. He is a bigger man than I remember, bespectacled, very welcoming. He has an open face, as if he could not hide a feeling if he wanted to. At the moment – and for the rest of my stay – he looks slightly perplexed, as if he does not know how to deal with what is happening to him. He apologizes for not talking to me at the trial. I say I was not surprised; I am sorry for what he and his wife had to endure. Mrs Frediani is sitting in the front seat, clutching a cushion to her stomach. She is recovering from a recent operation. 'I didn't tell Paul,' she says. 'I didn't want him to worry.'

We drive back through the suburbs, along wide streets lined with clapperboard houses set back from the road, mailboxes marking their spot like flamingo sentries. We pass the Fredianis' home. It is white with black shutters; the Stars and Stripes flutters from a flagpole in the front garden. They take me to a local restaurant for lunch, and we talk about the town, how it has changed. Paul slips naturally into the conversation, but we do not discuss his current plight. On the way back, they point out the school where he started in kindergarten and danced at the senior prom thirteen years later.

Their house is immaculate. Polished and ordered and comfortable, with treasured porcelain figurines on display in a dresser. While his wife has a rest, Mr Frediani gives me a guided tour of the family photographs, arranged on the mantelpiece, framed on the walls. They are a good-looking family: big-boned, apart from Donna, and strong-featured. In pictures of Donna's wedding her mother is handsome in pale grey satin and lace. Mr Frediani stares at the photographs of Paul, smiling with straight teeth, his hands on his sister's shoulders: 'Does he look like he belongs in prison?' he asks me. 'She's dead now, she has no family – so why does our family have to suffer, even if he is guilty?' I can see him thinking that perhaps he has slipped up. He quickly adds, 'Which I don't believe he is.

'I've been on anti-depressants since this all happened. That's what's kept me going. I went to see a therapist about it and she ended up crying. Before I started the pills, everything would make me cry. I would be watching TV and suddenly I would be bawling buckets.'

We walk out on to the long lawn, neatly mown in stripes, and he starts talking about Paul, what he was like when he was younger. When I ask whether I can take notes, he immediately clams up. 'Oh, I had better wait until my wife's awake,' he says. 'She's the smart one. I'm the dummy. I'm bound to say something wrong.' But he seems concerned that he might have upset me by this. I assure him that it is no problem. Despite what Paul told Diane about his family, right now Paul's mother appears very much in charge. She has the sharp brain, the ideas. He sensibly does what he is told, only occasionally, in a good-natured way, grumbling about how he is bullied. 'I couldn't live without her,' he confides.

'We haven't told anyone apart from our very closest friends about what has happened to Paul,' Mrs Frediani tells me. 'We can't. This is a very conservative community. We would be cut dead.' I instantly feel that I have already betrayed them, that I will be a part of their destruction.

That evening, their closest friends and Donna come round to dinner and we order take-away spaghetti and meatballs from a local Italian restaurant. It turns into a jolly night, full of happy reminiscences. It is cathartic for them to be able to talk about Paul, I sense. One by one, the old stories are rolled out: how he saved Steve from drowning, by diving into the pool with all his clothes on, and then asked, 'Who's watching this kid?' They repeat that line. It makes them laugh. How he hated mowing the lawn. How he flew over from California one weekend to take his father to a big football game. Donna is the centre of the party – she is lively and funny, affectionate to her parents and welcoming to me – so different from how she appeared at the trial, frozen to stone. They are obviously very proud of her: she has a postgraduate degree, a good job, a good marriage, lives on the smart side of the city, but still not far from home.

That night, I go to bed in the spare room, in a four-poster, with flowered sheets and matching scalloped pillowcases. In the book case, I find Agatha Christies, *The Godfather*, some old Dr Seusses and a pile of photograph albums. I flick through pictures of Paul, Donna and Steve growing up. In a later one, Paul has longer hair and is wearing a patterned shirt. He looks like a young Beatle. As I lie in bed, I cannot but wonder whether I am sleeping in his old room.

The next morning, after breakfast, I go with Mr Frediani to raise the flag in the front yard. 'I do this every morning, except when it's raining,' he tells me. 'Look, I had an eagle specially soldered on top of the pole.' He is a child of immigrants who adopted the values of the new world, only for his all-American oldest son to fall foul of its laws. Then we sit down to talk. As Mrs Frediani rehashes the case, she is close to tears. They are tears of anger, I think: her husband is bewildered, but she wants someone to blame.

'What I hated the most was what that prosecutor lady said in court about Paul murdering to avoid being shamed in front of his family,' Mr Frediani says. 'She was wrong. Whether he was guilty or not, we would stand behind him, whatever.'

When they drop me off at the airport, Mrs Frediani gives me a hug, and tearfully asks me to write to Paul. I say I will. These are good people. They are victims as much as Sydney Greenwood was. What has happened to their son has taken over their life and they are wading through it every day, terrified to think about his future – or theirs.

Meeting them, I feel, has brought me close to the end of my journey. I realize that this is a story whose ends cannot be neatly tied up and put to bed. There will always be questions in my mind: what was it really that drove Paul Frediani to take that one risk too far; what combination of life experiences, biological make-up and pure happenstance? Was there, hidden inside a tiny corner of his genome, some genetic force that pre-determined his behaviour, and catapulted him out of control?

I know that the time I have spent in this strange world of murder and molecules will never leave me. I will continue to correspond with Paul Frediani as long as he continues to reply. I will exchange e-mails with David Bartick, Laura Heilig and Martin Murray. When I am driving along the south coast of England, I will think of Sydney Greenwood, and at Christmas I will send the Fredianis our best wishes.

Paul's parents did what they could for their children. They are part of the story; in a way, their story is the root of mine. It is certainly the root of Paul's. Their DNA – 50 per cent from each – was found on Helena Greenwood's body. Their DNA sat in a box with the fingernail cuttings of a dead woman for fifteen years. Their lives have been brought down by the genetic codes that made them – and made their son who he is. And he was caught out by the very blueprint of his own destruction. He cannot claim poverty or drugs or blackmail drove him to murder. He cannot blame a harsh childhood, or friends who led him astray. Only a spiral of events, spinning off a much smaller spiral of his own.

Epilogue

In the mid-1990s, a scientist from Maryland set out to search for the 'thrill-seeking' gene. Dean Hamer had no idea what he would find. A few years earlier, he had caused a sensation when he claimed that he had sound evidence pointing towards a genetic explanation for sexual orientation: he had isolated, on the X chromosome, the so-called 'gay gene'. It was a controversial discovery, but one which was welcomed among the homosexual minority, and their families.

Hamer's search for what it was that made some people actively look for kicks led him to chromosome 11, to a gene related to the regulation of a certain chemical – dopamine – which controls the brain's activity or motivation. On this gene, Dean Hamer identified a variable minisatellite phrase – a stutter – forty-eight letters long. This phrase was repeated different numbers of times in different people, and Hamer noticed a correlation: the people with more copies of the minisatellite – more stutters – exhibited a greater desire for novelty. This was expressed in different ways: a desire for physical thrills, new experiences, danger, impulsiveness, a lack of inhibition and a willingness to take risks. It was not by any means the sole cause of this behaviour; Hamer estimated that this gene explained only 4 per cent of the urge to seek thrills, out of the approximately 40 per cent that could be ascribed to heritable factors. But there was a statistically significant relationship.

It was one of the first studies linking a personality trait to a specified genetic site. To an extent, it should not be surprising: it is taken for granted that children will look like members of their family, so why the resistance to the idea that they can act and feel like them too? As Hamer put it: 'You have about as much choice in some aspects of your personality as you do in the shape of your nose or the size of your feet.' Nurture – the environment – undeniably plays an important role in shaping a person's character, but it only has the clay to work with that nature supplies.

While the latest research suggests that many personality traits are inherited at birth, the study of the genetic root of behaviour still lags well behind that of the molecular causes of inherited diseases. From sickle-cell anaemia to cancer, genes have been identified that, at the least, contribute to the ailment, if not cause it. In the last few years, scientists have begun to link brain disorders such as epilepsy, schizophrenia and depression with specific genes. Diagnosis is the necessary first step towards the development of a cure. In the past, epileptics were cast out of society, locked up or punished; these days, the majority can be successfully treated.

There has been no research as yet into the genetic make-up of sexual compulsives – or the personality types known as 'sociopathic' or 'anti-social'. Without doubt, in the coming century there will be, just as there will be doctors and therapists of all different backgrounds and beliefs who will claim to be able to control this behaviour, whether by conventional medicine or otherwise. What is not certain is to what extent this genetic information will be predictive: will it be able to say that a person with eight stutters in the thrill-seeking gene will be twenty times more likely to commit indecent exposure than someone with three? Will it be able to assign a mathematical probability to this predisposition?

We are peering over the brink of an abyss. In the coming decades, there will be a monumental leap in our knowledge of the genetic locations of inherited diseases. And more and more genes will be discovered that link behaviour to the chemicals in our brains, and genes tied to our urges and emotions. Ever larger databases will gather our DNA, and more powerful computers will analyse it, in greater detail. The knowledge that this science will give cannot be unlearned once it is discovered. The genie cannot be put back in the box. It is what we do with that knowledge that will be crucial.

I have no idea what will happen: I doubt that the geneticists working in the field or the politicians who attempt to control the direction of their research do either. Over the past two years, through the microcosm of this murder story, I have become aware of the power that DNA holds over our lives. Every single person involved in this story has been affected by it somehow. Mendel, Crick and Watson, Mullis, Jeffreys and Gill have devoted their working lives to it. Helena Greenwood lived and died by DNA; Paul Frediani's freedom was curtailed by a microscopic particle of his DNA; but we have all been touched. Every tiny cell of the 100 trillion in our bodies is rippling with our unique DNA code. We cannot get away from it; it is not just the science that conquered this crime, it is the substance of human fallibility that committed the crime.

I am excited by the future of genetics; at the idea that we should – we will – be able to treat Parkinson's disease, Alzheimer's, a huge number of seriously debilitating conditions. But I would not like to know every gene, every potential flaw in my and my family's body, mind, character. I cannot help worrying about what the government or the insurance companies, or even my neighbours would do with that information if they had it. I do not believe that governments have any right to try to control or change people because of their genes – or any right to find out a person's genetic make-up. The individual must always have the freedom to choose what they find out, and what they do with this knowledge.

But the Frediani parents, with their congenitally sick children, could have been helped by some genetic foreknowledge. To know the genetic mutation that caused Paul to be born with a club foot and Steve with no colon, the chemical imbalance that gave Donna rheumatoid arthritis, would have been one step closer to relief from the pain these genes caused. If Paul had been low on dopamine receptors, for example, and they had known the potential problems it might cause, and there had been a drug that could have helped him, would they not have grasped that opportunity? Could a Helena Greenwood of the future be spared a terrible death thanks to the science she was so proud to be a part of?

After years of living with Helena, I think I know the direction she would take. She would point towards the brave new world of twenty-first-century genetics, and walk through its portals without a moment's hesitation.